Turkey

Informatics and Economic Modernization

The World Bank
Washington, D.C.

Copyright © 1993
The International Bank for Reconstruction
and Development/THE WORLD BANK
1818 H Street, N.W.
Washington, D.C. 20433, U.S.A.

World Bank Country Studies are among the many reports originally prepared for internal use as part of the continuing analysis by the Bank of the economic and related conditions of its developing member countries and of its dialogues with the governments. Some of the reports are published in this series with the least possible delay for the use of governments and the academic, business and financial, and development communities. The typescript of this paper therefore has not been prepared in accordance with the procedures appropriate to formal printed texts, and the World Bank accepts no responsibility for errors.

The World Bank does not guarantee the accuracy of the data included in this publication and accepts no responsibility whatsoever for any consequence of their use. Any maps that accompany the text have been prepared solely for the convenience of readers; the designations and presentation of material in them do not imply the expression of any opinion whatsoever on the part of the World Bank, its affiliates, or its Board or member countries concerning the legal status of any country, territory, city, or area or of the authorities thereof or concerning the delimitation of its boundaries or its national affiliation.

The material in this publication is copyrighted. Requests for permission to reproduce portions of it should be sent to the Office of the Publisher at the address shown in the copyright notice above. The World Bank encourages dissemination of its work and will normally give permission promptly and, when the reproduction is for noncommercial purposes, without asking a fee. Permission to copy portions for classroom use is granted through the Copyright Clearance Center, 27 Congress Street, Salem, Massachusetts 01970, U.S.A.

The complete backlist of publications from the World Bank is shown in the annual *Index of Publications*, which contains an alphabetical title list (with full ordering information) and indexes of subjects, authors, and countries and regions. The latest edition is available free of charge from the Distribution Unit, Office of the Publisher, Department F, The World Bank, 1818 H Street, N.W., Washington, D.C. 20433, U.S.A., or from Publications, The World Bank, 66, avenue d'Iéna, 75116 Paris, France.

ISSN: 0253-2123

Library of Congress Cataloging-in-Publication Data

Turkey : informatics and economic modernization.
        p.   cm. — (A World Bank country study, ISSN 0253-2123)
        Includes bibliographical references.
        ISBN 0-8213-2376-8
        1. Information technology—Turkey.   2. Turkey—Economic policy.
    I. World Bank.   II. Series.
    HC495.I55T87   1993
    338.9561—dc20

                                                                93-16706
                                                                     CIP

ACKNOWLEDGMENTS

This Report has been structured as a collaborative program between the World Bank and the Government of Turkey. It is the product of an extended dialogue on policy issues relating to technology development and economic modernization, and builds on the "new industrial policy" agenda of the Bank's Research Department. The World Bank team that visited Turkey (December, 1991 and May, 1992) and worked on this Report consisted of:

Jeremy Oppenheim, Task Manager (EC1CO)
Robert Schware, Senior IT Specialist (ASTIF)
Joel Brandon, Consultant (Computers)
Josephine Hykin, S&T Specialist
Yoram Alster, Consultant (Telecom)
Anne Branscomb, Consultant (Legal)
Ömer Karasapan, Consultant (Information Services)
Furuzan Batumlu, Resident Mission (Turkey)
David Tonge et. al., IBS Consultants

The team also benefitted from support and insights of: Mieko Nishimizu, Carl Dahlman, William McCleary, Carlos Ferreira, Flavia Fonseca, Eduardo Talero and Nagy Hanna. Jocelyn Dytang provided text, graphics and logistic support.

The Government team was coordinated by Treasury, and wrote eight Working Papers as input to the Report:

1. Research and Development on Information Technology (IT) in Turkey (TÜBITAK);

2. Public Sector Use of IT (Prime Ministry);

3. Public Sector Information Dissemination (SIS);

4. Legal Framework for Database Services (SIS);

5. International and Turkish IT Standardization (TSE);

6. Radio Spectrum Administration (TGM);

7. Software Specification, Maintenance and Training Standards (SPO/TÜBITAK); and

8. Market Research on Software Demand (SPO/TÜBITAK).

Detailed information and suggestions were also provided by: PTT, the Supreme Council for Radio and TV Broadcasting, the Ministry of Education, the Ministry of Culture, the Ministry of Justice, the National Productivity Council, YöK, the Turkish Informatics Association, the Middle East Technical University, and leading representatives from the private sector. The Bank team wishes to thank all those ministries and organizations that have supported this effort.

The views, interpretations and conclusions of the Report are strictly those of the World Bank. They should not be attributed to any individual member or institutional affiliation of the Government team.

GLOSSARY OF ABBREVIATIONS

AQAP	Allied Quality Assurance Program
ASIC	Application Specific Integrated Circuit
ATMs	Automatic Teller Machines
BCS	British Computer Society
CNN	Cable News Network
CRPG	Compound Rate of Productivity Growth
DAPRA	Defense Alliance Research Project Agency
FCC	Federal Communications Commission
GAAP	Generally Accepted Accounting Principles
GIS	Geographic Information System
GPO	Government Printing Office
GSA	General Service Administration
GUI	Graphical User Interface
IBE	Information-Based Economy
ICCP	Institute for Certification of Computer Professionals
IET	Industrial Economy in Transition
IIBK	Department of Labor Employment Service
IPRs	Intellectual Property Rights
IRMs	Information Resources Managers
ISDN	Integrated Services Digital Network
IT	Information Technology
KOSGEB	The Small Industry Development Organization
LANs	Local Area Networks
METU	Middle East Technical University
MOA	Ministry of Agriculture
MPAA	Motion Picture Association of America
MPM	National Productivity Center
NCB	National Computer Board
NIC	Newly Industrializing Countries
OECD	Organization for Economic Co-operation and Development
ONP	Open Network Provisions
PID	Personal Input Device
PTT	Post, Telegraph and Telephone
R&D	Research and Development
RTYK	Supreme Council for Radio and Television
SIS	State Institute of Statistics
SLAs	Service Level Agreements
SMT	Software Maintenance Training
SNS	Singapore Network Services
SRDC	Software Research and Development Center
TGM	Telsiz Genel Mudurlugu
TQM	Total Quality Management

TGM	Telsiz Genel Mudurlugu
TQM	Total Quality Management
TRT	Turkish Radio and Television
TSE	Turkish Standards Institute
TUBISAD	Association of Turkish Data-Processing Companies
TUBITAK	Scientific & Technical Research Council of Turkey
VAS	Value-Added Service
VSHEs	Vocational Schools of High Education
WANs	Wide-Area Networks
WIPO	World Intellectual Property Organization
YÖK	The Council for Higher Education

CURRENCY EQUIVALENTS

Currency Unit = Turkish Lira (TL)

Value of US$1.00

1987*	857.2
1988*	1422.3
1989*	2121.7
1990*	2629.0
1991*	4137.0
July 15, 1992	6944.8

----

*/ Annual average

TABLE OF CONTENTS

List of Annexes, Tables, Figures and Boxes

Annexes

Tables

Figures

Boxes

EXECUTIVE SUMMARY

Introduction

1.   Informatics is a technology set for information processing, storage, retrieval and transmission. Over the past 25 years, sustained technological change in the informatics sector has had an economy-wide impact on productivity growth, raising the information-intensity of private sector and government activities. In advanced economies, informatics now accounts for 5 - 6% of GNP, and by 1995 will be the single largest industrial sector. Policies that foster the supply, diffusion and efficient application of informatics have therefore become central to long run growth potential and to international competitiveness. However, not all consequences of informatics are guaranteed to be welfare-enhancing. Rather, informatics also poses new threats to civil liberties, creates significant costs of social and institutional adjustment, and is likely to have far-reaching implications for systems of governance. Hence, the interest of governments around the world in understanding the implications of informatics for social and economic progress, and in harnessing its benefits for national development.

2.   During the 1980s, Turkey laid the foundation for her transition to an information-based economy (IBE). A strategy for economic modernization predicated on open competitive markets forced the private sector to become more information-intensive. Growth in foreign trade and investment (direct and portfolio) increased the two-way flow of information between Turkey and the world economy. Massive public investment in an advanced communications network increased the economic return on informatics applications and, together with import liberalization, supported diffusion of this technology throughout the economy. Although the Government had no explicit informatics policy, a combination of market forces, technological change and infrastructure development provided the necessary climate for rapid expansion in the supply and demand for information goods, services and skills.

3.   Nevertheless, when compared to peer-group countries that targeted informatics as a catalyst for economic modernization, Turkey has not yet adequately developed the resource endowment for an IBE. Cross-country indicators suggest that Turkey is behind in:

- the markets for computer hardware and especially software;

- modernizing the framework for the communications sector;

- creating the human resources essential for an IBE; and

- developing a vigorous private information industry.

Longer term growth and international competitiveness will depend on measures that the Government takes to correct these deficits, and to mobilize private sector resources for productive use and supply of informatics.

Longer term growth and international competitiveness will depend on measures that the Government takes to correct these deficits, and to mobilize private sector resources for productive use and supply of informatics.

Existing Situation in Turkey: Diagnostic

4.   *Computer Hardware and Software.*   Despite rapid growth in hardware investment, Turkey is lagging behind comparator countries. First, allowing for relative income levels, the market for computer hardware and software in Turkey appears very small ($12 per capita) in comparison to countries such as Korea ($45 pc) or Spain ($110 pc), leaving aside the US or Japan ($400 pc). There is no local supply (except for a few PCs) of computers or informatics components. Second, the software industry is at an infant stage, compared to major competitors. The software-hardware investment ratio (14%) is significantly lower than in other countries (average 35%); exports are negligible; and there is no or little foreign investment. Third, massive investment by Government in computerization (over $500 million during the 1980s) does not appear to have achieved required productivity gains in public administration. In addition, informatics procurement has not been used effectively as an instrument for local technology capacity. Fourth, private sector development in informatics markets has been constrained by inadequate standards, a lack of copyright protection for the software industry, tax and regulatory constraints on financial instruments (e.g., venture capital), import barriers (tariff and non-tariff), and overall distortions in incentive policy.

5.   *Communications.* Since 1985, Turkey (through PTT) has invested almost 1% of GNP per annum to develop an advanced communications network that could support a competitive market-based economy. The network has expanded to the point where there is now universal geographic service. Over 50% of the network is digital, exceeding ratios achieved in most OECD countries. The terminal market has been substantially liberalized (though burdensome type approval and conformance testing regulations are still in place); and local industry supplies almost 90% of the public network's investment requirements. Perhaps the most striking aspect of this achievement is that over 85% of the investment program was financed from internally generated cash-flow. Nevertheless, it is not clear whether the formula for success in 1980s will prove adequate for the 1990s. First, the price of key telecom services for the business community is significantly above that of major trading partners, reducing international competitiveness and also Turkey's attractiveness as a location for direct foreign investment. Second, the sharp increase in the telecom profits has enabled PTT to mask a corresponding deterioration in its other businesses - especially the postal service. Third, the lack of competitive pressure on PTT has reduced operational and investment efficiency. Fourth, barriers to private sector entry into the communications sector have: (a) stifled an important source of innovation and consumer choice; and (b) left Turkey progressively out-of-line with regulatory and institutional modernization in other OECD/EC countries.

6.   *Human Capital.* Perhaps the most severe deficit that Turkey faces is in the area of human capital for an IBE. The formal education system has not been able to respond

adequately to broad shifts in occupational structure; nor to the need for a specialized informatics profession. Compared to more advanced countries, Turkey appears to be significantly behind in:

- the diffusion of computer literacy throughout the workforce;

- the supply of specialized informatics professionals - people to manage computerization, teams of skilled software engineers, and end-user support specialists for large organizations;

- the quality of these professionals in an international market that is demanding increasingly specialized skills; and

- the system for skills upgrading and retraining in the face of rapidly changing technology.

Despite growth of computer engineering departments, the universities graduate less students per million with degrees in computer-related subjects (160) than Mexico (230), Spain (550) or Korea (1100). Although universities attract the brightest 1% of students to their computer engineering departments, it is not clear whether graduates have the multi-disciplinary skills needed in the market. Nor has there been adequate (or efficient) investment in the diffusion of more general informatics skills throughout the workforce. Computer/student ratios (1:218) in the schools are significantly behind those in peer-group countries; and the regulatory framework for private computer schools reduces competition, and creates inadequate incentives for improved training performance. The challenge facing Turkey is therefore to turn her young population into a competitive resource in the international market, and to educate a new generation of informatics entrepreneurs.

7.   *Information Services*. Compared to more advanced economies, the private information industry in Turkey needs to attract resources and increase efficiency over the next decade. In other OECD economies, the private information industry (media, consulting, specialist information services) expanded rapidly during the 1980s, driven by both technological change and market liberalization. In Turkey, the industry remains highly fragmented; advertizing revenue (which drives the economics of private media) at $10 per capita is significantly below that of e.g., Spain ($151); there is little horizontal integration across the information industry; and growth has been only marginally greater than that of GNP. The main policy problems appear to be: (a) the existence of a de jure state monopoly in television and radio broadcasting; (b) poor dissemination of public sector data; (c) the inadequacy of standards related to information reliability (e.g., accounting principles) in the financial and consumer product markets; and (d) deficiencies in the legal framework for data-confidentiality.

Action Plan

8.   Turkey's strategy for an information-based economy (IBE) should be based on policy action in four main areas:

- *private sector development*: to foster an internationally competitive supply of informatics technology, goods and services (especially in communications);

- *human capital formation*: to align human resource strategy and education delivery mechanisms with the needs of an IBE;

- *public sector management*: to increase productivity and innovation in public sector services through better use of informatics; and

- *information regulation*: to safeguard civil liberties and consumer rights against risks created by informatics.

A public-private sector partnership that tackles this agenda can make informatics a catalyst for Turkey's economic modernization and a potent source of international competitiveness.

9.   ***Private Sector Development***. A competitive business climate is essential if Turkey is to accumulate informatics technology, attract foreign direct investment, and develop innovative information and communications services (more rapidly than competitors). Three main sets of policy action are required. First, the Government should reduce and progressively eliminate state monopolies in telecom, and television/radio broadcasting. While the latter reform is already underway, immediate action in the communications sector is needed to: (a) separate mail from telecom; (b) establish an independent regulatory body; and (c) increase private sector participation and competition. Second, policy and institutional barriers still constrain development of competitive informatics markets. In particular, tariff and non-tariff barriers to trade should be reduced, copyright protection for software introduced, international standards (especially for quality assurance) strengthened, and tax distortions on venture capital eliminated. Third, greater effort is required to stimulate technology development. The first best instrument to achieve this goal is improved public sector procurement of informatics, including unbundled specification of agency requirements for software and computer services. In addition, research and development support should be intensified especially for the software sector.

10.   ***Human Capital Formation***. Building an information workforce is the most important challenge confronting the Government. Turkey's young population is potentially the nation's greatest competitive asset, but only if the education system works and can be properly funded. To create the talent and skill-base central to an information-based economy, action is needed in three areas. First, the university supply of informatics professionals should be

strengthened through: (a) creation of separate Informatics Faculties; (b) actions to reinforce university-business linkages; (c) improved incentives for teaching staff and graduates in informatics disciplines; (d) establishment of a private fee-based Informatics Institute; and (e) integration of informatics into non-engineering curricula. Second, improvements in the university system are a necessary but insufficient condition for Turkey to close its informatics skill gap over the next decade. In addition, the private sector should be mobilized for the task. Key measures include: (a) introduction of occupational standards for informatics, test procedures and certification of private training schools to international norms; (b) regular surveys of the informatics labor market, and dissemination of the results; (c) elimination of non-productive regulations on the private training schools; and (d) a more rigorous approach to company training schemes. Third, Turkey needs to accelerate diffusion of general informatics skills in the workforce. More aggressive implementation of the Computer Assisted Education (CAE) program is essential with greater emphasis on: (a) teacher training; and (b) introduction of software tools. This school-based approach to computer literacy should be supplemented by phased implementation of a National "Bilgitel" Project, to create a nationwide network of inexpensive terminals along the lines of the French Minitel and other "information utilities" in OECD countries.

11.   *Public Sector Management*. The Government has made major investments in computer systems over the past decade, but with limited results in terms of public sector productivity and innovation. In addition to improved public procurement of informatics, two key steps should be taken: (a) design and implementation of a National Database and Information Policy; and (b) establishment of a mechanism to tackle inter-agency problems of computerization and related training requirements. A National Database and Information Policy would have three main objectives: (a) to facilitate data-sharing within the public sector and prevent duplicative investments; (b) to increase private access to public data, and to decentralize the channels for data dissemination; and (c) to improve system efficiency through the introduction of cost-recovery mechanisms. Action in this area would imply a significant modification to the State Institute of Statistics (SIS) law, with SIS assuming the role of a technical coordinating and advisory agency. A second key initiative for improved government computerization would be establishment of an small independent agency with the following functions: (a) to provide technical assistance to the agencies on informatics procurement and tender specification; (b) to negotiate special government prices for standard informatics goods and services; (c) to standardize public sector occupational streams for informatics professionals, and provide training support; and (d) to perform a technology watch function for the government. Once the agency has succeeded in this mandate, it could assume broader responsibilities on issues of procurement practices, and capacity planning for the public sector information system. The agency should have a small technical staff, broad public/private representation in the shareholder assembly, and an independent revenue source (possibly a 1% fee on public sector informatics procurements).

12.   *Information Regulation*. The transition towards an information-based economy creates potential welfare losses as well as gains. Technological change always poses new social

and economic risks, and informatics is no exception. Government action is required in three main areas to preempt these risks. First, the legal framework for informatics should be strengthened, particularly in the areas of data-confidentiality and computer crime. Turkish standards for data-protection are behind those in the EC and US, generating potential trade frictions and an immediate economic case for legal reform. With regard to computer crime, the Penal Code should be further strengthened (in addition to 1991 amendments) to cover cases of unauthorized access to computer facilities, as well as new classes of computer virus (unanticipated by the law). Second, the mandate of the Supreme Council on Television and Radio Broadcasting should be expanded to address issues related to information content for all electronic media. Third, there should be a concerted program to bring information standards in financial, consumer product and employment markets progressively in line with Turkey's OECD trading partners.

Implementation

13.   At present, Turkey possesses a decentralized institutional framework for implementing informatics policy. Almost every agency is involved in implementing various aspects of what in practice is an *implicit* informatics policy. Since a vast range of policies affect the speed and process by which Turkey's economy is becoming more information-intensive, this institutional decentralization is a natural (and desirable) outcome. Indeed, it is essential that each agency understand the implications of informatics for its own mission, and develop a corresponding set of programs and initiatives. As a result, policy design and implementation appears to have been more effective in those cases that require relatively limited inter-agency coordination (e.g., network modernization, import regulations, computer crime legislation). However in other cases (e.g., government computerization, procurement policy, public information policy, human capital development), policy implementation has been severely constrained by coordination failures. These issues must be tackled on a collective basis if Turkey is to accelerate her transition towards an information-based economy.

14.   In Turkey, development of an over-arching framework for informatics policy is likely to be a long-term task. In the short run, what may be more practical is the implementation of specific projects (contained in the Action Plan). These projects will by themselves generate much of the coordination necessary for effective action in the informatics sector, and will provide demonstrable concrete benefits for the economy. In the longer run, if additional coordination proves to be necessary, the Government has a number of possible vehicles including: (a) establishment of a Ministry for Communications and Informatics; (b) enlarging the scope of the proposed agency for government computerization; or (c) creation of a National Informatics Board with a broad mandate for coordinating sectoral initiatives. However, the case for such institutional change is not yet overwhelming; and there are significant risks that investment in creating new bureaucratic structures would substitute for real action in the sector.

Conclusions

15.   Even in the absence of an explicit informatics policy and accompanying institutions, Turkey appears to have made substantial progress towards an IBE. Indeed, it is likely that market and technological forces over the next decade will reinforce this trend without any significant change in government policy! A high rate of productivity growth in the informatics sector, greater experience in applications, the opportunity to catch-up with international practice, and competitive pressure in the market will be enough to ensure that informatics plays an increasing role in the Turkish economy.

16.   However, all OECD and middle-income countries are likely to benefit from these same market and technological forces. At best, the absence of an explicit informatics policy and action plan implies that Turkey will continue to lag behind the leaders and may fall further behind those countries that have targeted informatics as a strategic sector for overall economic performance. If Turkey aims to accumulate information assets at a faster rate than the competition and to catch-up with more advanced economies, then a more dedicated approach is essential. Turkey today has a choice: either to include the information-based economy as an explicit objective in the national development agenda or to make it a residual outcome of policy. The central message of this Report is that Turkey has the potential to become an active player in the informatics revolution and an information hub in the global economy. Realizing this potential will require a long-term partnership between enlightened government policy and private entrepreneurship.

CHAPTER 1

VISION, STRATEGY, AND CONSTRAINTS

" There are many steps between the availability of a higher performance chip and the achievement of more efficient information management in the economy as a whole. " (Jonscher 1983)

Vision

1.01   Advanced economies have become progressively specialized in the production, distribution and use of information. This specialization is the source of substantial welfare gains. First, good information is essential if competitive markets are to work as a mechanism for efficient resource allocation, and for the equitable distribution of wealth. Market economies have at their essence the concepts of individual choice and invisible coordination. When information on the key price, quality and technology variables is widely available, markets generate rational production and consumption choices, and provide powerful signals that coordinate economic activity. By contrast, information gaps and asymmetries create unemployment, misallocation of credit, economic rents, non-competitive technological choices, and policy mistakes. Second, information is the basic factor input for scientific and technological progress; and is therefore central to sustaining productivity growth throughout an economy. Information-based economies are therefore well-positioned to compete in research and development, in knowledge creation and as economic laboratories for business and government innovation. Finally, economies that invest heavily in information may enjoy higher long-run growth potential. Information cannot be perfectly copyrighted, patented or kept secret. Therefore, the creation of information by one firm (or by the government) inevitably benefits the production of other nearby firms. Given cross-border barriers to knowledge diffusion (e.g., language), this information externality may be an important source of the productivity gap between high and low income economies.

1.02   As demand for information has grown, the structure and occupational profile of advanced economies is undergoing significant change. First, the information sector itself - media, communications, consulting services, and the production of information technology - has grown very fast, and has also become increasingly specialized. Information sectors in advanced economies generate a high volume of internal trade in a manner highly analogous to sophisticated financial markets. The global market for information goods, services and technology is now estimated at over $1.2 trillion. Second (and more pervasively), all sectors of the economy have become more information-intensive, resulting in a gradual reengineering of business and government functions. Information has substituted for other inputs (e.g., labor, energy, inventory expenses), and information technology has become a vital intermediate input in the economy's aggregate production function. As a result, there is a high income elasticity of demand for this technological input; and improvements in its price/performance ratio are a significant source of economic growth. Third, the nature of work has changed. In many OECD economies, employees whose primary task is to collect, process or transmit information now account for over 50% of the workforce.

1.03   This economic transformation in advanced economies has been fuelled by rapid advances in information technology.   The past 25 years have witnessed the emergence of technological paradigm - informatics - that radically reduces the cost of information acquisition, storage, processing and dissemination. Informatics technology - semiconductor chips, computer hardware and software, and communications systems - is based on a simple scientific insight: that all information, whether text, voice or image, can be translated into a digital language of ones and zeros, and then handled in a common electronic environment. Informatics therefore liberates information-handling from earlier technologies that separated the various media for printing text, broadcasting images (i.e., television), and communicating voice-messages (telephones). Moreover, informatics permits information-processing capability to be embedded into a vast range of manufacturing equipment and domestic appliances. For example, the average car already contains $200 of chips[1] and electronic circuitry. The impact of informatics has therefore not been restricted to the information-handling sector of the economy. Rather, it is transforming process and productivity across all sectors: manufacturing, agriculture, services and public administration. The result is that a growing proportion of economic activity is becoming information-based.

1.04   For the Turkish economy, this informatics "revolution" is crucial to growth and development prospects over the next decade. During the 1980s, Turkey laid the foundation for her transition to an information-based economy.   A strategy for economic modernization predicated   upon   competitive   open   markets   replaced   policies   of   import-substituting industrialization that had been pursued in the 1960s and 1970s.   Financial markets were liberalized; the capital account was opened up; and the Government introduced an attractive regime for direct foreign investment. Despite continued inflationary pressure and stop-go fiscal policies, the economy responded positively to the policy reform. Growth accelerated to over 6% per annum; the private sector grew much faster than the public sector; manufactured exports increased from $1 billion in 1980 to over $10 billion by 1990; foreign direct investment grew ten-fold; and generally, industry diversified into higher value-added products, and became better-equipped to compete in OECD markets.

1.05   A key challenge facing the Government during the 1990s will be to design and implement policies that permit a further increase in the long-term growth potential of the economy. Within the productive sectors (agriculture and industry), there remain a number of policy and institutional constraints on growth: the excessive size and low productivity of the state-owned enterprise sector; distortionary tax and incentive policies; barriers to competition; and a persistently high rate of inflation. These issues need to be tackled decisively if Turkey is to catch-up with her main OECD/EC trading partners. However, longer term growth will also depend on the speed and efficiency with which Turkey can become an advanced user and

---

[1] described by Japanese commentators as "industrial rice".

producer of information. This relationship between productivity growth and information resources holds for every sector of the economy. First, in industry and agriculture, Turkish firms need to shift from price-sensitive commodity markets to differentiated product markets. If Turkish producers lack strategic information for technology, customer and competitive analysis, export performance will be "caught in the middle", progressively squeezed between low-wage suppliers (in the commodity markets) and information-driven producers (in high value-added markets). Second, information is a vital resource for the public sector to overcome its productivity problems; and to improve the efficiency of government interventions designed to correct market imperfections and failures. In many cases, market problems (i.e., unemployment in the labor market, credit rationing in the financial markets) are the result of information gaps; and the least cost intervention will be one that deals directly with the underlying information problem rather than its symptom. Third, information is a basic input into the delivery of educational services; and informatics offers an opportunity for Turkey to mobilize additional resources for human capital formation.

1.06   Most fundamentally, information and ideas are the lifeblood of development. The speed with which Turkey joins the ranks of leading OECD economies (and achieves economic integration with Europe) will be largely determined by her participation in the global information market-place. A policy and institutional framework that encourages citizens and organizations to access, exploit and contribute to the stock of global knowledge, can therefore be the handmaiden to overall economic and social progress. Early investment in that framework - while not a substitute for necessary reforms elsewhere in the economy - will have a high return for Turkey.

1.07   This introductory Chapter is organized in four main sections. Section 1 reviews the development of information technology, and the emergence of a unified technological paradigm for information collection, processing and transmission: informatics. Section 2 analyzes the impact of informatics on the transformation of advanced economies. Section 3 assesses the success with which Turkey has taken advantage of informatics; and also some of the constraints on further structural transformation towards an information-based economy. Section 4 outlines the elements of an informatics strategy.

Information Technology: From Paper to Informatics

1.08   Information resources and information technology have always been central to the process of economic modernization. Early Chinese civilization flourished (in part) because of its leadership in paper production and calligraphy. This information technology permitted development of the legal and bureaucratic structures essential to the Chinese empire; and was central to the accumulation and dissemination of social and technical knowledge. In the 15th century, the development of the printing press (first in Korea, and then modified by Guttenberg in Germany) transformed economic structures in Europe, and laid the basis for scientific rationality to displace feudalism as the organizing principle of economic life. Over the subsequent four centuries, printing and paper-making technologies experienced slow but steady increases in productivity; and the costs of information-intensive activities gradually declined.

1.09   It was the development of electricity in the late 18th and early 19th century that paved the way for modern information technology.   The early devices for electrical communication were primitive: the telegraph and morse code.   However, they represented a radical change in the relationship between distance and time; and were instrumental in opening up new geographic markets (e.g., the US hinterlands), and in separating production activities from investment decisions (i.e., the basis for financial capitalism).   The telegraph soon paved the way for a range of more productive information technologies (based on the same fundamental insights into the transmission properties of electro-magnetism): the telephone, telex, radio and ultimately T.V.   Since T.V. requires the transmission of much more information than the telephone, it is no surprise that this technology was the last to be commercialized.   Each successive advance in information technology has broadened cognitive horizons, encouraged the spread of knowledge, and oiled the wheels of social and economic change.

Figure 1.1: Productivity Growth in Information Technology

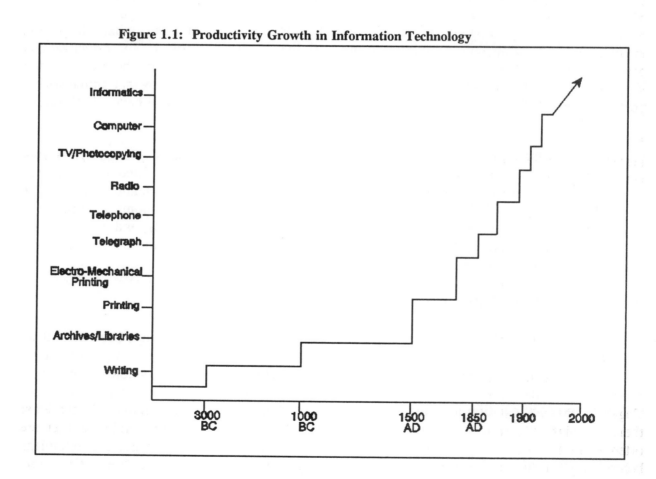

1.10   Over the past 25 years, the pace of change in information technology has dramatically accelerated. As a result, there has been a parallel increase in the rate at which advanced economies are becoming information-intensive. The new information technology is *informatics*; a unified and increasingly powerful technological paradigm for information processing, storage, retrieval and transmission.

1.11   At the heart of informatics (and its basic commodity input) is the semi-conductor chip. A semi-conductor chip is a device (made out of silicon wafer) for conducting electronic signals. Because of special properties inherent to silicon, a semi-conductor chip can store data in the form of electronic bits (where each bit is a positive or negative electronic impulse). In this form, chips can store not only data but also programs of instructions. And chips can be combined into computers (which is an assembly of chips for different information processing operations), or into any other equipment which operates on the basis of systematic and repeated logic. The performance of these chips has improved exponentially over the past two decades, with an approximate doubling of speed and memory size every 3 years. From a technical perspective, the result is that personal computers today have the performance specifications of a 1965 mainframe computer. However, the consequence of technological change is not restricted to the production of computer hardware. Rather the most significant impact of informatics is that chips are now an intermediate input into production equipment and consumption goods throughout the economy. As chips become cheaper and more powerful, they will be integrated into an increasing number of products - improving their performance and permitting customization for specialized market niches.

1.12   Improvements in chip performance (and computer architecture) have dramatically increased information processing power. They have also created demand for innovation in a whole range of complementary skills and technologies, such as:

• lithography and wafer fabrication for chip manufacture;

• packaged and customized software;

• peripherals for data-entry, printing, storage, systems interface, and computer-security;

• visual display units, graphics boards and multimedia devices; and

• data-communications and network equipment.

Together, these industries form the informatics sector. They thrive off each other's innovations; there is a high volume of inter- and intra-industry trade (and vertical integration); and they are often at similar stages in firm and product life-cycle. When one industry within the sector lags behind (e.g., software development), this constrains growth and innovation for the whole sector. The dynamism and cross-fertilization of ideas that characterizes the informatics sector is perhaps without parallel. The sector thrives on a high rate of inter-firm learning, generating geographic clusters of firms that both compete and cooperate. As firms copy ideas, clone the market-leader's products, poach staff and share know-how with each other, they create a unique engine for innovation and growth. The benefits of this innovation spill over into the rest of the economy.

1.13   The continued pace of technological change in informatics poses complex problems for policy-makers, both in advanced and in developing countries. First, the technology has rapidly become so specialized that it is hard for laypeople to understand; and is therefore likely to be subject to ill-informed policy debate (or worse, left to the scientists). Second, the speed of technological change makes longer-term planning difficult. Mis-timed investment decisions - especially for larger projects - may result in costly and premature technological obsolescence. The same problem also occurs in the education sector, where technological uncertainty often results in manpower planning for yesterday's economy. Third, the technological potential of informatics has become progressively at odds with market and institutional reality. Most users of personal computers utilize only a small fraction of their processing capability. Office technology has not replaced support staff; nor has electronic mail been more than a partial substitute for faxes and paper mail. Most consumers prefer cheques to the promise of electronic banking (Box 1.1). Finally, there is a temptation to ignore that the same economic principles apply to informatics as to other industrial sectors. Even in the most

---

Box 1.1: Social Barriers to New Information Technology

When the printing press was introduced in the 1500s, it did not immediately displace earlier forms of information technology. Indeed, monastic scribes continued to reproduce the key religious texts by hand; and the new printers produced mainly the same books, such as the Bible, that were readily available to the tiny minority of the population who was literate. Hand copying continued to be competitive until the early 17th century; and in the region of Paris and Orleans alone, about 10,000 scribes held onto their jobs. Often these scribes copied printed books when the first edition ran out, since it was more economical to meet residual demand by hand. Ultimately, the bourgeois printers prevailed; and gradually overcame Church censorship to produce controversial secular material that is the basis of modern society. Similar problems were experienced in the Ottoman Empire, where the introduction of printing was long resisted by devout Moslems.

The parallel between the introduction of printing and that of informatics is very clear. As in the case of print technology, informatics:

- co-exists alongside earlier information technology;
- initially produced very similar outputs;
- has high initial setup and learning costs;
- is constrained by a lack of literacy;
- is viewed by many as a threat to job security, civil liberties and social discourse; but
- will in the long run generate equally fundamental social and economic change.

advanced economies (i.e., USA, Japan), it is no longer possible to maintain technological leadership in all fields. Hence, international trade is essential to permit economies of specialization that would justify the sector's large research expenditures. Voluntary restraint agreements (e.g., on semiconductor chips), public procurement that favors national champions, and other anti-competitive policies typically undermine rather than foster the intended beneficiary.

Toward an Information-Based Economy

1.14   The pervasive impact of informatics creates the technological environment for an information-based economy (IBE). However, this development will not take place overnight, but is likely to be constrained by the slower evolution of economic structure, cultural mores and public policy. The experience to date of the advanced economies suggests that transition towards an IBE - one in which informatics is ubiquitous - will take place in three main (somewhat stylized) "strategic eras"[2] (Figure 1.2):

- *industrial economy in transition*: in which informatics is largely used in the information-intensive sectors (with marginal uses in other productive sectors);

- *limited information economy*: in which informatics is used to increase the efficiency of existing economic structures; and

- *information-based economy*: in which economic structures are determined largely by their information efficiency.

This economic transformation will inevitably generate certain social costs of adjustment. To foster social acceptance of the transition, governments must provide retraining opportunities for workers whose skills are devalued by informatics, and deal with the very real threat to civil liberties that informatics may create.

1.15   *Industrial Economy in Transition (IET)*. During the first strategic era, information demand growth is concentrated in a small number of economic sectors: e.g., banking, international trade, government administration of tax and security. Investments in information technology and communications infrastructure pick up; but economic returns are constrained by a lack of complementary software, by human capital shortages and by institutional

---

[2] Transition towards an IBE is inevitably a dynamic process, imperfectly captured by a comparative static presentation of "strategic eras". However, the framework presents a practical tool for: (a) cross-country comparisons on key variables; and (b) identifying policy and behavioral constraints on productive use of informatics.

Figure 1.2: Strategic Eras in Transition to Information-Based Economy

	Industrial Economy in Transition	Limited Information Economy	Information Based Economy (IBE)
Information Technology (IT)	Informatics partially substitute for other IT inputs	Informatics partial substitute for other factor inputs (e.g., energy, labor, time)	Informatics becomes an invisible part of economic and social life
Communications	Network Expansion National PTTs manage system	Digital Network Value-added Services liberalized Mobile Communications	Electronic Highway for multi-media information delivery All services liberalized Global Communications System
Human Capital	Development of Informatics Profession Shift to white-collar jobs	Specialization of informatics profession into sub-disciplines	Diffusion of informatics literacy throughout workforce
Information Services	Government major player Rapid growth in private industry	Government as regulator Better access to public data Industry structure consolidates	Further deregulation as industry globalizes Universal access to information as entitlement
Legal System	Intellectual Property Rights (IPRs) enter statute books Existing laws extended to cover computer crimes and privacy	Enforcement of IPRs Data Protection Measures Separate class of computer crimes Informatics as productivity tool for legal profession	Civil Liberties in IBE Informatics changes rules of legal procedures New forms of civil liability
Economic Impact	Informatics investments increase production costs; few measurable benefits Informatics investments mainly in finance, public admin, etc.	Limited productivity growth; but still large gap between performance and potential of informatics Manufacturing, agriculture and retailing invest in informatics	Organizations become information-driven; and realize benefits of informatics investments Faster productivity growth through diffusion of knowledge

failures. Government control of broadcasting (TV and radio) permits information dissemination in support of national educational and cultural goals, but at the expense of a stronger and more innovative private media industry. Information has little legal protection, and the private information industry is slow to modernize. Education systems emphasize rote-learning, and focus on supply of workers more appropriate for a traditional industrial economy. Information gaps and imperfections continue to impose large welfare losses on the economy.

1.16   *Limited Information Economy*. During the second strategic era, informatics becomes more widely diffused through the economy. Lagging sectors (e.g., manufacturing and retailing) rapidly catch-up in their use of informatics; while leading sectors (e.g., financial services) begin to experience a more profound transformation of institutional and market structures. The communications system (both telecom and broadcasting) is liberalized; and there is a burst of private investment in information and media services. Legal protection for information is protected by statute; though this does little to change behavioral patterns. The education system improves its performance in supplying informatics specialists; but the system remains conservative on pedagogical method and curriculum content. The transition towards an IBE remains blocked by a number of institutional and policy constraints. These include: (a) constraints on private access to government information resources; (b) residual monopolistic behavior by the telecom authority; (c) coordination failures in the fields of technical standards and network infrastructure; and (d) institutional and individual barriers to behavioral change.

1.17   *Information-Based Economy (IBE)*. The transition from the second to third strategic era implies a profound structural transformation of the economy. An IBE is not a fantasy world of robotically-controlled "factories of the future" nor of farming communities in Eastern Anatolia electronically browsing through the Library of Congress for latest crop technologies (though some of both may happen). Rather in an IBE, a discrete shift in the information supply curve creates pressure to reorganize private and public sectors of the economy. In the product markets, an IBE may see changes in the optimal size of the firm. As transaction and information costs fall, markets may substitute for firms,[3] reversing the process of 100 years of corporate consolidation in the major capitalist economies. At the same time, distribution systems are likely to experience structural change, as direct marketing techniques (based on customer information databases) allow manufacturers to substitute for more traditional retailing channels.

1.18   Factor markets will also undergo significant change; and indeed, the financial sector in more advanced economies already provides an early case-study of the transition towards IBE (Box 1.2). Similar developments are likely in the labor, land and knowledge markets in which more complete information flows are likely to reduce search costs, sub-optimal resource allocation, and price stickiness. Institutions that evolved as a response to information scarcity

---

[3] See Williamson Markets and Hierarchies: 1985. Practical examples of this phenomenon include: (a) above-average growth rate of the US small business sector; (b) increase in subcontracting in the global auto-industry; and (c) increase in management buy-out activities in the 1980s.

and imperfections (e.g., commercial banks, trade unions, universities) will need to become more organizationally transparent if they are to flourish in an IBE. Moreover, direct government interventions (e.g., employment agencies) in the factor markets will need to be reoriented so that they can more efficiently address the underlying information problem. More generally, government will increasingly see its role in information terms, leaving the private sector to the physical delivery of goods and services (even in the social sectors).

Box 1.2: Information Efficiency in the Financial Sector

Over the past decade, capital markets in advanced economies have grown significantly faster than commercial banks. In part, this can be attributed to the over-exposure of banks to certain types of credit-risk (i.e., Third World debt, commercial real estate in the US). However, it is also due to informational advantages enjoyed by capital markets. Banks are highly non-transparent institutions. It is hard to assess the market value of their asset portfolio; product pricing contains significant cross-subsidies; and financial engineering lowers the information content of audits and other financial statements. By contrast, capital markets: (a) react rapidly to news through changes in market values; (b) do not permit sustained cross-subsidization (even in the delivery of services to small investors); and (c) provide information very efficiently to investors through financial asset prices. However, the growth of capital markets has not been problem free:

- they may be too volatile with regard to information;

- there are severe problems of inside information;

- the large institutional investors may be as non-transparent as the banks in the way they conduct affairs; and

- the information demands placed by capital markets on public companies (i.e., quarterly statements) may be counter-productive to longer-term planning and investment.

Informational efficiency does not appear to correlate in any simple way with economic performance.

1.19   The speed of adjustment from the second to third strategic era is likely to be in inverse relation to the high economic costs of change. Even in the more advanced economies, the change is only beginning. The real problems of adjustment lie not only in (as yet) unresolved technical issues, in the costs of an enabling communications infrastructure, or in the social costs of adjustment. Rather, the problems are ones of deeply ingrained habits, cultural mores and assumptions about the way to do business. An IBE will provide an environment for information entrepreneurs: people who supply new goods and services through combining the unique resources of an IBE in imaginative and efficient ways. The creative skills essential for this task are not well-known; but may not be acquired through mimicking the behavioral traits of individuals with successful career and business strategies in today's economy. Rather, the problem is more likely to be solved through inter-generational skill transformation. It is the children that grow up with informatics that will be best able to negotiate their economic lives in an information-based economy.

1.20   While the broad outlines of an IBE and the necessary transition path are relatively well-defined, many of the details remain to be articulated and are likely to be highly culturally specific. In the USA, for example, the evolving IBE is structured around a vigorous private sector providing competing information goods and services. Government's role is regulatory (especially in the communications sector), to supply data[4] which it is uniquely positioned to collect and store, and to provide funding for research and development efforts. In more centrally planned market economies (e.g., France), the Government is playing a more expanded role in supplying the communications infrastructure, defining and producing the technology, and in supplying information services. The two models have competing merits. A market-based strategy for transition toward an IBE takes advantage of private sector dynamism to provide innovative information-based goods and services; but suffers from problems of technical incompatibilities and barriers to change (because of vested interests in a fragmented media industry structure). On the other hand, a greater injection of central planning can accelerate investment in more advanced infrastructure (e.g., a fibre-optics network) and can impose common technical standards; but at a potential cost of less innovation, greater concentration of risk and reduced specialization. The key for Turkey will be to increase the efficiency of her own learning by copying the best elements of both models.

Evolution of Turkey's Information Economy

1.21   *Historic Evolution.* Until 1980, a combination of central planning and policy barriers to competition (both domestic and foreign trade-based) limited private sector demand for information (and derivatively for information technology). Because competition was restricted, private sector agents could still earn high profits without investing either in techno-commercial information or in a management tier, specialized in corporate strategy, marketing, finance, R&D, etc. As a result, most information-intensive activities were concentrated within the public sector: planning in the central government, project appraisal in the state enterprises and ministries, and (to some extent) credit analysis in the public sector banks. Continued growth of the public sector through the 1960s and 1970s created the basis for further expansion of information-based employment; however without accompanying productivity gains.[5]

---

[4] Information is data with value-added of processing, marketing and distribution. The private information industry in the USA argues that these value-added services are properly carried out in the market, and that the public sector role should be restricted to data collection and storage (since data not information is a true public good).

[5] Growth of an information-based economy is therefore *not* necessarily welfare-enhancing. Public sector expansion is not the only problem. Recent evidence from the US suggests that excessive corporate overheads (associate primarily with growth in management occupations) has been a tax on productivity growth since the 1970s. See Katz, The Information Society: An International Perspective (Praeger, 1988).

1.22   The beginning of the policy reform process occurred in 1981. As the government reduced policy-related distortions and barriers in the product and factor markets, private demand for information (and for information technology) slowly began to respond. The response was not however instantaneous; and rather a number of factors led the private sector to delay its response. First, it was not initially clear whether the policy reforms were irreversible; or that therefore private companies should change investment strategy and operational behavior. Second, poor communications infrastructure reduced the return on investments in informatics relative to other resource allocations. This problem was compounded by high rates of taxation on computers and other forms of information technology (which unlike other capital equipment was not exempt from customs duty until 1986). Third, development of a professional (i.e., information-processing) class is a longer-term project for the corporate sector, and even today requires considerable investment in human capital and organizational change. Institutional stickiness in the private sector therefore constrained the speed with which market-based demand for information increased in the early 1980s.

Figure 1.3: Informatics Investment (1981-90) $ millions

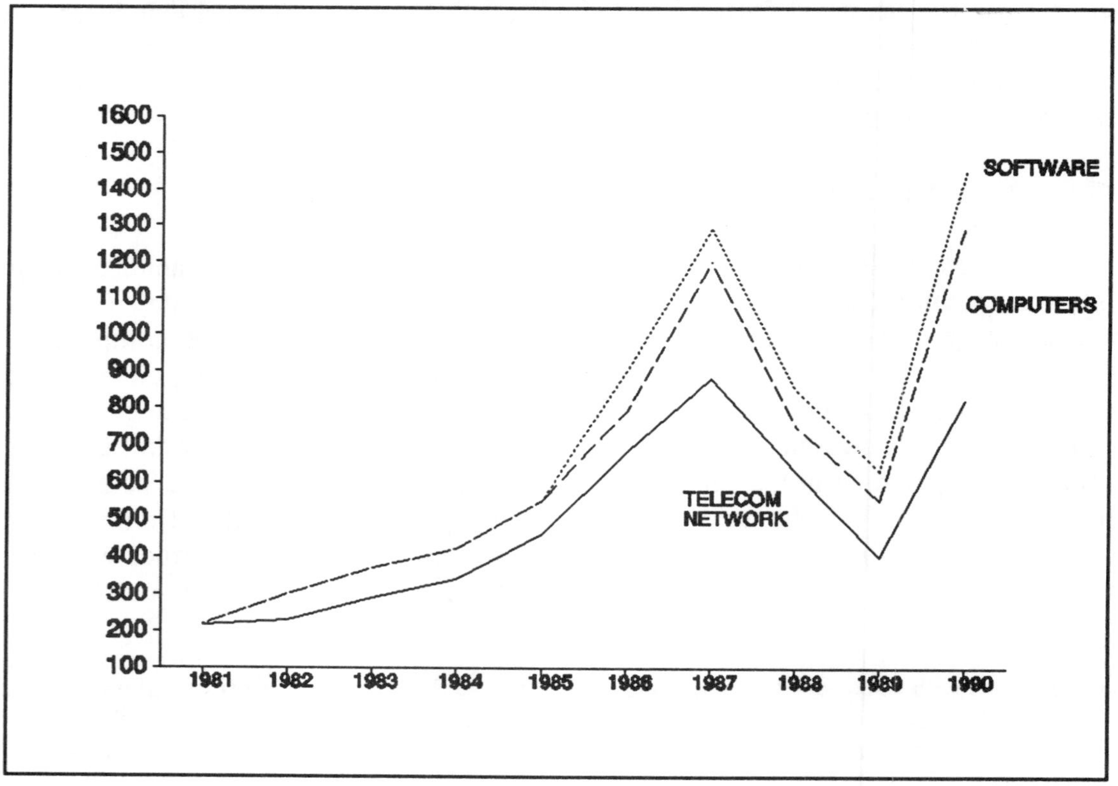

1.23   After 1985, investment in informatics picked up sharply both in the public and private sectors. Three main forces were at work. First, government decided to increase public investment in the communications infrastructure. PTT (which previously had been starved of resources) embarked on a sustained investment program; and over the remainder of the decade invested almost 1% of GNP per annum (equivalent to approximately 4% of total capital formation in the Turkish economy). This investment both stimulated a significant supply response from Turkish private industry but also served to catalyze large complementary investments in terminal and computer equipment. Second, the tariff on computer equipment was dropped from over 50% to a duty- exempt category (albeit that the equipment is still subject to a range of other import "special levies", which raise its price above international levels). Moreover, as the informatics market in Turkey grew and became more attractive to international suppliers, Turkey benefited from increasing price competition, product differentiation and improved vendor services. The result of these open market policies is that Turkish companies have unrestricted access to globally competitive informatics technology.

1.24   Investment in informatics has remained relatively concentrated in sectors of the economy that are intrinsically information-intensive: certain aspects of central government, financial sector, travel (i.e., airlines and international hotel reservations), higher education, and select operations of large companies (especially the multinationals). In these fields, informatics has been used to increase productivity; but without challenging basic assumptions about how the organizations should function. For example, the commercial banks (repeating the experience of many OECD countries) have invested heavily in state-of-the-art ATMS. But customer service remains poor; many transactions still require human interfacing; there has been only limited success to reduce costs through more extensive applications of electronic banking (e.g., debit cards); and commercial bank profitability does not appear to have improved as a direct result of the investments. Similarly, many central government investments in informatics have generated below-forecast returns as a result of: (a) inadequate investment in complementary human capital; (b) poor integration of informatics with agency missions; and (c) software development problems.

1.25   In other sectors of the economy - manufacturing, agriculture, distribution services - the informatics penetration rate still appears to be low (compared with other OECD economies). To a large extent, manufacturing investment in informatics appears to be concentrated in the automation of payroll and of other administrative functions, rather than in the production process itself. With a small number of exceptions, informatics has not become integral to corporate strategy; and information technology professionals are isolated from the corporate management stream. The vast majority of small and medium enterprises make no (or very little) use of informatics. A similar pattern predominates in the agricultural and retail sectors. These sectors are still highly fragmented (largely because of land market rigidities); and have yet to go through the cycle of consolidation and modernization experienced in other OECD economies. The result is that these sectors (with certain exceptions) have been protected from the pressure to upgrade technologically and to become more information-intensive.

1.26   Informatics demand remains concentrated in a relatively narrow range of goods and services. Telecom network equipment and informatics hardware are the largest market segments; and there is a revealed reluctance to pay for informatics intangibles and services. As a result, the software, computer services, systems integration, and electronic information services markets all lag behind the degree of technological sophistication attained in the hardware segment. Where these services are purchased, they are often bundled into hardware contracts to minimize their perceived cost. And frequently, the absence of legal protection for intellectual property results in software piracy, stealing of trade secrets, employee poaching, and breaches of copyright for information copying (both in paper and electronic formats). If Turkey is to follow international experience, increased supply of intangible informatics services is a prerequisite for graduation to an IBE.

1.27   Despite economic liberalization during the 1980s, the public sector still plays a dominant role in Turkey's information economy. The public sector is the largest purchaser of informatics goods and services, especially of major systems. The Government retains control over the telecommunication network, and (with diminishing resolve) the broadcasting system for radio and television. New communications media - mobile telephony, data transmission services, cable TV - which could have been an opportunity for private business (without undermining network externalities) have not yet been liberalized. In addition, there are inadequacies in the institutional and technical framework for disseminating public sector information. As a result, the private information industry - from publishers through marketing consultants to the accountancy profession - has not yet moved up the growth/learning curve of rapid employment expansion, knowledge accumulation and horizontal integration.

1.28   In the 1980s, Turkey succeeded in taking a short-cut to a more information-based economy. Growth in information demand was concentrated in core government functions and Turkey's top 100 corporations. Informatics was managed as a highly specialized business: the preserve of mainframe installations, electronic data-processing centers and computer scientists and engineers. Much of the equipment could be imported, and human capital constraints overcome by a small cadre of specialized professionals. However, it is the transition towards a more sophisticated information-based economy that is proving more difficult: one based on highly decentralized uses of information, informatics applications distributed throughout organizations, and a vigorous private information industry.

1.29   *Cross-Country Comparisons.* Turkey has made impressive progress over the past 5 years in the supply and applications of informatics. In the most dynamic sectors of the economy (i.e., finance), informatics applications are on or close to the international technology frontier. However, in a number of critical respects, Turkey continues to lag behind the competition - and has further steps to take in order to catch-up. The importance of informatics catch-up is not merely to build market share in the informatics markets themselves. Rather, as the global economy becomes more information-based, the competitive supply and use of informatics is likely to be an important factor determining overall economic performance.

1.30   Table 1.1 compares Turkey with other OECD and NIC economies along a number of variables that are indicators of the *information-intensity of the economy*. These indicators capture the extent to which economies have:

●   become advanced users of informatics (computer hardware and software investment per capita; percentage of this investment spent on software);

●   developed and are allocating resources to their telecommunications infrastructure (telephone lines per 100; telecom investment/GNP);

Table 1.1: Cross-Country Informatics Indicators
1985-90

	USA	Japan	Spain	Mexico	Korea	Turkey (85)	Turkey (90)
Informatics Market							
IT Investment per Capita (1)	400	400	110	14	45	3	12
Software as % of IT (%)	42	35	31	36	24	7	13
PCs/Total Computers (%)	45	30	50	55	40	17	44
* IT Exports (Hardware) $B	21	17	n.a.	0.5	3.5	0	0.02
Communications Infrastructure							
Telephone Lines per 100	52	41	31	6	29	5	14
Telecom Investment /GDCF (%)	2.8	1.9	2.4	0.5	4.5	4.4	3.4
Human Capital							
White Collar/Total Workforce	67	55	43	33	44	22	23
Professional & Technical/T.W.	16	11	9	7	8	4	5
Computer Student/Million (2)	1000	830	550	230	1100	130	160
R&D/GNP (%)	2.9	2.9	0.7	0.4	1.8	0.1	0.2
Information Services							
Newspaper/1000	259	566	75	124	208	67	70
Televisions/1000	812	589	380	124	203	159	172
Advertising Revenue per Capita	479	281	151	n.a.	n.a.	4	11

Note: (1)   IT equals hardware and software expenditures
         (2)   Computer students includes degrees in computer science services & related engineering fields [estimates]
         (3)   Where numbers are in values; they are US$ estimates
         (4)   Data is from 1988-1990

Sources: OECD, NSF, UNESCO, World Bank Data.

- shifted human resources towards information-handling activities (white collar and professionals/total workforce, computer students/million);

- invested in the production of knowledge (R&D/GNP); and

- a vibrant private information industry (newspaper circulation/1000; advertizing revenues per capita).

The indicators suggest that Turkey is catching up with its peer group of OECD/NIC economies; but still has significant requirements in terms of capital investment and resource reallocation.

1.31   *Computer Hardware and Software.*   Despite rapid growth in hardware investment, Turkey continues to experience a number of deficits with respect to comparator countries.   First, IT investment per capita is very low and appears to be a reflection of: (a) structural differences between Turkey and other OECD economies (i.e., high share of agriculture); (b) scarce public sector investment funds; and (c) scarcity of qualified personnel, which reduces return on hardware investments.   Second, the software industry remains in an infant stage compared to major competitors.   The software-IT investment ratio is substantially lower than in other countries; exports are insignificant; there is no or little foreign investment (because inter alia of inadequate legal protection); and the industry is still dominated by hardware vendors who bundle software products into their complete system.   Third, there is no local supply (except of PCs) of computers or IT components.   In many respects, this situation is highly advantageous for Turkey, which can capture the benefits from international investment (frequently OECD government subsidized) in informatics research and development.   Moreover, local buyers of computer hardware can source frontier informatics technology globally without any "moral suasion" to buy from a more restricted set of national vendors.   Nevertheless, a strategic issue for the Government is whether targeted programs to stimulate a competitive local supply in selective informatics market niches may generate benefits for the economy as a whole.

1.32   *Telecom.*   Turkey has achieved striking success in catching up in the telecom sector.   The network coverage has increased significantly; and service quality has also improved due to the introduction of advanced digital transmission and switching technology.   While the low number of lines per 100 population still points to a lack of universal service, there appears to be no major deficiency with regard to key users in the productive and administrative sectors of the economy.   Given the geographically dispersed nature of the population in Turkey (and low revealed demand for telecom services in rural areas), it is unlikely that universal service will be achieved in the next decade.   The main challenge for the Government will be to capitalize on the communications assets created during the 1980s through policies designed to strengthen the international competitiveness of PTT's service, and to create new opportunities for private sector investment.

1.33   *Human Capital*. Perhaps the most severe deficit that Turkey faces is in the area of human capital for an information-based economy. The formal education system has not been able to respond adequately to the shift in occupational structure; nor to the need for a specialized informatics workforce. Compared to more advanced economies, Turkey appears to be falling behind in:

- the diffusion of computer literacy throughout the workforce;

- the supply of specialized informatics professionals - people to run the mainframes, write software, and design information networks for large organization;

- the quality of these professionals in a market that is demanding increasingly specialized skills; and

- the system for skills upgrading and retraining in the face of a rapid changing set of technologies.

Turkey produces less informatics professionals than Singapore - a country with only 2.2 million people. Although universities attract the brightest 1% of students to their computer engineering departments, it is not clear whether this talent is properly developed. Graduates rarely have the multi-disciplinary skills necessary to combine technical know-how with business insights. Nor does it seem that Turkey is adequately positioning herself to educate a new generation of workers and citizens as informatics users and information entrepreneurs.

1.34   *Information Services*. Compared to societies that have progressed further towards an information-based economy, the private information industry in Turkey has a catch-up opportunity over the next decade. In other OECD economies, the private information industry expanded rapidly during the 1980s, driven by both technological change and market liberalization (though the pace of change clearly varied across countries). In additional to rapid growth, the industry in more advanced economies enjoyed an era of: (a) horizontal integration across previously disparate information media and services; (b) growing cross-border investments and acquisitions by international media companies; and (c) emergence of a proliferation of small information providers as technological change lowered (investment cost) barriers to entry. In Turkey, the private information industry has not so far evolved along these lines; and is not yet positioned to support transformation of the Turkish economy. The industry remains fragmented; advertizing ratios suggest limited demand for consumer information; there is little integration across information services; and growth has been only marginally greater than that of GNP. Television broadcasting is the most active segment of the industry (given high rates of TV penetration); but regulatory uncertainty continues to postpone large-scale private investment.

1.35   *Conclusions*. Over the past decade, Turkey has been able to develop some of the resources for an information-based economy. With respect to *traded informatics goods* -

computers, communications equipment, capital equipment with embedded chips and software - Turkish organizations have been able to buy the latest technology at competitive prices. Public and private organizations have been able to capture the benefit of open market policies; and to close the productivity gap with the international competition. Given the pace of change in the informatics sector, Turkey may have benefited by coming late to the technology.

1.36   However, Turkey is less well-positioned to combine traded informatics goods with the *non-traded* complementary inputs that are essential for world-class applications. What Turkey principally lacks is not access to the latest technology, but the other less mobile factors of production for an information-based economy (Figure 1.4):

Figure 1.4: Complementary Inputs for an Information-Based Economy

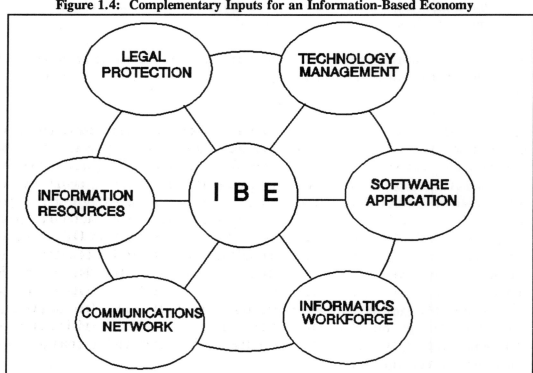

- the technical and management skill-base essential to be a superior computer user;

- the software and computer services industry that can customize informatics to local market conditions;

- an education and training system that can deliver: (a) a broadly computer literate workforce; (b) informatics specialists in line with market requirements; and (c) retraining opportunities;

- an innovative communications sector that creates competitive advantage for the business sector through unique configurations of network resources;

- a private information industry that provides services specifically tailored to the needs of the domestic suppliers, consumers and potential foreign investors; and

- a legal framework that balances public and private interests as they evolve in an information-based economy.

These non-traded inputs cannot be bought; but have to be created domestically through superior policies and the reform of institutional arrangements rendered obsolete and inefficient by informatics.

1.37   As competitive advantage in international markets becomes increasingly a function of superior information resources, it is essential that Turkey catch-up with competitors in developing these non-tradeable assets to complement the technological hardware. However, the quantitative indicators in Table 1.1 provide only a partial account of the difficulties that Turkey faces in accomplishing this objective. A more profound constraint is likely to be represented by Turkey's overall stage of development. Despite the economic modernization that took place in the 1980s, there are still significant differences between Turkey and other OECD economies. These include: (a) the large proportion of the population that lives in the countryside; (b) the relatively small formal employment sector; (c) a demographic profile that is significantly younger than that of other OECD countries; (d) more recent accumulation of private industrial/financial capital; (e) widespread perception of information as a free or public good; and (f) the relatively greater role of the public sector in the economy. The vision of Turkey as an information-based economy needs to recognize these differences; and to consciously model strategies that take advantage of them.

Strategy

1.38   The single most important policy for an information-based economy is commitment to open competitive markets. These create the pressure for increased productivity, and thereby for investment in information and in advanced applications of informatics. Within this framework, this Report would propose a strategy for IBE development based on four main focus areas:

- *harnessing the private sector*: to foster competitive domestic suppliers in the markets for information technology, goods and services;

- *informing the workforce*: to align human resource strategy and education delivery mechanisms with the needs of an information-based economy;

- *modernizing the public sector*: to increase productivity and innovation in public sector services through better use of information technology.

- *regulating information*: to safeguard civil liberties and consumer choice against risks created by informatics.

These focus areas mirror the four major stakeholders in an information-based economy: enterprises, the workforce, citizens/consumers and the government. They therefore provide an agenda that addresses the relationship between informatics and economic modernization, but without ignoring the social consequences. As in other cases of technological change, informatics creates the potential for significant but unevenly distributed welfare gains. A key role for the Government is therefore to support equitable distribution of informatics-generated benefits through investment in complementary human capital, protection of civil liberties, regulation of monopolies (in markets for information services) and improved delivery of public services.

1.39   *Private Sector Development*. Technological change and innovation takes place largely at the enterprise (or agency) level. The informatics markets exhibit an exceptionally high rate of inter-firm technology diffusion, and vendor-user interactive learning. The communications sector is experiencing an era of rapid technological change as more competitive market structures substitute for state monopolies over telecom services. Within the private information industry, the lines between broadcasting, printing and publishing, telecom services and information search/retrieval activities have become increasingly blurred, as innovations in one media market spill over into the others. Productivity growth in all these markets is largely the consequence of competitive pressure, and of private enterprise initiative. If Turkey is to accelerate her transition towards an IBE, the policy framework must therefore support: (a) private investment in complementary inputs (para. 1.36); (b) a reduced direct role for the state in the information and communications sector; and (c) direct foreign investment for technology transfer. This implies implementation of reforms in the communications sector (Chapter 5), in TV and radio broadcasting (Chapter 6), in intellectual property rights (Chapters 3 and 7), and in the framework for private sector technology development (Chapters 2 and 3).

1.40   *Human Resource Strategy*. Further development of an information-based economy during the 1990s will be progressively human-capital intensive. The essence of an IBE is a diffused application of informatics throughout the Turkish economy; and the substitution of knowledge and information (much of which will be embodied in informatics) for low-skill labor and other inputs. In realizing this vision, Turkey's main constraint today is not the technology, but rather the supply of professionals with *specific skills* in informatics and the diffusion of *general skills* in information-handling throughout the workforce. In certain respects, Turkey has a natural advantage over other OECD economies in development of an IBE-compatible workforce. The age structure of Turkey's population is significantly lower than that of other OECD economies; and the gap is likely to grow over the next two decades. This means that Turkish industry should enjoy a wage-cost advantage over EC economies, but only if human capital investments close the productivity gap. A key set of issues (addressed in Chapter 4) is therefore how the Government can: (a) enhance the responsiveness of the higher education system to market demand for informatics professionals; (b) increase private sector resource allocation to informatics training; and (c) foster behavioral change among the younger generation to create a new class of information entrepreneurs.

1.41   *Public Sector Management.* The Government has invested massively (over $500 million) in computer systems over the past decade, but with limited results in terms of cost efficiency and innovation. Despite various attempts to coordinate investment, improve procurement practices and develop complementary human resources, computerization does not appear to have resulted in any measurable increase in public sector productivity. Nor has the Government been able to exploit the potential externalities from its investments for technological development and skills formation in the private sector. In addition, there appear to be severe problems in using informatics to facilitate the flow of information between agencies, and between the public and private sectors. Again, the problem is not technological. Rather, it is one of reengineering government to capture the potential efficiency gains generated by informatics. The challenge for the public sector (addressed in Chapters 2, 3 and 6) is to find new ways to: (a) strengthen government information flows (inter-agency and with the private sector); (b) use informatics as a productivity tool and as a platform for improved service quality; and (c) deploy government's buying power in the informatics markets as an instrument for efficient industrial development.

1.42   *Regulation to Protect Citizen Rights.* The transition towards an information-based economy (IBE) creates potential welfare losses as well as gains. Technological change always poses new social and economic risks, and informatics is no exception. First, informatics provides the technological platform for new intrusions on civil liberty as public (and private) organizations process increasing volumes of sensitive personal information. Informatics also creates the potential for new classes of crime (e.g., through unauthorized entry into computerized bank accounts), the generation of misleading information (e.g., through manipulation of digital images), and new standards of civil liability (as computer-related failures impose large economic losses on society). Second, informatics permits the introduction of new information services (e.g., cable TV, electronic bulletin boards, 1-900 telephone services) which need to be subject to a consistent regulatory framework, especially with regard to information content. More generally, market behavior does not always create incentives for appropriate disclosure of information. Rather, even advanced economies experience repeated instances of information gaps (often at the expense of shareholders and creditors), false or misleading advertizing (at the expense of consumers), and information over-supply (e.g., in insurance contracts) (para. 6.48). If Turkey is to accelerate her transition to an IBE, it is important that the Government take preemptive action to reduce risks associated with informatics and information imperfections. A major fraud or abuse of privacy could set back the social acceptance of informatics by years. Measures are therefore needed to: (a) strengthen the legal framework for informatics, particularly in the areas of data-confidentiality and computer crime (Chapter 7); (b) develop a consistent regulatory framework on issues of information content (Chapter 5); and (c) enforce better information standards in the market-place (Chapter 6).

1.43   The success of this IBE strategy will ultimately depend on the overall economic framework of the Government. Policies that foster greater competition, create a stable environment for investment and innovation, and strengthen human resources are per se conducive of further progress towards an IBE. Assuming that these factors are in place, it is likely that Turkey will continue to accumulate "complementary inputs" even in the absence of a more targeted strategy. However, if Turkey is to catch up, to attract foreign investment into the informatics sector and to build a competitive supply of informatics goods and services, she must accumulate these complementary inputs at a rate faster than competitors. Turkey's potential to be a supplier - as well as a user - of informatics technology will depend on government's ability to implement the principles of "new industrial policy", firmly grounded in competitive markets, human capital, innovation mechanisms, sophisticated demand-side pressures, regulation and standards. A dedicated strategy around which key stakeholders in Turkey's information economy can plan and invest should contribute significantly to realizing that target.

1.44   *Organization of Report*. This Report is organized in six main chapters which together articulate a strategy for Turkey's transition to an information-based economy. Chapter 2 focuses primarily on the constraints to best practice computer use in Turkey, but also on the potential for Turkish suppliers to enter international computer markets. Chapter 3 assesses the opportunity for Turkey to become an internationally competitive supplier of software services; and the policies and institutions needed to achieve that target. Chapter 4 turns to the central issue of human capital formation, and examines ways to improve the supply response of the education system to rapidly evolving market demand for informatics specialists and general computer literacy. Chapter 5 addresses the need for a strategic shift in the communications sector to build upon successes enjoyed in the 1980s. Chapter 6 outlines the potential for policy reform to foster a dynamic and creative private information industry; while Chapter 7 considers the need for further modifications to the legal framework in light of the economic and social changes induced by informatics. Chapter 8 develops an IBE action plan (drawing upon the main recommendation of the Report), and compares institutional options for effective implementation.

CHAPTER 2

CREATING COMPUTER ADVANTAGE

Introduction

2.01   Computers are a core technological input into information-based economies. Global investment in computers and related information technology has grown rapidly over the past decade, and is now equivalent to 2% of global GNP. By 2000 this percentage is forecast to double. It is far less clear however, that these investments have translated into commensurate increase in productivity. Rather, the performance of computer technology appears to have outstripped the capability (and perceived requirements) of most computer users. Over the next decade, international competitiveness and productivity growth will largely depend on the effectiveness with which computers can be applied across the economy. Policies that help to close the gap between computer potential and performance will generate a high economic return.

2.02   The computer industry is itself viewed by policymakers in many advanced economies as a "strategic industry". Japan and the European Community both have explicit programs to support research into next-generation computing techniques. The US Government, so long opposed to active industrial policy, also deploys a range of research and procurement instruments to provide support to its computer industries. There are a number of standard justifications offered for these subsidies. These include: (a) national security; (b) the externalities from technological progress in the computer industry; and (c) trade balance considerations. The computer industry has replaced steel and autos as a benchmark of economic competitiveness. Surprisingly, much less government support has been provided to the community of computer users, where in large part the productivity problems lie. This policy omission provides an opportunity for countries, such as Turkey, to differentiate their strategy for computerization.

2.03   In Turkey, the market-based strategy for economic modernization adopted in the 1980s has resulted in rapid adoption of computer technology. Trade barriers are low, direct foreign investment is encouraged, and there is no public sector bias towards locally supplied computer hardware. In all these respects, Turkey's policy environment has been diametrically opposed to that of e.g., Brazil, which attempted to attain a high degree of informatics self-sufficiency. The policy has been highly successful, and the Turkish economy has captured benefits from the subsidies provided by other OECD governments to their computer industries. Annual investment has grown from $85 million in 1985 to over $500 million by 1990. Turkey is taking advantage of being a latecomer; and the 3 year average vintage of its computer park compares favorably with all other OECD nations.

2.04   Over the next decade, Turkey can look forward to growing investment in information technology. Further integration with the global economy together with competitive pressure will be sufficient conditions for increased computerization. There will be a further diffusion of computers to the social, small business and residential sectors. And improvements will take place in the way that private and public organizations use their computer assets. However, if Turkey is to become a world-class user of computers, and a competitive supplier, then a more aggressive strategy needs to be designed and implemented. First, the public sector can have a significant and positive impact on productivity of computer use. The public sector is the single largest user of computers, and therefore its procurement and computer management practices affect the behavior of computer vendors, facilitate the introduction of consistent technical standards, and influence best practice in the private sector. Second, government policy is central to the development of a local computer (and related IT hardware) industry. At a general level, the policies of low inflation, product market competition, and efficient financial markets apply to computer production in the same way as in other industrial sectors. However, the research and development intensity of computers, the rate of technological and market change, and implications of local supply for productive use create the analytic basis for catalytic interventions by government.

2.05   This Chapter is organized in three main sections, which reflect policy sequencing consistent with Turkey's progression from competitive user to supplier of computers (and related product family). Section one therefore examines key technological developments in computer hardware over the last decade, and reviews state-of-the-art user practices. Section two looks to the Turkish market, and assesses the success of the public and private sector as computer users. A central message of this section is that the Government, by facilitating more productive use of computers, can differentiate Turkey from other OECD countries, whose policy focus has been principally on the supply-side. Section three then turns to the prospects for Turkish companies as suppliers in the international hardware markets. An annex provides a technical overview of hardware technology, and considers specific opportunities for Turkish industry.

Technological Development and Best Practice Computer Use

2.06   Rapid declines in the cost of hardware over the past 25 years have resulted in computerization of advanced societies. Initially employed only for scientific and engineering calculations and later for certain business data processing calculations, computer technology has now diffused throughout the manufacturing, education, communications, agriculture, medicine and defence sectors. In the world of business, data-processing machines that were once confined to payroll and accounting now form the core of modern corporations. They are increasingly relied upon to help create documents, route messages, analyze financial data, conduct banking transactions, handle airline reservations, run the telephone system, determine marketing strategies, manage manufacturing process, and gain access to vast amounts of information stored in electronic databases. In the world of scientific calculation, computers are now a key productivity tool for research and are used to design transportation vehicles, guide satellites, predict the weather, explore for oil, increase food production, develop new pharmaceuticals, investigate the atom, and map the human genome. In the public sector, computers play a major role not only in defence, but also in handling the information flows, which are the main input (and largest cost) to the delivery of public services, and design of efficient policies. In short, computers have become indispensable.

2.07   A series of technological innovations has driven this process of computerization (Figure 2.1). In the 1960s time sharing, which distributes computer power from a single mainframe machine among dozens of users in numerous locations, became commercially viable. In the 1970s, very large scale integrated (VLSI) circuits made possible the processor on a chip, which in turn made computers ubiquitous, faster, cheaper and more powerful, while computer memories grew bigger, cheaper, and more reliable.   These chips are now incorporated (invisibly) into a vast array of manufacturing equipment, consumer products, construction materials, vehicles, and measurement devices.   In the 1980s, the personal computer has captivated millions of people through easy-to-learn programs for spreadsheets, word-processing, databases, and business graphics.   At the same time, computer networks have become more widespread, interconnecting many personal and time-shared machines, thereby redefining computer architecture within and between organizations.   In the 1990s, miniaturization of computer components has made the technology mobile.

Figure 2.1: Decentralizing the Computer

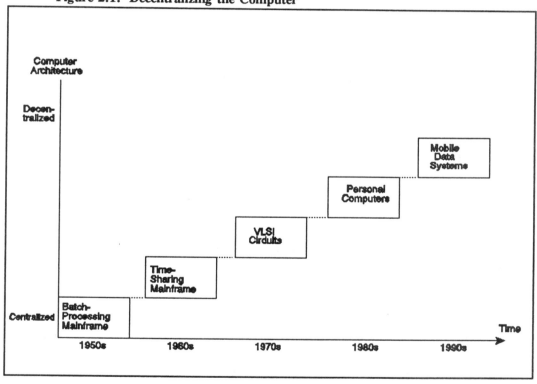

2.08   Current technological trends suggest continuation, if not acceleration, in the rate of technological progress accompanied by even more useful and powerful applications. There are two areas in which major advances can be expected over the next decade. First, commercial applications of multi-processor technology are beginning to appear. With the introduction of multiprocessors technology, mainframes, mid-size computers, and PCs would all be based on the same chips and a unified computer architecture. This will permit configurations of data-processing power that are economical, scalable, and potentially more powerful than those available today. That power should help multiprocessors achieve ambitious new applications of artificial intelligence (e.g., real-time speech translation, machine vision, and computer learning); and also expand the research possibilities of physical science through massive computer simulations (e.g., of the greenhouse effect). Second, the technology for computer interfaces and graphical visualization will see further advances. Direct manipulation of objects on the screen is already replacing traditional, much less user-friendly interaction via typed command languages. In the future, there will be voice recognition and pen-based interfaces, thereby increasing the cognitive and behavioral ease with which computers can be used.

2.09   Despite these impressive technological accomplishments, the productivity with which computers are used and the techniques for computer management have not kept pace. The potential benefits of computer investments are many: increased responsiveness to clients, reduced time-based costs, lower coordination and transaction costs, and enhanced competitive

---

Box 2.1: Computers in Banking

During the 1970s and 1980s, US Banks invested massively in information technology (IT). They account for 20% of total US expenditure on IT; and outside the communications sector, they are the most IT-intensive businesses. By 1989, IT accounted for 45% of the banking sector's fixed assets. Although service customer quality has improved, financial performance has not:

- employment growth slowed only marginally from 1% to 0.3% per annum, suggesting only limited IT-labor substitution;

- non-performing loans increased as a percentage of total assets, despite the introduction of expert systems for credit-analysis;

- the introduction of Automatic Teller Machines (ATMs) added to costs rather than profits, since no bank could translate this IT into a sustainable competitive advantage; and

- banks have had only limited success in using IT (e.g., debit cards) to reduce the 50 billion check-based transactions in the US, each of which costs approximately $1 to process.

The potential of IT cannot be realized in regulatory framework for the banking sector that inhibits competition and encourages low-quality lending. In the US regulatory framework, IT cannot increase banking efficiency through scale economies in data-processing. Rather, IT investments have added to the banking sector's fixed costs, and thereby contributed to the sector's vulnerable financial position.

advantage. However, in practice, most public and private organizations appear to generate only a fraction of these benefits and belatedly discover that computers add more to costs than to profits. A number of recent studies provide compelling evidence that unless properly managed, investments in information technology may be both unproductive and unprofitable. The MIT Center for Advanced Engineering analyzed a large sample of corporations, and found no correlation between computer investments and improvement in profit. A well-known study carried out by the senior economist of Morgan Guaranty demonstrates that productivity in the service sector - which is the largest investor in information technology - barely increased during the 1980s.[1] Despite massive investments in computers, the financial position of the US banking sector (and that in a number of other OECD countries) appears to have deteriorated during the last decade. Moreover, the rate of productivity growth in the Japanese economy has been much greater than that in the US, despite US lead as a supplier and investor in computer hardware and software.

2.10   This gap between computer potential and performance is alarming; and appears to be explained by two main factors. First, effective use of information technology requires an integration of technical know-how with detailed business understanding. Computers add value when they support business reengineering along more efficient lines i.e., eliminating layers of management and internal paper-trails that slow down response-time. In the absence of accompanying organizational change, computers only result in marginal process improvements. Second, introduction of computer technology has high associated management and support cost. The technology cannot simply be plugged into the nearest electrical socket, and then switched on. Rather, effective use of computer requires a set of complementary investments in the process of: (a) defining system requirements; (b) information flow reengineering; (c) system and software design; (d) implementation and unit testing; (e) end-user training; and (f) staffing, operation and maintenance (Figure 2.2). The same MIT study also found profit improvement in those companies that spend a large proportion (about half) of their computer and office technology budgets on support and implementation.[2]

2.11   *Computers and Business Reengineering*. When computers are used merely to automate existing business processes, the return on investment is very limited. Organizations that are effective computer users have seized the opportunity to redesign business processes

---

[1] Technology and the Services Sector: The Hidden Competitive Challenge; Steven Roach, Technological Forecasting and Social Change, 34, 287-403 (1988).

[2] Paul Strassman in The Business Value of Computers (1990) estimates the first year cost of a personal computer at $12,000, of which only $2,000 can be directly attributed to computer hardware. Related technology costs (i.e., software, data-com, LAN services) account for a further $3,000; while organizational costs (training, support staff, reorganization expenses) amount to $7,000.

Figure 2.2: Managing Computers

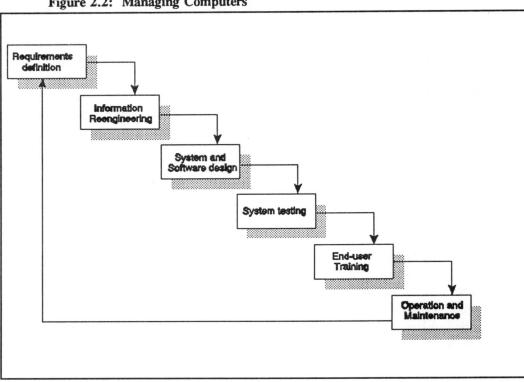

around their computer investments, rather than vice versa.[3]   Successful users are able to radically shorten the product-cycle, improve product and service quality, move towards flexible manufacturing systems, implement just-in-time production scheduling, restructure their relations with suppliers and distributors, enter new markets and reshape customer purchasing habits (Box 2.2). However, the number of success stories is quite small; and there are at least as many problem cases in which system development projects have been scrapped after multi-million dollar investments, there has been no substitution of computers for other factors of production, or massive information technology investments have failed to reverse declines in profitability or market share. One example is General Motors, which is the largest corporate user of computers outside the information industry. Despite acquisition of a specialized information technology subsidiary (EDS), GM continues to experience problems in its core product market: autos. The main lesson appears to be that computers can enhance companies' competitive advantage; but they cannot substitute for a failed business strategy.

---

[3] The first formal study of the management of computer was made by Booze, Allen and Hamilton in the mid-1950s, subsequently published under the title Managing to Manage the Computer. This Report first pointed out the consistent patterns of organization, management and use that evolved around the computer. Computerization could therefore be used by organizations as a tool to force improved management techniques.

Box 2.2: Computers for Competitive Advantage

Many companies have been successful in enhancing their competitive position through the introduction of new computer systems. Businesses that have added value through computing include:

- SABRE: American Airline's seat reservation system revolutionized the airline business and, by making it easier for travel agents to buy seats on American, boosted the airline's market share;

- FEDERAL EXPRESS: Fedex backed its skills in moving packages with a computer system that can tell customers the exact location of their package at any time. Fedex now manage's much of IBM's spare parts inventory;

- AMERICAN HOSPITALS SUPPLY increased its share of the market for medical and other hospital products through a system that allows hospitals directly to place order through a terminal-based system; and

- McDONNELL-DOUGLAS cut the cost of producing new aircraft by 40% by re-engineering its design and production systems to take advantage of information technology.

2.12   The rules governing successful computer implementation apply just as much in the public as in the private sector. The most important step is analysis of the public sector agency mission; then the design of a supportive computer strategy that includes complementary organizational restructuring. In certain respects, this process is much harder to follow in the public sector. In many cases, public sector agencies have multiple (or unclearly defined) missions. The lack of a competitive benchmark makes it hard to assess agency performance, or to measure improvements that computers may have facilitated. If the agency mission is unrealistic or economically unjustified, computers may help to entrench unproductive public sector activities. And in those cases where the agency mission makes sense, and there is a clear linkages between mission and computer strategy, general public administration rules may prevent the necessary organizational changes. Public administration is notorious for unnecessary paperwork, excessively hierarchical management structures, long response lags to changing social demands, and inflexible personnel policies. In many countries, these problems are not specific to a particular agency, but are endemic to the whole public sector. Progressive agencies with forward-looking computer strategies may therefore find it impossible to optimize their own processes because of system-wide administrative constraints.

2.13   *Managing Computerization.* Public and private organizations that are successful computer users also face a number of more technical implementation issues. These can be classified into 4 main categories:

- *designing systems architecture*: which has undergone significant change with a shift towards distributed computing networks, and provides the basis for hardware procurement, organizational information-flows, and system compatibility;

- *managing mainframe platforms*: where the difference between best and average practice can amount to 33% of total costs over the investment lifetime (Box 2.3);

Box 2.3: Key Success Factors in Datacenter Management

Requirements analysis and capacity planning: a set of methods for quantifying the data-processing requirements of an organization. The results are used to determine data-management requirements (i.e., databases, database tools, data-storage facilities) and to analyze work-flow computer needs (i.e., processing capacity, user terminals and PCs, communications capabilities).

Procurement and installation: this phase of computer management includes: (a) determination of computer requirements; (b) a competitive tender process; and (c) installation support, even for smaller systems.

Facilities management: the process of controlling the physical environment (heating, electrical power, chilled water, fire prevention systems, air-conditioning, etc.), protecting computer security, ensuring efficient operations and minimum downtime (including back-up systems), and allocating computer-time through various chargeback systems.

Communications and Notebook Management: requirements specification, procurement and operation of communications facilities that link end-users to all the computing servers, and to each other.

Human capital Development: requirements in this area are for fewer, more technically qualified staff. A medium-sized data-center would have 1 to 2 operators per shift (3 shifts per day), 1 to 2 production control clerks, and 2 to 4 technical specialists in the systems programming and communications groups. These figures represent a 50% reduction over 1980, due to increased system reliability and the availability of software that has automated many operator functions. Data-centers are largely comprised of non-degreed staff, many of whom have diplomas from specialized vocational training schools. Computer engineering graduates are mainly recruited for management positions.

Financing instruments: originally mainframes were rented from the vendors. Today, greater vendor competition, together with tax and product life-cycle considerations, is accelerating a shift towards vendor and third-party leases that permit flexible upgrading arrangements. Development of a second hand and forward market for computers has created significant arbitrage opportunities for aggressive buyers.

- *creating a networked environment*: in which distribution of data-processing power is creating organizational pressure to decentralize technical support and management, with centralized standards for technology and data interchange; and

- *containing technological risk*: by minimizing exposure to unproven products, by using off-the-shelf software and systems where possible, and analyzing latest trends to lower probability of premature technological obsolescence.

In addition, computer management still faces substantial problems of investment appraisal. Frequently, the benefits are hard to quantify (or at least to attribute), and depend on factors outside the control of the data-processing center. Recurrent cost implications are equally difficult to assess. Potential cost-savings (through employment reduction) are rarely achieved; and incremental costs of training, end-user support, and work-process redesign are often understated. These evaluation problems have been compounded with the shift towards computer networks (from which there is rarely a baseline to measure improvement).

2.14   As computer technology changes, the problems of implementation have become progressively more complex. Before personal computers, computer management was the domain of a small number of technicians and specialized personnel. The number of potential points of system failure were small. And "users" had limited access to the computer system; their requests were often batch-processed through the intermediation of dedicated software programmers. Today, the networked personal computer environment of large organizations poses a more complex set of implementation issues. There are multiple points of system failure; data-management is more difficult, not least because so much data is being generated; and inter-operability of many systems that coexist in large organizations, is far from fool-proof. However, best practices are evolving in all three aspects of computer management, and significantly influence the performance of computer investments.

2.15   *Public Sector Issues.* Public sector organizations (including defence) buy over 40% of the informatics hardware that is sold worldwide. This should give governments considerable leverage on price, terms and equipment functionality issues, helping to offset other computer management problems (para. 2.12). The US Government has been particularly aggressive in negotiating with vendors, and typically achieves significant improvements over vendors' list price and terms. The US Government has also been uniquely successful in influencing the design of computer hardware, and its procurement rules have influenced specification of international standards.

2.16   *Conclusions.* The scale of computer investments, high rate of technological change, and difficulties in bridging the potential-performance gap are encouraging the

---

Box 2.4: US Government Procurement Practice

US Government procurement of computer hardware is coordinated by the General Service Administration (GSA). GSA uses its sole procurement authority to: (a) negotiate a specific hardware purchase for a government agency; (b) negotiate a schedule of price and terms for off-the-shelf equipment, which any agency may use without further GSA approval; and (c) delegate procurement authority to agencies. In the third case, agencies seeking delegated procurement authority must obtain GSA approval for the procedures that they would follow. The GSA schedule contains prices and terms that must be the lowest prices offered to any customer by each vendor. Vendors are motivated to negotiate with GSA because agency procurement from the schedules is very simple and is almost certain to generate revenues. The terms are almost as important as the price. The equipment must be demonstrated to work before the government is required to make any payments. GSA leases may always be cancelled at the end of each year without penalty.

---

introduction of new computer management techniques. First, there is growing interest in applying the concepts of Total Quality Management (TQM) to computer operations. Mainframe facilities and decentralized office systems are challenges to any form of quality assurance, due to difficulties in setting performance standards. In the past, quality was measured only by service availability. More recently, advanced organizations introduced Service Level Agreements (SLAs) that are essentially negotiated contracts between the use and data-center for levels and types of service. However, it is becoming increasingly difficult to define and performance targets (and monitor their achievement) in networked computing environments. Organizations are also investing in "technology watch functions", which aim to manage technological risk by assessing the relevance of technological developments for future computing needs and for solutions to computer management problems.

Computer Applications in Turkey

2.17   The use of computers in Turkey as old as the technology itself. Telephones and unit-record accounting machines were installed as soon as they became available in Europe. However, as of 1937 only two organizations - TEKEL and Ziraat Bank - had automation equipment, and the first digital computer was installed in 1960 (in the Highway Authority). By 1980, there were only around 300 data-processing centers in the country. In the 1980s following the introduction of more liberal economic policies, Turkey experienced a sharp increase in the investment demand for computers. Demand gradually picked up in the early 1980s and, as investors became convinced that the policy reforms would not be reversed, accelerated in the 1985 - 1990 period (Table 2.1). Investment growth has averaged 35% per annum and, given rapidly increasing cost/performance ratios for computer equipment, the growth in capacity has been very significant.

Table 2.1: The Hardware Market in Turkey
($ millions, end-user prices)

	1985	1986	1987	1988	1989	1990
Total Sales	85.7	176.9	228.6	287.5	333.9	516.9
Larger Systems	50.7	110.7	149.4	192.2	200.3	270.9
Personal Computers	10.4	24.6	41.7	52.9	87.5	216.1
Others (1)	24.6	41.6	37.5	42.4	46.1	29.9
Import Percent (2)	73%	72%	83%	78%	62%	67%
Percent of total capital investment (3)	0.7%	1.3%	1.7%	2.3%	2.8%	3.7%

(1)   includes memory units, communications devices, and other peripherals not captured by larger systems category.
(2)   cif prices
(3)   excludes housing investment

Source: World Bank Estimates.

2.18   The public sector accounts for approximately two-fifths of the market for larger systems; and significantly less of the personal computer market (Table 2.2). Public sector hardware investments have traditionally been biased towards larger and more expensive systems; and in 1990 accounted for almost 60% of the hardware computer park for systems valued at over $700,000. In 1991, the government is proposing 64 computer projects whose value is over $1 million (per project), pointing to the continued significance of public procurement in this segment of the market.[4] The structure of public sector computer investments inevitably creates a step-function in computer implementation and utilization. Whereas private organizations tend to take an incrementalist approach to computer investments (i.e., adding extra PCs to the network), public investments are much more discrete. As a result, effective utilization of public sector computer systems depends on upfront actions to define the agency mission, assess computing requirements, design system architecture and review work-processes and information flows. Without this advance planning, it becomes difficult for agencies to absorb investments in advanced computing environments.

---

[4] The 1991 Investment budget proposed 5 computer investments over $5 million: by Ziraat Bank ($35 million), the Police Commission ($14 million), HalkBank ($6 million), PTT ($5 million), and Turkish Railways ($5 million). It should be noted that public computer procurements includes that of the state enterprises, distorting comparisons with other OECD countries.

**Table 2.2: Composition of Larger System Computer Park
Public versus Private Sector**

	1985	1986	1987	1988	1989	1990
Total value ($m)	205.3	255.9	405.4	597.4	757.8	1102.8
Public Share (%)	56.2	63.9	62.0	64.7	60.4	55.3
Private Share (%)	43.8	36.1	38.0	35.3	39.6	44.7

Source: Bilgisayar Magazine.

2.19   The sectoral distribution of computers by end-user suggests a pattern in Turkey that is very similar to that of other OECD countries.   As elsewhere, computer use is concentrated in finance and banking (approximately 32%), public administration (25%) and manufacturing (12%). These are the most information-intensive activities within the economy. In other OECD countries, there has been a trend towards increased manufacturing sector investment in computers with a corresponding decrease by the financial services sector. However, this development is not yet evident in Turkey. Indeed, much of the manufacturing sector's investment in computers appears to be in office rather than in factory automation. The sectoral composition of computer use in Turkey also reveals a number of lagging sectors. In particular, it appears that the distribution sector (wholesale and retail) has been slow to computcrize operations, and that computer penetration of the health and education sectors remains exceptionally low (less than 5% of total computer use). Over the next decade, these sectors can be expected to catch-up as competition (in the case of distribution) and demographic factors create pressure for increased productivity.

2.20   The process of diffusing computers to smaller users is only now beginning in Turkey. In 1991, the top 50 users accounted for almost 50% of cumulative investment in larger systems. However, explosive growth in personal computer sales since 1989 has significantly increased computer penetration in the small businesses and household segment. In 1990, 47% of PC users were small companies (employing less than 50 personnel), 31% were medium-size (51-500 personnel), and 22% were large companies (more than 500 personnel).[5] Despite improvements in the distribution of computer use, the pattern in Turkey is an exaggerated replica of the S-curve found in other OECD countries. It is estimated that less than 5% of approximately

---

[5] Bilgisayar Magazine, April 1991.

Figure 2.3: Sectoral Composition of Computer Use

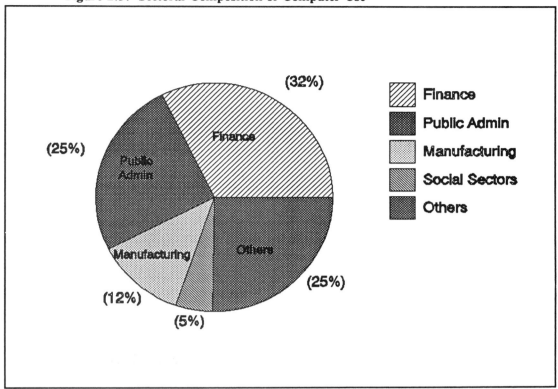

600,000 small businesses in Turkey use computers. And in general, computer use mirrors the highly skewed size distribution of firms.

2.21   In certain important respects, Turkey has benefitted from its status as a computer latecomer. First, relatively late adoption of computers means that Turkey suffers less from the problem of technological obsolescence. In other OECD countries, early adopters of computer technology are finding that they are now locked into outdated systems, and suffer from high maintenance and software development costs. Since most computer technology in Turkey is less than 5 years old, organizations should be well-positioned to stay close to the computer productivity frontier. Second, the late computerization of the Turkish economy means that many users have leapfrogged mainframe-based computer architecture straight to distributed networks of personal computers. These networks offer superior performance in many applications because of their ease-of-use, data-sharing functionality, and advanced communications facilities. Third, Turkey benefits from having no national "computer champion" which might distort public procurement decisions, or create a political lobby in favor of import restrictions. Rather,

Turkey has an open market for hardware; customs duty was reduced to zero in 1987; and there is a highly competitive supply offered by all the international vendors.[6]

2.22   Both public and private sectors possess role-models of superior computer management. In large part, this is due to a competitive market structure which has encouraged vendors to provide after-sales services and training. However, the success is also home-grown. Massive investment in a modern communications infrastructure (Chapter V), top management commitment to computer investments, the establishment by certain private organizations of independent computing services subsidiaries, and the demonstration effect from sustained public investment in computers are now beginning to pay off. Companies and public agencies have found innovative ways to take advantage of their new computing facilities. Success stories in the public sector include:

Figure 2.4: Comparing US and Turkish Datacenter Management

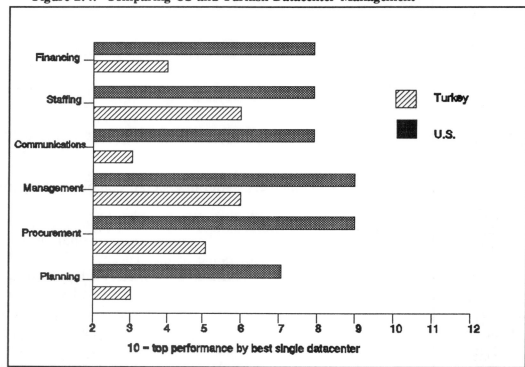

Source: World Bank Estimates.

---

[6] Nevertheless, it should be pointed out that special levies for transport infrastructure and mass housing add 8% to the import cost. In addition, the Ministry of Industry has recently acquired regulatory authority to pre-authorize all computer imports. The stated policy objective is to prevent dumping of obsolete and inadequately serviced computers. However, the regulation is a highly inefficient instrument for this purpose, and should be replaced with a licensed dealership approach.

- the *Ministry of Agriculture* automated on- and off-track horse betting system that generates substantial profits used to subsidize breeding investments; and

- the development by *Treasury* of an advanced computing environment that has evolved from a mainframe-based data management system to the latest generation computer architecture for centralized data control and distributed processing.

In the private sector, advanced computer management techniques have been adopted in the major conglomerates, and in the banking sector. The establishment of independent computer services subsidiaries (by certain Holding Groups) is an institutionally transparent approach, paralleled by only a small number of US corporations. The wide-area-networks (WANs) of the retail banks have efficiency and functionality ratings that match those found in the US and Europe. When demand and competitive pressure is present, Turkish organizations have the capacity to be superior computer users.

2.23   However, there are also a number of ways in which Turkey is failing to take advantage of its growing investment in computers. First, there are issues related to the effectiveness with which public sector computer investments are planned and implemented. Second, the government has not yet exploited the potential externalities from its procurement activities for market. Third, despite rapid growth in the PC market, both public and private sector computer users appear to be lagging behind latest techniques for networking applications. Fourth, there has been only limited introduction of the formal and documented computer management techniques that are central to Total Quality Management. Fifth, there are shortages in the supply of informatics personnel, especially in more specialized fields of systems analysis, capacity requirement planning, etc. Sixth, there is mixed evidence regarding the impact of computerization on business practice. As in other countries, management culture is resistant to technological modernization.

2.24   *Public sector computer use appears to suffer from systemic problems in three main areas: requirements analysis, procurement, and agency reengineering* (paras. 2.12 - 2.16). In the other areas of mainframe management (e.g., human capital, facilities maintenance), the picture is much more mixed, and appears to depend on the organization and commitment of specific agencies. There are examples where agencies have been successful in recruiting and retaining high quality staff (despite salary differential vis-a-vis the private sector[7]). Large public sector projects provide challenging work opportunities, and may offer younger staff a steeper learning curve than would be available in (higher wage) private sector jobs. The physical arrangements for mainframe facilities are primarily a function of the age of the host building. In more recently constructed computer facilities (e.g., Treasury), systems for power, air-conditioning, alarm systems, fire protection and physical computer security appear to be up-

---

[7] See Chapter IV: Human Capital for an Information Economy.

to-date. However, many government buildings (e.g., the Prime Ministry) are more than fifty years old. Despite modifications and upgrading, some of the older buildings cannot provide fully controlled environments for mainframes, and present substantial obstacles to wiring arrangements for computer networks.

2.25   *Requirements analysis* is the first step in the process of buying computers. Mis-specification of requirements is extremely costly. It results either in unnecessary "gold-plating" of computer investments or in costly modifications to computer architecture, once implementation efforts have exposed original specifications as inadequate. A recent survey carried out by the Prime Ministry[8] suggests that almost half of computer installation in the public sector have either excess or insufficient (disk and/or memory) capacity. The Government has long recognized the importance of this step, and until 1986 required that all major projects clear requirements analyses through a committee, chaired by the State Planning Organization. However, this committee was disbanded on the basis that it excessively centralized decision-making and added little of technical value to the proposals. Nor did this committee establish any common principles or standards regarding scope of proposal, hardware choices, communications protocols, implementation procedures, etc. As a result, little inter-agency learning appears to have taken place, slowing down the speed with which best practice diffused through the public sector. By 1991, the Government realized that the computer procurement and management arrangements had become too decentralized, resulting in a proliferation of equipment types, communications problems and incompatible data formats. The Prime Ministry therefore established an inter-agency committee, whose first initiative has been to develop a base-line database of computer hardware and software in the central government. In addition, the committee has approved the X.25 communications protocol and TS5881 Turkish character set as government standards. However, no decision has as yet been taken regarding the review powers, or management authority of this committee, creating a significant vacuum in the institutional framework for public sector computerization.

2.26   In 1986, the Government recognized that *computer procurement* needed to be treated on an exceptional basis, and that it should therefore be exempt from the "low-bid wins" requirement (under Public Tender Law 2886).   Given the complexities of computer implementation, training requirements, after-sales service and work-process redesign, price could not be the only criteria for selection. Despite this exemption, procurement practice suffers from two main problems.[9] First, in most cases price appears to be the decisive factor, rather than technical merit or the quality of service. The result is neither efficient nor ironically is it always least cost. Rather, successful companies often: (a) provide inadequate implementation support, reducing the benefits of computerization; and (b) restore profit margins through higher charges

---

[8] Public Sector Use of Information Technology (1992), a Working Paper prepared by Associate Professor Ismail Erdem on behalf of the Prime Ministry.

[9] See Chapter III: Competing in Software for a further discussion of procurement problems, in particular as they affect the software industry.

for after-sales service, spare parts and maintenance. Second, most tender documents are biased towards highly technical description of hardware requirements. Conversely, they inadequately specify both the objectives of the computerization program, and related requirements for software, training, implementation support, etc. This approach to the tender documents generates a number of costs. First, it reduces competition since the technical specifications are frequently so detailed that only a small number of vendors can apply. Second, it reduces the ability of computer vendors to find more creative solutions that might address agencies' underlying information problems (as opposed to their stated computer requirements). Third, it distorts the selection process by focusing attention on upfront costs (i.e., of hardware) rather than on computer lifecycle costs, including those costs associated with organizational change.

2.27   One potential benefit of government procurement activities is their impact on technical standardization (para. 2.20). In the past, a small number of hardware manufacturers established proprietary computer standards, which acted as a barrier to competition. More recently, national governments and international organizations[10] have been defining "open standards" for computer architecture that will strengthen competition and system inter-operability. However, these allegedly open standards are incomplete. There are many cases of multiple open standards for the same computer functions. For example, both Ethernet and Token Ring are ISO standards for local area networks (LANs), but are incompatible with each other. Standards rarely specify the computing situations to which they best apply, creating significant buyer (and product designer) information problems. Furthermore, the standards are often insufficiently detailed to preclude cases in which two products meet the same standard but are incompatible. This situation makes compatibility and inter-operability difficult goals for data-centers. The Government can help, as in the US case, by selecting a single uniform set of standards and providing conformance testing for them.

2.28   In Turkey, the Government has not used the procurement process to support migration towards any particular set of technical standards (whether open or not). Across the public sector, computers are using different operating, software applications, data and communications standards, compounding the problem of inter-agency coordination and information-sharing.[11] For example, there are over 10 different database packages (mainframe and PC-based) currently used by government agencies, creating significant problems of inter-operability and data-sharing.[12] By adopting consistent technical standards in the procurement process, the Government would reduce information problems in the market and improve the returns on its own computer investments. The standard need not be a legal requirement outside

---

[10] These organizations include International Standards Organization (ISO), European Community Commission and European Computer Manufacturers' Association (ECMA), and the non-profit Open Standards Foundation (OSF). It should be noted that large manufacturers exercise significant influence over these organizations, with the result that there are competing versions of supposedly open standards (e.g., UNIX).

[11] See Chapter 3 and 6 for further discussion of standardization problems.

[12] For further details, see the Prime Ministry Working Paper, Public Sector Use of Information Technology (1992).

the public sector. In Turkey, the public sector is a large enough client that vendors will assure compliance with the government standard. Private sector clients will specify the government standards if: (a) they make technical and business sense; and (b) there are benefits from system compatibility with the government. Government selection of a uniform set of standards will require a significant research and documentation effort; but will have a pay-back period of under 3 years.

2.29   Computerization works best when the physical investments are accompanied by changes in work-process and management structure. In many countries, these changes are hard to introduce, particularly in the public sector (para. 2.13). Turkey is no exception. Surveys from 1984 and 1992 show a consistent picture: of sub-optimal computer utilization, of limited intra-agency information flows despite the introduction of personal computers, and of massive internal paper-trails coexisting with data-communications facilities. There do not appear to be many (if any) agencies that have consciously examined their work-patterns to see how computers can: (a) reduce information-processing time; (b) minimize unnecessary bureaucracy; (c) eliminate management layers; (d) improve client service; or (e) redefine appropriate scope of the agency's actions. Rather, the objectives of many government computerization projects appear to be internally focussed; there are few inter-agency projects that would reduce duplicative transactions with the private sector; and only exceptional projects in which computerization has quantifiable targets in terms of time-saving or efficiency gains for the private sector. As a result, key economic activities (e.g., foreign trade, company registration) remain hamstrung by red-tape and multiple form-filling requirements. The costs of e.g., customs delays are very real, and could be avoided through a more market-driven use of computers in the public sector.

2.30   As computers become increasingly central to the government function, there will be substantial benefits from dealing with systemic problems of requirements planning, procurement and broader computerization objectives (including quantifiable targets). This requires an institutional framework that: (a) maintains initiative and implementation responsibility at the agency level; but (b) strengthens coordination for those aspects of computer use on which there are high economic returns from collective action. Key functions that should be centralized are:

- oversight of procurement to ensure consistent practice on requirements planning, and design of tender specifications for both hardware and non-hardware project elements;

- publication of standardized tender documents for contracts of computer equipment and services;

Box 2.5: Computerization of International Trade

Turkey's foreign trade equalled approximately $40 billion in 1990. Delays in clearing customs average 3 weeks, creating a real cost to the economy of $140 million per annum (assuming 6% real interest rate).

In Singapore, the Government has established a joint stock company: Singapore Network Services (SNS). SNS has worked with the Singapore Port Authority, public agencies that regulate international trade, and major importers/exporters to implement the TradeNet System. Tradenet allows the foreign trade sector to clear all trade documents electronically with the relevant import and export authorities, thereby greatly speeding up the documentation and cargo clearance process. TradeNet functions 24 hours a day all-year-round, thereby freeing business from the restrictions of normal government hours. The subscribers include importers and exporters, manufacturers, freight forwarders, air cargo agents, shipping agents, courier service operators, and all relevant government agencies. Most cargo clears the Singapore Port in less than 72 hours. In 1989, Singapore received the "Partners in Leadership" award from the US Society for Information Management for its success in creating national competitive advantage through TradeNet.

If Turkey could use computer networks to reengineer the customs process, the economy would gain a minimum of $100 million per annum. This does not include the additional revenues that Turkish firms could earn if enabled to enter faster-response market segments (i.e., high fashion, perishable fruits).

- development of standards for computing and communications, including procedures for conformance testing;

- negotiation of special government prices for off-the-shelf computer products (Box 2.3);

- standardization of government occupational streams for informatics personnel; and information supply on personnel requirements as feedback for universities and vocational training schools;

- development of standards to disseminate best government practice inter alia on computer budgeting, computer security (Chapter VII), chargeback systems, software development, and office technology management;

- a technology watch function for the government (with findings disseminated to the private sector);

- introduction of standards for government data-management, and dissemination.[13/]

2.31   The agency chosen as central coordinator of informatics should enlist the representation and active participation of the main public sector users *and* suppliers, including universities, TSE, TÜBITAK, MPM, SIS and PTT. International experience points to the risk that such an agency or committee may become a regulator rather than facilitator of best practice. Such a development would undermine the coordination effort, since line ministries ultimately find ways to bypass unproductive central procedures. However, this risk can be minimized (Box 2.6) if the agency: (a) works through a user committee; (b) provides optional technical assistance at an early phase in computer project appraisal; and (c) emphasizes development of

---

Box 2.6: Singapore's National Computer Board

Established in 1981 as a statutory body under the Ministry of Finance, the National Computer Board (NCB) spearheads implementation of Singapore's National Information Technology Plan. With a professional staff of 650, NCB has 3 main responsibilities:

- The *Civil Service Computerization Program* aims to turn the civil service into a world-class user of information technology. The NCB provides technical assistance to government agencies in determining requirements, preparing tenders, and in the initial implementation period. NCB also coordinates investment in the public sector data network, which is designed around data-hubs with common data-formats and communications protocols.

- *IT Applications Program* aims to diffuse best practice computer use throughout the economy. NCB prepares and disseminates standards for total quality management; conducts annual surveys into IT use and penetration; organizes an annual Applications Mega-Conference to spread awareness about IT goods and services; selects the winners of national IT awards for outstanding applications; provides technical assistance on computerization to small enterprises; and develops electronic information networks (Box 2.3);

- *IT Industrial Development* through incentives for direct foreign investment, an IT research framework, software quality improvement programs, and management of market-based system for manpower planning (including use of labor market surveys and formal certification procedures).

The real lesson of Singapore has been its success in using IT to enhance its existing competitive advantage: as a communications hub for south-east Asia and as an export platform for multinational companies.

[13/] For more details on public sector information dissemination, see Chapter VI: Reducing Uncertainty - The Role of Information.

standards that provide an objective point of reference for project appraisal and support diffusion of best practice. Over time, the development and dissemination of standards should substitute for the agency's procurement oversight function (except for large-scale projects with inter-agency dimensions or where exemption from standards is requested).

2.32   In addition, there are three aspects of computer use, in which problems appear to be common across the public and private sectors: (a) communications and networking; (b) total quality management; and (c) human capital constraints.[14] To some extent, these aspects of computer use will improve automatically as the technology matures, greater experience translates into learning, and diffusion of best-practice in the public sector provides demonstration effects for the whole economy. However, progress on these issues will also require policy initiative and collective action.

2.33   Public and private organizations are adopting *networked* computer technology relatively slowly. Computer architectures are still mainframe-oriented, and networks largely permit communications between PCs and the mainframe (rather than between PCs). The main problem appears to be local area networks (i.e., within a single location) rather than wide area networks (i.e,. between many locations). Wide area networking is well-developed (para. 2.27), and PTT can offer data-communication services through dedicated circuits and its packet-switched network that will meet demand over the medium term. However, PTT's dominance in the communications field may also explain the slow development of private sector expertise on local area networking. In other OECD economies with more liberal telecom regimes (Chapter V), there has been rapid growth of companies specialized in designing and managing corporate networks. Large telecom operators (e.g., ATT, BT, MCI) today have dedicated subsidiaries that service the entire communications requirements of large corporate clients. In addition, there are a range of smaller companies providing communications support and consulting services. In Turkey, PTT provides only limited assistance to companies that have internal networking problems; PTT employs the majority of communications engineers; and private companies are not in a position to manage integrated communications networks. Developments in this area are likely to be delayed until regulatory and institutional change creates a more commercial environment for communications.

2.34   There appears to be little application of techniques for *total quality management* of computer installations, either in the public or private sector. Few data-processing centers have developed a systematic approach to requirements analysis or capacity planning, use chargeback systems or computer budgeting procedures, have entered into service level agreements with users, or are establishing a technology watch function. There is inadequate

---

[14] An additional area that Government is already addressing is financing instruments for computers. At present, operating leases are for a minimum of 4 years, effectively limiting their value for computer investments (which have an above-average rate of obsolescence). There are now proposals to reduce minimum lease life to 3 years, thereby increasing external sources of finance for computer investments.

documentation of computer management processes. Only limited attention paid to the requirements for personnel development and skills upgrading. Financing relies on internal sources of funds, with marginal use of operating leases. In sum, data-centers in Turkey have yet to adopt the formalized methods of computer management. As computers represent a growing percentage of total investment and information becomes a strategic corporate resource, techniques to increase computer efficiency, measure performance and improve service quality are likely to assume growing economic significance. In this respect, standards for total quality management of computers are central to closing the gap between best and average practice; and will help computer management in Turkey to be an internationally competitive business function. The Turkish Standards Institute therefore needs to take a lead (in collaboration with key users and vendors) in developing standards for total quality management of computers, and in certifying qualifying users.

2.35   *Human Capital constraints* are addressed in more detail in Chapter IV. In the hardware field, the main skills shortages appear to be in the disciplines of: (a) computer networking and communications; and (b) computer management techniques. These problems are most pronounced in the public sector where severe salary compression (for specialists and experienced personnel) make it hard to retain more talented informatics staff.[15] There also appear to be weaknesses in the supply of refresher courses for mid-career informatics professionals, and of skills upgrading courses for computer programmers (as new technology automates low-level programming). In the future, distributed computer networks will create demand for a new class of informatics personnel, specialized in end-user support. Current occupational classifications (developed by the Turkish Informatics Association) focus on data-processing center staff, and will therefore need to be updated as computing moves away from the mainframe. Given the high rate of technological progress in computers, training institutions (both public and private) need to become more adept in anticipating its impact on requirements for informatics personnel. However, inadequate information on both computer technology trends and market dynamics for informatics skills prevents adequate personnel planning by users and training organizations. Building on existing efforts by the Turkish Informatics Association, these information problems might be best addressed through a joint public-private initiative that integrates technology watch and labor market analysis functions.

2.36   *Conclusions.* Since 1985, organizations in Turkey have moved rapidly up the learning curve of computer use and management. Already, there are examples of world-class computer management; and a competitive hardware market generates appropriate incentives for vendors to support the latest applications. There are even cases in which Turkey has been the pilot market for new computer models, or for vendor development of applications (especially in banking) that have subsequently been replicated in other OECD countries. Nevertheless, the gap between best and average practice in computer use is large. First, there are a number of

---

[15] For example, the Prime Ministry Working Paper indicates: (a) $600 per month as the highest salary for a government informatics professional (only twice that of a junior data-entry operator); and (b) a total of 64 communications experts across all government agencies.

weaknesses in the public sector's use of computers, which reduce productivity and fail to capitalize on the wider benefits that efficient government procurement can generate. Second, computer use continues to lag in a number of key sectors including distribution, factory automation (i.e., manufacturing), education and health. In distribution and manufacturing, efficient computerization is likely to be the result of policy initiatives that lower remaining barriers to competition. In the social sectors, public investment in computerization could be a key instrument to increase productivity, but only if accompanied by necessary institutional reforms. Third, the progress that Turkey has demonstrated in the communication sector (Chapter V) needs to be replicated in corporate as well as public networking.

2.37   Turkey has a number of advantages in pursuing and realizing the objective of superior computer use throughout the economy. In addition to the benefits of late adoption and a competitive computer market, Turkey now possesses an advanced communications infrastructure that can provide all the services demanded by corporate and public sector users. Perhaps most important, relatively late modernization of the economy means that (at least in the private sector) Turkey has not accumulated management hierarchies or business practices that resist computerization. For example, unlike the US and most of Europe, Turkey is not a check-based economy. Most transactions are by cash, with a growing number of credit card users. If the banking sector could move rapidly to a payments system based on debit cards and other forms of electronic payments (including home and direct business banking services), the economy would realize substantial efficiency gains. Similarly, distributed computer networks may help the industrial sector (in which small enterprises predominate) to miss the mass-production era and move straight to a mass customization modes of production, based on flexible networks of small specialized producers.[16] Competitive pressure in the productive sectors, open informatics markets, an efficient strategy for human capital development, and a systematic approach to government computer procurement will make Turkey a superior computer user, and thereby lay the basis for a dynamic local hardware industry.

Competing in the International Hardware Markets

2.38   *Policy Rationale.* The primary objective of government policy should be to increase productivity of computer use. However, there are also reasons why policy cannot ignore the production of computers and related information technology products. First, there are strong forward linkages from a dynamic vendor industry to advanced computer applications in the rest of the economy. Second, rapid growth in the global market for computers (and other informatics goods and services) offers a potentially attractive export opportunity for Turkish industry. While Turkey cannot be expected to compete across the whole product range (nor can the US or Japan), market restructuring over the next decade will provide entry opportunities for well-positioned companies.

---

[16] This market structure and strategy (combined with efficient information flows) is central to the competitiveness of Italian textile and ceramics industries.

2.39   The economics of innovation in computer applications provide an inherent advantage to those computer vendors that both produce and distribute the equipment. The computer industry is an extreme example of reciprocal learning between vendors and users. Vendors learn of the need for new computer products and services through intensive interaction with clients, and sustained after-sales involvement in systems implementation. Advanced computer users learn from the vendors new methods of business and information management, embodied in the latest generations of hardware and software. Vendors with production capability have a strong incentive to use their clients as a "laboratory" for new applications and computer architectures. Successful innovation can be embodied in the next generation of products, and its cost spread over the product life-cycle. By contrast, a vendor industry that provides only distribution services may have a greater incentive to imitate rather than innovate. Lacking any production capability, innovations become once-off exercises in client service, generating only limited externalities for future clients in the same industry sector. A vendor industry that has minimal local production capabilities may therefore constrain Turkey's development as an outstanding user of computers.

2.40   Worldwide, computer hardware and peripherals is a US$300 billion business (Table 2.3). Sustained market growth (at over 10% per annum) is the result of: (a) rapid increases in hardware performance; (b) proliferation of new products; and (c) horizontal integration of consumer electronics, communications, and computer products. The computer industry is becoming much more competitive in terms of market structure (Figure 2.5). Only a few years ago, the computer hardware industry was highly concentrated. In 1984, the top vendor (IBM) accounted for over 21% of the market. Since 1980 however, this dominance has been progressively eroded; and the industry is going through a period of rapid structural change. IBM (which today accounts for 12% of the market) is reengineering its own business to get closer to the markets, and has entered into a profusion of "strategic alliances" with Apple, Siemens, and most recently Honeywell-Bull. Other suppliers (American, Japanese, and European) can compete effectively with IBM across the product range, including mainframes. Technological barriers to market entry have also been eroded by the development of personal computers, and the widespread availability of the basic components. Horizontal and vertical integration is creating electronics conglomerates (e.g., Matsushita, Samsung, Daewoo) and computer/communications mergers (e.g., ATT, Siemens). Although market entry has become easier, sustaining growth requires that smaller companies manage the transition from low-cost assembly to more design and research-intensive operations.

2.41   Computer hardware is an internationally traded product. Much hardware can be sold anywhere, with the exception of items that have language related components, like keyboards. Hardware, for the most part, adheres to international standards and requires little modification from country to country. By contrast, software requires much greater local customization than hardware (Chapter III), requiring conformance to local languages, laws and standards. It is predictable therefore that leading hardware manufacturers have geographically diversified sources of revenue. The only exception is local assembly of PCs from imported

Table 2.3: Global Market for Computer Goods and Services
$ billions

	1985	1990	1995
Mainframes	69	90	120
PCs and Workstations	36	75	181
Peripherals	62	117	212
Software & Services	76	208	399
Total: Information Systems	243	490	912
Semiconductors	32	70	125
Industrial Automation	60	118	180

Source: World Bank Estimates from Price Waterhouse & IDC.

components. This propensity to export suggests that if a manufacturer can build a successful product, it will be exported (given trade restrictions). As Turkish industry develops hardware production capability, it must therefore be with the global rather than domestic market in mind. Whether as OEM or own-brand suppliers, producers in Turkey will need to base their product strategies on:

- a comprehensive understanding of emerging *market niches*;

- *competitor analysis* to identify and maximize sources of cost advantage;

- advantages of *small-scale* production and proximity to European markets, including better product timing and flexibility; and

- development of *competitive distribution* channels (including for the new markets in C.I.S. nations).

Given the cost of capital in Turkey, companies cannot afford to compete in mass-production of basic components (e.g., memory chips). Nor does the level of technological sophistication permit head-to-head competition with e.g., IBM or DEC. Rather, the strategy for Turkish export success is more likely to look to strategic partnerships, joint ventures, and entry into

Figure 2.5: Competitive Dynamics in Computer Market

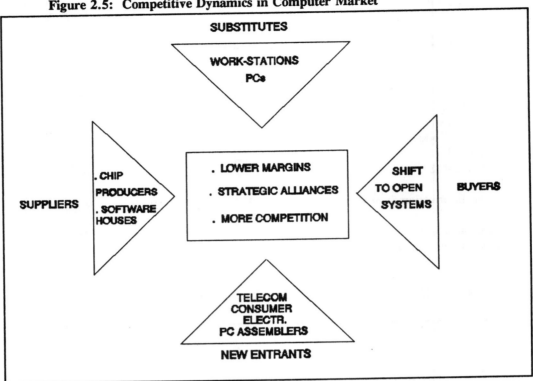

market niches for highly differentiated computer products. This approach requires minimal intervention by Government, and rather is predicated on the proven ability of Turkish firms to optimize their production and marketing capabilities.

2.42   *Policy, Structure and Performance.* Government policy has been to maintain an open market for computer hardware, and to create competitive market conditions. The result has been a steady reduction in IBM's market share, and the emergence of a more competitive market structure. IBM retains over 40% of the larger system market (i.e., over $10,000), and over 70% of the mainframe market for systems over $700,000. However, rapid growth in the market for personal computer technology has created a less skewed industry structure (Figure 2.6). All the major international suppliers are represented in Turkey, through a combination of wholly-owned subsidiaries, sole-source representatives, and multi-vendor dealer networks.

2.43   Computer manufacture in Turkey is today limited to PC assembly operations. These are small, and no market leader has emerged. There is a high rate of market entry and exit. Out of six larger companies operating in 1988, only four were still in business by 1990 (Table 2.4). Given their limited scale of operation and barriers to growth experienced by PC assemblers in other countries, these companies are unlikely to form the basis of Turkey's hardware export sector. The incentive to produce even for domestic market is undermined by a tariff structure that perversely taxes imported PC components more highly than the finished product.

**Figure 2.6: Concentration in the Computer Market
Turkey, 1987-90**

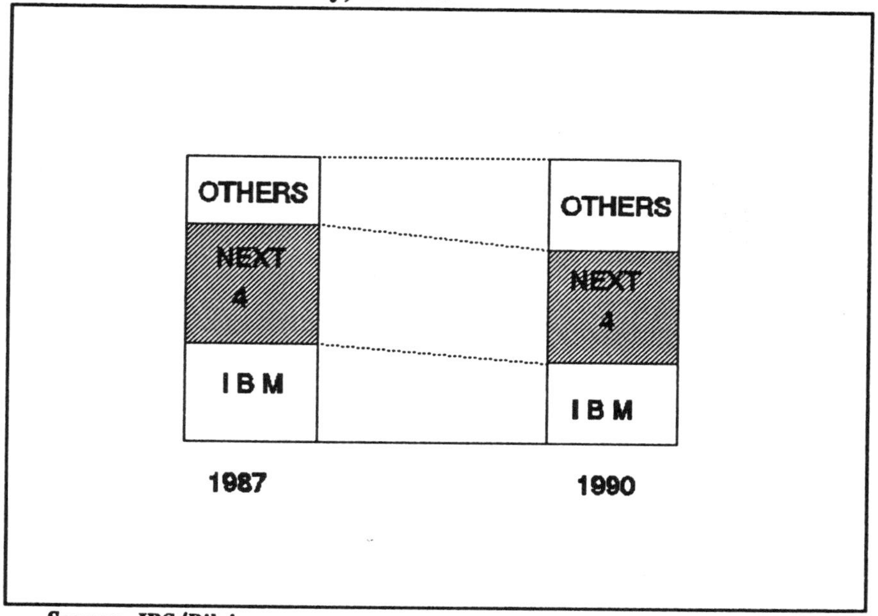

Source: IBS/Bilgisayar.

**Table 2.4: PC Assembly Operations
1987-90**

Company	Range	1987	1988	1989	1990
BEST	PC, XT, AT, 286	1000	2000	2200	0
KAREL	XT, XT30, 386	490	1500	1800	1550
SISTEM	XT, AT, Laptop	750	1000	1200	-
PALS	XT, AT	240	850	0	0
BITON	PC, XT, AT, 286, 386	350	400	850	0
BILGI	PC	1000	1500	2800	4000
IST	XT, AT, 386, 486	-	-	380	2800
TELETEKNIK	PC				
TOTAL		3830	7250	9230	

Source: Company interviews by IBS.

2.44   Better prospects may emerge from Turkey's success in building a competitive consumer electronics and communications industry. Over the past five years, a number of substantial private companies have been established with growing domestic and export revenues (Table 2.5). It is interesting to note that there are now 6 electronics companies in Turkey's Top 150 industrial concerns, and that all are either under private or mixed ownership (but with private control).

Table 2.5: Leading Electronics Suppliers: Turkey 1990

Companies	Rank in Top 500	Public/Private	Sales	Value-Added	Exports($M)
Bekoteknik	13	Private	442	131	50
Vestel	14	Private	361	99	89
Profilo Electronic	37	Private	190	37	16
Teletas	46	Mixed	165	72	9
Netas	53	Mixed	153	65	3
Aselan	124	Private	76	52	12
TOTAL			1387	456	179

On the communications side, these include Netas, Teletas, Aselsan, and the local subsidiary of Siemens-Nixdorf. Turkey has also recently become a significant supplier of color TVs and monitors as a result of investments by Vestel, and Bekoteknik. These companies are increasing resource allocation towards product design and development, and have established an Electronics Foundation at Istanbul Technical University, whose objective is to master Application Specific Integrated Circuit (ASIC) technology (para. 2.07). Total exports of computer equipment (largely monitors), communications hardware and consumer electronics increased from $50 million in 1986 to over $400 million by 1991 (Table 2.6). The speed with which Turkish companies have been able to penetrate international markets (especially in consumer electronics) suggests that there are few structural barriers to export growth. Indeed, Turkey may be in a position to compete effectively for sources of foreign direct investment in its electronics industries (especially from the Far East), as international suppliers look for ways to enter the C.I.S. markets.

2.45   *Incentive Framework*. The basic policy rules for development of an informatics hardware industry are not unique. Rather, efficient industrialization in this sector (as in others) depends on stable macroeconomic conditions, the elimination of tax distortions, and a large dose of competition.   International evidence does not appear to demonstrate high returns from government policies that pick national champions, reduce competition (e.g., through liberal anti-

Table 2.6: Electronics Exports
1986-91

$ millions

Sector	1986	1987	1988	1989	1990	1991
Integrated Circuitry	5.5	16.8	15.3	6.7	17.5	21.0
Consumer Electronics	13.1	22.9	105.5	131.4	259.0	290.9
Telecom. Equipment	10.1	19.0	14.6	27.4	57.8	59.8
Other Prof. and Industrial Eqpt.	7.5	8.5	1.8	3.9	8.1	3.8
Military Electronics	14.0	12.0	8.0	9.0	10.0	11.0
Computers	-	-	-	7.5	18.4	14.6
Total	50.2	71.2	145.3	186.4	370.1	401.2

Source: Electronics Association of Turkey.

trust policies), or provide tax subsidies. Indeed, the experience of many European Community countries points in the opposite direction. Already in Turkey, the Government deploys a vast range of tax incentives whose primary effect is to hand windfall profits to companies rather than influence investment decisions. An optimal incentive policy for informatics hardware is therefore one based on creation of a more neutral tax framework through reduction of existing incentives and tax holidays. This would support the development of an internationally competitive industry, whose profitability depended on design, manufacturing, and marketing value-added rather than on tax-breaks and investment subsidies.

2.46   *Specific Interventions*. Within a more neutral incentive framework, there is however a strong case for specific government interventions. First, the rate of technological progress in the computer (and related informatics) industry has a broad impact on productivity growth across the economy. Hence, the social returns on informatics research and development are larger than private profits on this investment. Second, even within the informatics industry, it is very hard for private companies to capture the full benefit of their investment. The speed of knowledge diffusion within the industry is very high through product imitation strategies (e.g., IBM PC clones) and through inter-firm mobility of highly skilled professionals and scientists. Third, there are very high risks associated with research activities in this field. The international technology frontier is moving quickly, the required capital investments are large (especially in enabling technologies such as chip production), and the user-base is often under-developed. These factors tend to shorten companies' time-horizons, and discourage the pre-commercial investments necessary for more fundamental breakthroughs. Fourth, there are certain "strategic" technologies which are monopolized by a small number of companies, creating substantial market imperfections.

2.47   Governments in most advanced economies have responded with substantial public financing for informatics research and development (R&D). In 1990, global expenditure on informatics R&D amounted to almost $100 billion (up from $40 billion in 1985). 55% of this expenditure is based in the US, 27% is Japanese and 18% is invested by European Community nations. European Community research programs for informatics (e.g., ESPRIT, and RACE) received $2.7 billion in funding for 1990-1994; and cover the fields of chip and integrated circuit technology, new computer architectures, office-automation, computer-integrated manufacturing, and broadband communications. In addition, each national Government has informatics research programs, which (aggregated) more than double available research funding from the public sector. Japan has a similar set of programs (under the general framework of Fifth Generation Computing) that aims to develop knowledge-based systems and high performance computers, based on a parallel processing architecture. In the US, the research funding system is more decentralized. Key agencies that provide long-term funding include Department of Defence, DARPA,[17/] the National Science Foundation, the Department of Energy, the National Institutes of Health, and NASA. DARPA's contribution has been particularly significant; and has resulted in landmark innovations in artificial intelligence, computer graphics, VLSI design tools, packet-switched networks (i.e., ARPANET that links all the major universities in the US), and parallel processing computers. The National Science Foundation has focused more on advances in theoretical and experimental computer science, and in upgrading university computing and network facilities.

2.48   The main lesson from these programs is that their success depends on the overall commercial environment for innovation. The programs appear to have been more effective in the US and Japan, where there is a strong industrial base in information technologies and (in particularly in the US case) a pool of private risk-capital (i.e., venture capital). In Europe, the informatics hardware industry remains fragmented and, with certain exceptions lacks the resources to compete in research-intensive products. Despite massive government funding for research and development in informatics, the Europe Community experienced an informatics trade deficit of over $40 billion in 1990. The US and Japan continue to enjoy leadership in the next generation technologies of artificial intelligence, high-performance computing, graphical interfaces, and opto-electronics. In more mature markets, European producers face increased

---

[17/] The Defence Advance Research Projects Agency. DARPA's mission is to invest in technologies that have both military and civilian applications. The strategy has emphasized funding for a few high-risk visionary projects, and the building of a critical mass of research talent at relatively few locations.

competition from East Asian NIC suppliers of semiconductor chips, consumer electronics, personal computers, and peripherals.

2.49   Research funding in Turkey for informatics is limited, but growing in significance. By 1991, informatics R&D expenditure amounted to over $30 million, of which more than 80% came from the private sector (Table 2.7).[18/] The majority of this expenditure is concentrated in the communications industry (PTT, Netas, and Teletas).

Table 2.7: Distribution of Research Personnel and Expenditure: 1991
Informatics Sector Compared with Total Research Activities

Percentage

	Personnel		Expenditure	
	Total	Informatics	Total	Informatics
Universities	86	38	62	1
Public	12	18	29	18
Private	2	44	9	81

Source: TÜBITAK.

In line with informatic's growing significance as a meta-technology, the Scientific and Industrial Research Council (TÜBITAK) created an Electrical, Electronics and Informatics Research Group in 1991, and has started to fund a growing research agenda. Further efforts in this field are being supported by the Defence Industries Administration, a number of Ministries (for sector-specific applications), and the universities. There are also a number of projects with private sponsors that are being supported by the Technology Development Foundation.[19/] However, there is no overall framework for public research support (whether through explicit research funding or procurement), individual projects are very small, and the research community continues to suffer from significant brain-drain and inadequate computer facilities (Chapter IV).

2.50   Even with substantially increased research funding, Turkey will not be able to compete across-the-board in informatics technology. This is neither a realistic nor desirable

---

[18/] For further information, see Research and Development on Information Technology in Turkey (TÜBITAK Working Paper, 1992).

[19/] This Foundation was established in 1991 as part of a World Bank financed Technology Development Project (9097-TU). The Foundation provides matching grants for competitively selected industrial research projects.

policy objective. Both the US and Japan are large importers as well as exporters of informatics hardware; and the laws of specialization and dynamic comparative advantage apply within the $300 billion global market for the products. However, it is equally realistic to believe that Turkish industry can become a competitive supplier in a small number of informatics market niches. Since each of these "niches" may represent a global market of $3 billion (i.e., 1% of the 1990 market), achieving 10% share of 5 niche markets would put Turkey on the informatics map. To achieve this target, the Government - together with the private sector - needs to put in place a market-driven program that: (a) mobilizes long-term resources for research; (b) focuses on a small number of enabling technologies at the pre-competitive stage; and (c) builds private sector mechanisms for commercial exploitation of the results through an appropriate framework for intellectual property rights and venture capital.[20] An important benefit of this program is the signal that it would send to foreign investors. Turkey is a potentially attractive country for inwards investment in the informatics sector. The domestic market is open and growing fast; skilled labor is relatively inexpensive; a preferential trade agreement exists with the European community; and there are potential markets in the C.I.S. for which Turkey would be an efficient manufacturing location. A research program that was open to international as well as domestic suppliers could catalyze substantial technology transfer and foreign investment.

2.51   The basis for such a research program already exists in Turkey. The Technology Development Foundation has a mandate (and resources) to finance privately-sponsored research projects, and to promote business-academic collaboration. TÜBITAK is also increasing its support for projects that have a strong market-orientation and an effective private sector sponsor. However, neither institution has as yet prepared a dedicated program of research and exploitation for informatics. To make progress on this initiative, there are a number of key analytic steps:

- assess competitive position of Turkish informatics industry (consumer electronics, components, communications, etc.);

- define key user segments in the domestic market, with high potential demand for new applications (e.g., agriculture, education, office technology);

- determine size, growth and competitive structure of global market niches in these product categories;

- distinguish key competitive success factors to determine where Turkish-based production might have sustainable cost advantages;

---

[20] On intellectual property rights, see Chapter 7. With regard to venture capital, development of the industry remains constrained by: (a) taxation of nominal capital gains in a high inflation environment; and (b) lack of a regulatory framework. These issues are also being addressed under the Technology Development Project.

Box 2.7: Informatics Development Projects

Turkey has many sectors for which unique informatics applications (with significant domestic value-added) could be developed and potentially exported. For example, there are immediate opportunities in:

- The *Small Business Retail Sector*. Retailing in Turkey (as in many countries) remains a highly fragmented industry. No single small business can afford the development costs of a new dedicated informatics support package; but the sector as a whole would realize efficiency gains from such a product. One possible project would as its goal to produce an affordable informatics system that would support all the functions of a small retail business: (i) simple accounting; (ii) inventory; (iii) order processing; (iv) credit; (v) collections; (vi) payments; (vii) tax; (viii) small business planning; and (ix) cash register. The system could also support FX conversion, and foreign language assistance for shop-floor support.

- *Textile - Net*. Modelled after Singapore's TradeNet (Box 2.5), this initiative would aim to provide Electronics Data Interchange (EDI) services for key transactions across the entire spectrum of commerce. Given the importance of the textile industry to Turkey's export performance, this could be one logical place to start the EDI system. A generic EDI system could be developed, using the TURPAK packet-switched data network; and then customized modules developed for the textile industry (as a pilot vehicle for the system).

- *Agri-Informatics*. The agricultural sector still employs almost 50% of the civilian workforce. However, the information resources of the sector are extremely poor; and constrain the ability of farmers to make appropriate business decision. Currently, the Ministry of Agriculture (MOA) is one of the least computerized segments of the Government - although agricultural information has a very high public good contact. There is no wide-area-network (WAN) that links Ankara with the field offices; and very little data (flowing in either direction). The MOA could be a showpiece for agency modernization through a systematic program to define information requirement, restructure work-patterns and create an enabling technological environment, based on field, office PCs, a WAN, and remote-sensing satellite data acquisition system.

- identify key enabling technologies; and

- estimate program funding envelope, and identify available funding sources.

This program development effort could be financed from the strategic studies program under the Technology Development Foundation.

2.52   *Conclusions.* Turkey has the potential to become a competitive (albeit niche) supplier of informatics hardware. While this potential is limited to modest shares of global markets, the revenues would be significant to the Turkish economy, and the externalities will also be very beneficial. There is already a sizeable local industry supplying and exporting communications equipment, consumer electronics, and advanced military electronics. The international markets are large, technologically volatile and growing at a speed that permits market entry. The private sector is beginning to invest in research and development, and further government support may accelerate this effort and catalyze foreign investment into the industry. However, public research funding and other sectoral initiatives cannot substitute for policy measures to remove distortions in the incentive framework, and to create greater financial stability. They also need to be part of a broader informatics agenda that improves computer use (especially in the public sector), fosters development of a competitive software industry (Chapter III), mobilizes human capital for informatics (Chapter IV), and increases productivity and innovation in the communications sector (Chapter V). Strong complementarities within the informatics sector make progress in one field (i.e., computers) highly dependent on all the others. The lesson of more advanced information economies is that success in global markets depends on domestic policies for competition across the informatics sector, and for superior computer use.

CHAPTER 3

COMPETING IN SOFTWARE

Introduction

3.01   During the 1980s, the global software industry experienced phenomenal rates of growth: over 20% per annum. As advanced economies (including that of Turkey) became more information-intensive, this translated into a high elasticity of demand for software goods and services. Initially, this demand was fuelled by growing investments in informatics hardware (Chapter 2). However, more recently expansion of the software market has continued despite decelerating growth in informatics hardware sales. On the supply side, the software industry has experienced substantial gains in productivity that have reduced costs, shortened the life-cycle, and increased product range. On the demand side, organizations (especially those that have invested heavily in informatics) are looking to maximize return on their information resources through new applications and increasingly sophisticated software tools.

3.02   The software industry is becoming increasingly international. Many software products and services are traded; the major companies are establishing a presence in key markets; and the industry is experiencing a phase of consolidation on a world-wide basis. However, software is not a traded good in the same way as (for example) computers or communications equipment. Rather, software is a "product" that provides customized solutions to the particular information problems of an organization or activity. Efficient design and implementation of software products (at least for more complex applications) is subject to: (a) high transaction costs between the software supplier and client; and (b) significant information costs in terms of local market conditions, culturally-specific barriers to implementation of software solutions, and cross-country differences in internal reporting requirements, data security regulations, accounting rules, etc. The result is that software know-how - albeit internationally traded through packaged software and mobile consulting firms - has a high *non-traded* component. If Turkey is to realize potential welfare gains from informatics investments, then an internationally competitive software industry is a necessary (if insufficient) condition.

3.03   Turkey's market for software has already grown rapidly over the past 5 years in line with overall investment in information technology. Starting from a very low base in 1985, the market has grown at almost 70% per annum and is today valued at $76 million. This however represents less than 0.05% of the global software market that is today estimated at approximately $150 billion. (By comparison, Turkey's GNP is equivalent to 0.4% of global GNP i.e., ten times larger). Exports are minimal; and imported packages account for 2/3 of the market. None of the international software houses have established a permanent presence in Turkey; and industry structure is still dominated by the hardware vendors. There is a long tail of small independent software houses; but only one or two have the financial and human resources essential for longer term profitability and growth.

3.04   If the software industry is to catch-up with the international competition and become a source for productivity growth throughout the economy, action is required. The Government has already designated the software industry as a "priority sector" in the Sixth Five Year Plan (1990 -1994). Despite a number of small initiatives to support product development and design, the overall policy and environment remains hostile to the industry's growth. There is a shortage of human capital; defects in the legal framework; imperfections in the capital markets that preclude external financing; a lack of standards; and problems in the crucial field of public procurement.   This last issue is a particularly significant constraint since the government accounts for approximately 40% of the total software market.

3.05   This Chapter is organized in four main sections. Section one provides a more detailed discussion of the economic and business significance of software.   Against this backdrop, Section two reviews developments in the Turkish software market since 1985, and assesses its competitive positioning for the 1990s. Section three assesses the policy framework in Turkey, and compares existing measures with those adopted in more advanced economies. Section four develops a possible action agenda for the industry.

Definition and Economics of Software

3.06   Computer software has become the "lifeblood" of business, industry, and government. Some six years ago--about three generations in the fast-changing software industry--the U.S. Office of Technology Assessment concluded that:

> *"Of all the information technology services, telecommunications and computer software are most important for United States competitiveness in other industries ... Competitiveness in computer hardware, and indeed in all high technology industries, increasingly depends on software.* "[1]

3.07   The term software refers both to the instructions that direct the operation of computer equipment and the information content, or data, that computers manipulate. There are two general types of software: *systems software*, which is used to manage the components of a computer system--for example, computer operating systems that control input and output operations--and *applications software*, which is designed to apply computer power to the performance of tasks such as materials and facilities management in hospitals, budget and payroll administration, or computer-aided design of turbines and pumps. In the 1980s there was an explosion in the number and types of applications of software in organizations ranging from back-office record keeping, front-office clerical support, to highly specialized and technical scientific and engineering systems. A noteworthy aspect of software and hardware design efforts

---

[1] U.S. Office of Technology Assessment, <u>International Competition in Services</u>, Washington, D.C., July, 1987, pp. 21-22.

has been in the area of *systems integration*, which is the process of identifying and bringing together various technologies in order to define and deliver a complete information package.[2]

3.08   The software industry is a source of substantial economic benefits. As the software industry has grown, innovated and become more specialized, this dynamism has spilled over into productivity gains throughout manufacturing, agriculture and the service industries (both public and private). Embedded software[3] is at the core of the machine tool and vehicle control industries, as well as of power generation and distribution, and electronic products and telecommunications. Customized software has grown in importance as banks, government services, and management of large institutions depend more and more on computer-based technologies for routine operations and management. Further, packaged software has driven the development of the personal computer sector and continues to be the principal source of its diversity in such areas as office automation, productivity tools, and computer-aided design, engineering, education and manufacturing. Increasingly, work processes, management structures, products and service modes are all reflected in the software systems of more advanced organizations. Software use and production can be described as an "overriding activity" which (like mechanical engineering) cuts across many different sectors, requiring a new range of skills and know-how.

3.09   Worldwide, software is a booming industry, and in the advanced economies is a leading source of employment creation and economic growth. The software industry offers an example of a vigorous economic sector: strong competition, rapid sales growth, a diverse mixture of firms, rapid commercial innovation, strong performance in international markets, and, over the past twenty-five years, low barriers to entry. The world software goods and services market was around $100 billion in 1987 and is estimated to exceed $400 billion in 1995 (Table 3.1). There are hundreds of thousands of independent software companies (some 8,000 in the U.S. alone), typically small in size, with a handful of developers writing new applications. Increasingly, the world's leading hardware manufactures are becoming software companies, in part because of the blurring of boundaries between hardware and software, and in part because of the general move to products with greater utility. For example, ICL and Bull claim 50 percent of their revenue in 1991 came from software and services. Revenue from software is growing faster than revenue from hardware, in spite of the fact that software functions are continuously integrated into new hardware designs. In a mirror image of earlier practice, software is today defining how computers are designed, built, and applied.

---

[2] Systems integration refers to the integration of hitherto disparate components of an information system, including, for example, large and small computers from different manufacturers, ancillary equipment also from different manufacturers, and packaged and custom-designed software. Systems integration has existed since systems with distinct components have been available. In the recent past, however, systems integrators have been relieving clients of the burden of data processing and of planning, developing, and implementing new applications by taking over its clients' systems and running them itself, thereby providing single solutions from a single source.

[3] Other examples of devices with considerable embedded software include: production robots, numerical control machines, diagnostic devices, quality monitoring and testing meters, and materials handling equipment.

Box 3.1:   The Strategic Importance of Software

Consider the following examples from various different sectors:

"E.F. Hutton decided to build a highly sophisticated, comprehensive, and competitively significant software system for processing trading transactions, rather than to purchase a vendor's tested but more limited system. The in-house software development project was never completed and added to the firm's multimillion dollar losses that hastened its demise.

Wells Fargo Bank lost a lawsuit for not advising a customer to place a large, low-interest savings account deposit into a higher-yield product. Such advice could have been provided easily if the bank had software capable of scanning for such situations.

Financial problems at Bank of America were exacerbated by the lack of software capable of identifying critical levels of bad debt."1/

Defective computer programs at the United Education & Software Co. may cost banks $650 million in unaccounted student loans. Switching to a new system in 1987 was not properly tested and resulted in the introduction of major software errors.2/

An error in a hospital radiation device resulted in a 63-year old patient undergoing radiation treatment at the Kennestone Oncology Center in Georgia to mistakenly receive two bursts of radiation that were 125 times greater than prescribed. The perilous extra pulses burned a hole in the patient's chest, destroyed a nerve controlling the left hand and required a mastectomy.3/

A faulty modification to a software program which was supposed to speed up the transmission of signals between computers resulted in the world's largest and technically most expert computer network—AT&T's interstate and international network—not fully functioning for nine hours on January 15, 1990.4/

The 1989 Lincoln Continental [automobile] has 83,517 lines of code that required 35 person-years of programming at a development cost of $1.8 million. Check-out machines [at supermarkets] typically have over 90,000 lines of code that require 58 person-years of programming.5/

Notes: 1/   S. Rosenthal, H. Salman, "Hard Choices about Software: The Pitfalls of Procurement," Sloan Management Review, Summer 1990, p. 81

2/   "United Education's Computer Blunders," Wall Street Journal, March 10, 1989, p. A6.

3/   A. Kornel, "When Computerized Disaster Strikes," Computerworld, June 4, 1990, p. 90. Other software horror stories can usually be found in the monthly issue of the technical journal ACM SIGSOFT Software Engineering Notes.

4/   "The Day that Every Phone Seemed Off the Hook," Business Week, January 29, 1990.

5/   B.R. Schlender, "How to Break the Software Logjam," Fortune, September 25, 1989.

**Table 3.1 Growth in Software Industry Revenues
1985-95, $ billions**

	1985	1990	1995
Total	93	213	442
USA	50	90	172
Western Europe	25	65	134
Japan	9	30	66
Other	9	28	70

Note: Operating systems and basic applications packages account for approx. half the market; and do not provide realistic entry opportunities for smaller companies.

Source: World Bank Estimates.

3.10   As relative hardware costs continue to fall,[4] software accounts for an increasing proportion of informatics investments. Depending on the type of investment, costs for hardware and software have followed a neat 'S-shaped curve' over time: whereas in 1955, software cost typically only about 10% of a project, now it is the hardware that is only 10%, as illustrated in Figure 3.1. The dramatic growth of software costs can also be seen in the U.S. Electronic Industries Associations' regular surveys of the computer industry. For example, software costs increased 250% from 1980 to 1985 and an estimated 680% between 1980 and 1990 compared to that of hardware costs, which increased 110% from 1980 to 1985 and an estimated 340% between 1980 and 1990 for embedded software development in the U.S. Department of Defense.[5]

3.11   The world of software has changed dramatically, particularly since the emergence of personal computers in the early 1980s when the best of the industry's output was assembled in "garage-like" settings. Today in the largest firms, software products comprising millions of lines of code are produced in industrial environments against committed plans for function, cost, and date of delivery. Today's software is increasingly based on widely accepted industry standards, formal design methods, standard components, and supplementary aids such as computer-aided systems engineering (CASE). As the structure of the industry has matured,

---

[4] Unit costs for hardware (i.e., for information storage, processing and transmission) are estimated to have fallen in real terms at a compound rate exceeding 20% per annum since the 1950s. A recent study suggests that costs for a 1987 system and its parts may be expected to be reduced by a factor of 145 from 1987 to 2000. Al Cutaia, Technology Projection Modeling of Future Computer Systems, Englewood Cliffs, NJ, Yourdon Press/Prentice Hall, 1990.

[5] Electronics Industries Associations, DoD Computing Activities and Programs: 1985 Specific Market Survey, Washington, D.C. 1985.

firms have established themselves and customers have come to rely on continuous, incremental improvement of their applications, as well as on secure and knowledgeable service and support. The magnitude of the up-front investments required to create competitive software products, and of the down-stream investments needed to sell and support them, has also increased dramatically.

Figure 3.1: Changes in the Relative Costs of Hardware and Software

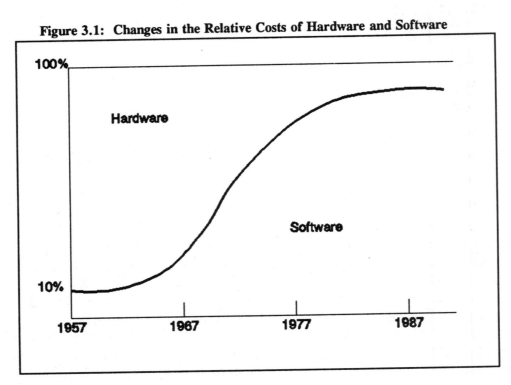

Source: **D. Bell, T. Morry, J. Push, <u>Software Engineering</u>, Prentice Hall International, Englewood Cliffs, NJ, 1987.**

The Turkish Software Market

3.12   *Demand*. The growth of Turkey's software market has been spectacular; at an annual rate of 70% between 1985 and 1990 (Figure 3.2).[6] This rate of growth is faster than for the U.S. software industry during its "boom" period between 1981 and 1983. It is also considerably faster than the rates in the United States and in Western Europe during 1984-87,

---

[6] It should be noted that there is no generally accepted data series on the size of the Turkish software market. Further discussion of the different methodologies used in obtaining estimates and differences between estimates can be found in the International Business Services background report to this study, "The Software Market in Turkey," Istanbul, November, 1991. In this survey, software development includes packaged software sales and contract programming services. It does not include companies' expenditures on in-house software activities. This non-marketed activity is significant in Turkey, particularly in large corporations and in government.

which was 15% and 32% respectively. The Turkish software market is currently valued at $78.6 million. Employment in the industry is showing strong growth, with an annual increase of around 35-40% per year over the last five years.

Figure 3.2: Growth Rate of the Turkish Software Industry ($ millions)

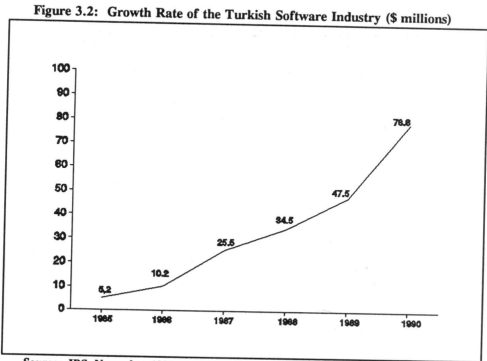

Source: IBS, November 1991.

3.13   The software market is only the visible (and probably smaller) component of the overall demand for software goods and services.   There are three respects in which observable market data understate the true level and composition of demand.   First, many of the larger public and private organizations have established electronic data processing (EDP) departments departments that provide in-house software services.   These internal EDP departments are responsible for meeting the customized software requirements of their corporate parents, and make relatively little use of external software houses[7]. Despite potential gains from external supply of specialized software services, internal provision appears to be driven by: (a) confidentiality requirements; (b) limited supplier capability; and (c) high monitoring and transaction costs in dealing with external suppliers. The result is that for the Top 36 Informatics Users, revealed software expenditure is equivalent to only 7% of hardware sales (Table 3.2). This compares with a ratio of closer to 50% in information-intensive companies in the more advanced economies.   Second, a high proportion of software sales is still bundled with

---

[7] Market information is available only for four EDP departments that have been established as independent subsidiaries by the Holding Companies: Bimsa, Eczacibasi, Aknet, and Bilpa.

investments in large computer systems. Frequently, there is no separate price defined for software systems, training, after-sales service, and maintenance. This price and service bundling is particularly evident in the case of public procurement (which represents over 50% of the large system market). Third, there appears to be a growing incidence of software piracy, which has been intensified by the shift from mainframes towards PCs (para. 3.11). Estimates suggest that only 10% of generic word-processing, database and spreadsheet programs are legally obtained.

Table 3.2: Composition of Software Sales by End-User

$ Million	Public	Private	Total
Cumulative Sales (CS)	77	125	202
Sales to Top 36	18	13	31
Percentage of CS	23%	10%	15%
Software/Hardware	9.6%	5.2%	7.4%

Source: Bilgisayar.

3.14   The composition of demand (as revealed by market transactions) by user group remains fairly concentrated. The top 36 (public and private) informatics users in Turkey account for almost 15% of the total market (Table 3.2). This is however significantly less than their share of the hardware market for larger systems (35%), implying that the large in-house EDP departments carry out substantial software development activities. In addition, the public sector accounts for almost 40% of the software market. This share is broadly in line with the public sector share of the hardware market, and presents the government with a significant opportunity to influence industry standards and capabilities through its procurement activities.

3.15   Recent estimates suggest that software applications (mostly packages) account for 60% of expenditures (of the $78.6 million), operating systems account for 20%, and custom software development for the remaining 20%. Turkish domestic consumption of software is overwhelmingly dominated by software packages. Almost all accounting and related commercial packages are developed locally. Unlike in some countries, such as India, the software industry in Turkey recognized early on that there was no point in reinventing readily available international software applications. Thus, manufacturing (computer-aided design and engineering), networking, and decision-support applications (including databases, spreadsheets, etc.) are nearly all imported as packages. Custom software services have not been developed for a number of reasons that partially reflect Turkish management attitudes towards software: (a) software, being intangible, does not enjoy the same prestige as hardware--it has no visible form; (b) most of the large and medium-sized user firms have their own EDP departments to provide customized software; and (c) software specifications are inadequately defined in public procurements. In most cases they are eclipsed by lengthy hardware specifications.

3.16   *Supply.* The Turkish software industry comprises three main supply segments. The first dominating the industry are the hardware vendors (which represent approximately 40% of the recorded industry sales). The second comprises the in-house EDP departments of a small number of more advanced informatics users in the corporate market (11% market share). Third is a long tail of small independent software houses (whose numbers range from 100 to 200) that together represent 15% market share, of which 2/3 is supplied by the top six software producers. Other software suppliers include: (a) local distributors of imported hardware which also supply compatible software (9% market share); (b) local distributors of imported packages (7% market share); and (c) foreign companies that are providing site licenses to Turkish organizations (16%). Local value added in the software market appears to be significantly less than 40% (of total sales).

3.17   The Turkish software industry is dominated by the large computer producers-- particularly IBM, KOC-UNISYS, NCR, DEC, and Siemens Nixdorf. These firms provide much of the software that is used with their hardware, either as representatives of international software producers, or through custom programming for local conditions and requirements (mostly related to differences in accounting principles). Within this group, IBM is by far the leading player in the market. Clearly, the hardware vendors provide a significant transfer of know-how to the software industry through training, quality standards and procedures, and exposure to best international practice. However, these benefits need to be balanced against the barriers to entry and competition that hardware vendors often create through proprietary software and systems. A particular problem is that hardware vendors often bundle their sales of software and maintenance into the total sales price for a system (a practice which is further encouraged by public procurement practices (para. 3.37)). The practical consequence is that hardware vendors are able to cross-subsidize their software sales, and thereby prevent fair competition from the independent software houses. Development of a productive software industry in Turkey will require an industry structure that is more balanced between hardware vendors and independent software houses.

3.18   In-house EDP departments play a large and important role in the industry. Even excluding the non-marketed activities of most EDP departments, the four that have been established as independent subsidiaries already account for 11% of the market. These companies have significant competitive advantages vis-a-vis the other software houses in Turkey. First, they possess a parent "with deep pockets", able to finance investments in personnel, more complex product development, and in quality. Second, they have access to a captive market for their services, thereby offsetting the significant market uncertainties that accompany product development by the independent houses. Third, they provide mainly services that are vertically integrated (i.e., that are tailored to the information problems of a particular industry sector such

Table 3.3: Industry Segments (1990)

	Recorded Sales ($m)	Market Share
H/W Vendors	32.7	41%
of which IBM	20.4	26%
Site Licenses (1)	12.6	16%
In-House EDP Depts.	8.9	11%
Software Producers	8.4	11%
H/W Distributors	7.0	9%
Software Distributors	5.5	7%
Micro-Suppliers (2)	3.5	4%
TOTAL	78.6	

Notes: (1) Residual estimate of unrecorded software imports in the form of aide license fees.
(2) There are approximately 100 micro-suppliers, each of which have less than 0.05% market share.

Source: IBS/Bilgisayar.

as finance). The better EDP departments are gaining experience in line with the international learning curve of the software industry. More and more, successful software companies will have a sector-specialization (i.e., for government services, finance, or manufacturing).[8] Provided that the implicit protection afforded to in-house EDP departments is temporary and balanced with out-sourced suppliers, experience of other OECD countries suggests that this industry segment: (a) will become increasingly organized as independent companies with a sectoral focus; and (b) will gain market share.

3.19   There are between 100 and 150 smaller companies in Turkey involved in selling and producing software. Many small companies have entered the market in the past few years because of the relatively low cost of initial entry to the market (in terms of capital requirements). These start-up and small software firms come and go--often due to the scarcity of long-term risk capital that offsets revenue fluctuations--and a reduction in their number can be anticipated as the industry consolidates. Most of the companies have less than 15 professionals, of whom only about one-third of these are working on software-related activities. To diversify revenue sources, many of these companies are also in the business of distributing imported hardware and software (which on average accounts for 50% of revenues). Very few of the products supplied by these companies represent original or creative design. Rather, the smaller companies survive

---

[8] An example borrowed from Singapore illustrates this point. Singapore, with the fourth largest deep-water port in the world and a track record of experience and expertise in port management, is now capturing that expertise in computerized expert systems, which it hopes to export to other major ports around the world.

by supplying Turkish adaptations of generic software (that is internationally available), and by developing commercial and accounting packages that conform with the specifics of Turkish legislation and accounting practices. As Turkey modernizes her accounting rules in line with international standards (Box 6.3), this industry segment will lose a significant proportion of its existing customer base.[9]

3.20   There are only a handful of independent software suppliers whose principal activity is software development and sales, and which have established credibility and demonstrable achievement within the local market. Indeed 6 companies account for over 1/3 of the market revenues attributed to the independent company segment of the industry. However, even these companies are small by international standards. In 1991, the largest had revenues had revenues only slightly greater than $3 million, which was earned on a small number of large projects. The main business of these companies is customization of foreign software for local application. Development of new more specialized software packages is seen as too risky in light of: (a) the companies' limited capital base and access to external financing; (b) the rampant copying of software packages in Turkey; and (c) considerable market uncertainties and information problems in forecasting demand.

3.21   Only one foreign software company has established an independent subsidiary in Turkey. A number of companies have provided services on a transactional basis, particularly in the financial services sector.[10] However, these are isolated examples and do not appear to have resulted in a broader commitment to the Turkish market. The contrast with the hardware industry is striking. All the major hardware vendors are represented in Turkey through local subsidiaries; and they have played a crucial role in the formation of an informatics profession and in diffusing state-of-the-art technology. Although Turkey is not a major producer of computer equipment, its highly competitive supply structure ensures that users have access to the latest technology at international prices. In the software market, however, the absence of international software houses is slowing down the speed with which local industry is increasing productivity and improving service. In part, this problem results from small market size (para 3.12). However, it is also the result of very specific defects in the legal framework whose adverse impact is much greater for software than for hardware companies[11] (para. 3.55).

---

[9] An estimated 90% of organizations in Turkey use computers and software mostly for accounting purposes. See PIAR-ANKARA Research Company's Working Paper on "The Determination of Software Needs of Organizations," prepared for TÜBITAK, Vol. 1, November 1991.

[10] e.g., Systematics is supporting Akbank's branch automation; Logica is working on the Central Bank's network configuration; Kirschman has been contracted to assist in Emlak Bank's automation.

[11] Hardware companies typically protect their most strategic intellectual property through trade secrets and internal security measures; and are therefore less reliant on protection from the legal framework.

3.22   At present, performance in the software industry appears to be significantly below that in other economies. While there is no single way to measure performance, a number of indicators point to industry lack of competitiveness:

- very limited exports;

- low revenues per employee (as proxy for labor productivity);

- low software to hardware sales ratio; and

- slow diffusion of software productivity tools.

3.23   Limited software exports have taken place since 1985. Measuring the amount of software exports is hampered by the lack of data and problems of definition. According to official statistics from the Undersecretary of Treasury and Foreign Trade, software sales outside Turkey amounted to: $761,000 in 1987; US$16,100 in 1988; US$10,400 in 1989; US$26,500 in 1990; and jumped to over $125,000 in 1991.[12] Surveys of companies have identified a few software packages being exported--Software AG has developed an airflight package that has been sold to the Portuguese airlines, Hachi has developed a multi-function office package that is being distributed through IBM. It is clear that Turkish software firms have a long way to go to establish and market themselves in the highly competitive and quality-conscious markets of OECD countries.

3.24   Revenues per employee in the software industry appear to occupy a very wide range: from over $60,000 per capita to $4,000 per capita in the companies.[13] Among the leading independent software houses (para. 3.21), revenues per employee average $30,000. In part, this wide range stems from inter-firm differences in capital stock. The companies that have higher per employee revenues are the in-house EDP subsidiaries that are providing both computer and software services. However, the wide range also indicates certain barriers to competition and exit. Even at the top end of the industry, revenues per employee are substantially below those earned by the international software houses. Major companies such as Microsoft or Lotus expect to earn $200,000 per employee; and smaller specialist houses with lower overhead and marketing costs may earn even more. In part, low labor productivity can be explained by the small size of the domestic market etc., and by widespread software piracy (that effectively sets a product price ceiling). But it is also an indication of more systemic weaknesses in the industry. First, it points to problems of low skills, and limited value added

---

[12] Again, official data may not reflect exports of software only, or sufficiently explain the drop between 1987 and 1988, and the jump from 1990 to 1991. The export figure of $761,000 in 1987 has been difficult to verify. See IBS, "The Software Market in Turkey," Istanbul, November, 1991, p. 45.

[13] This range excludes the hardware vendors for whom separate software revenues per employee are not available.

incorporated in domestic software products. Second, it suggests that there may be a problem of excess competition in the market. Since there are no product standards, low barriers to entry and a high ease of product copying, marginal firms are able to enter the market and drive down prices for the more established companies. While consumers may appear to benefit in the short run from lower prices, the medium and longer term implications are less positive. As a result of marginal firm competition, average industry investment in training, after-sales service, quality and new products is likely to decline. Short run cost savings are therefore traded off against a medium term decline in service and product performance.

3.25   Software to hardware sales ratios in Turkey lag significantly behind those in other OECD economies. The ratio has increased marginally since 1985 (Table 3.4); however it remains surprisingly low especially given the speed with which Turkey has increased its investment in hardware. To some extent, the low ratio in Turkey is an accounting artifact. Software industry structure in Turkey is still based on a high proportion of hardware vendor sales and in-house EDP departments. As a result, much software industry activity is non-marketed, and therefore not captured by sales data. Over time, system unbundling and establishment of separate EDP subsidiaries (paras. 3.18) will increase the marketed proportion of the software industry.

Figure 3.3: Ratio of Software to Total IT Sales Percentage (1990-91)

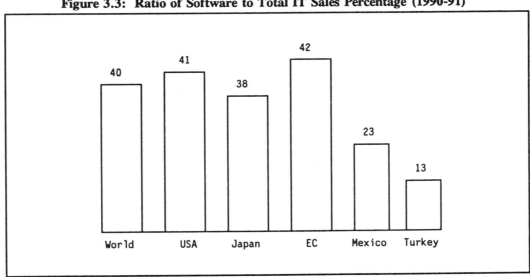

3.26   However, the problem also reflects demand and supply weaknesses. On the demand side, there still appears to be a reluctance to attach the same weight to software/maintenance/training (S/M/T) investments as to hardware procurement. This is true both in the private and public sector. Tender documents rarely devote equal attention to S/M/T issues. The composition of revenues from a sample of software companies reveals that maintenance and training activities are poorly rewarded, even when companies make the investment in the necessary human capital. Similarly, accounts receivable are largely comprised of overdue payments for these services.[14/] The problem is not however simply one of unsophisticated demand. There are also a range of supply-side weaknesses that discourage potential clients. A lack of appropriately trained informatics specialists and end users within organizations leads to computer under-utilization and poor in-house applications services.[15/] The lack of industry standards creates unevenness in the product, service and documentation quality, creating significant information problems for customers. In addition, there are substantial gaps in industry product range. It appears that there are only 300 packages available in Turkey, compared with thousands in more advanced economies.[16/] While the market for commercial and accounting applications is very competitive, there is little supply either of customization services or of specialized application packages (e.g., for scientific and technical applications, or for manufacturing). The software industry has made only modest efforts to expand the market for these more advanced services through e.g., investment in personnel training, marketing and client education.

3.27   Tools and techniques for increasing the productivity of software development have diffused only slowly through the Turkish software industry. Very few companies make use of specific applications packages for Computer Assisted Software Engineering (CASE); and therefore are subject to both higher risks of program design flaws and increased costs for program de-bugging. Second, software products are seldom developed according to international standards. These quality management standards (e.g., ISO 9000/9001, EN29001) provide detailed guidelines for each stage of the software product lifecycle: design, quality assurance, production, maintenance, documentation, product upgrades, etc. The standards can have a significant impact on industry efficiency and rate of productivity growth. They define minimum levels of customer service. They correct client/supplier information asymmetries, and thereby support market growth. And they embody and the accelerate the diffusion of best industry practice. The formal adoption and dissemination of software standards would address a number of constraints on medium term industry growth and competitiveness.[17/]

3.28   *Conclusion*. The Turkish software industry has displayed considerable dynamism since 1985. Annual growth rates have reached almost 70%. The industry has experienced rapid firm turnover. A small number of companies have become established as industry leaders; and

---

[14/] In the case of one company, three-quarters of maintenance and training fees were in arrears.

[15/] As documented for a wide range of sectors in the Working Paper prepared by PIAR-Ankara Research Company, "The Determination of Software Needs of Organizations," TÜBITAK, November 1991.

[16/] Based on a survey of all application packages advertized in Bilgisayar Magazine between July 1990 and July 1991.

[17/] It should be noted that software productivity tools and standards have also diffused relatively slowly in more advanced economies.

are investing in skills, client relations, and product and service diversity. Nevertheless, software is still an "infant industry," lagging 5-10 years in production of the kind of large, sophisticated software products that are found in OECD countries. One stylized model of software industry development points to four strategic but overlapping eras (Box 3.2). More advanced economies are today located between eras three (the "shrink-wrapped" package era) and four (systems integration era). The industry in Turkey is however approximately five years behind the frontier: between eras one (bundled software) and two (in-house customized software). While the model abstracts from the texture and complexity of software industry development, it clearly points to the productivity gap that Turkey needs to close.

Box 3.2: International Software Industry - Strategic Eras

Era 1: hardware makers did much of the basic software design work in-house and contracted out only the coding and programming work to their affiliated software companies. Software was not widely regarded as a separate product in its own right--it is simply included in hardware sales. In the late 1970s, following IBM's lead a decade earlier, most hardware vendors "unbundled" their software, separating prices for software products.

Era 2: rapid growth in customized software, developed by domestic computer and software producers and users in large organizations. Software applications become distributed throughout organizations. Service industries, which depend on the storage, processing, and retrieval of information to a larger extent than other industries, become the largest purchasers of software and services.

Era 3: dominated by "shrink wrapped," software packages. These packages offer economies of scale to vendors, who can focus on market niches and meet growing demand for more sophisticated technical and support services related to the product. Demand for packages increases because of the scarcity of experienced human resources and the risks in custom development projects. At the same time, software copying is rampant, particularly for two of the most common software applications— word processing and spreadsheets. Software firms adopt legal and commercial strategies to protect investment.

Era 4: information systems become larger, more integrated, and more complex, requiring systems integration services. These services can include project management, requirements analysis and design, contract programming, subsystem integration, education and training, and ongoing system support and maintenance. This era is marked by: large investments in and absorption of new technologies for software production; using software to solve domestic productivity problems; a priority in developing technically trained software engineers; data processing organizations shifting to "programming in the large" with larger shops typically employing over a thousand data processing professionals; monitoring, analyzing, and responding to trends in the worldwide industry; and an intellectual property protection system that protects software and encourages innovation in the industry. A rather powerful strategic inversion can be noticed at this stage, as the once dominant computer hardware manufacturers (in stage one) become leading suppliers of software and systems integration services.

Figure 3.4: Evolution of Software Market

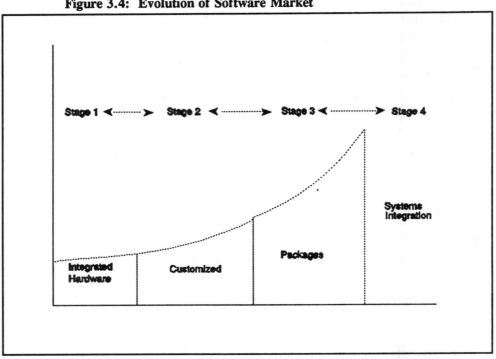

3.29   There are no short-cuts to this process. Rather, the policy and institutional framework must support industry efforts to mobilize resources for an increasingly complex and specialized business with large projects, large systems, sophisticated telecommunications networks, distributed systems, and the like. From one strategic era to the next, the industry becomes progressively more capital and skill intensive, dependent on multiple levels of intellectual property protection, and professionalized in terms of organization, management, and and standards in software production. If the Turkish software industry is to move rapidly up the product development ladder and to become internationally competitive, it needs to start by building sub-contracting relationships with international systems integrators and hardware vendors. These relationships would expose Turkish software houses to best practice on the key aspects of software development: cost control, quality assurance, demonstrated compliance with standards, project management skills, and data-security.

Policy and Institutional Framework

3.30   Free-rider problems, externalities and market imperfections are rampant in the software industry. The main source of the problem lies in the extreme economies of scale to which software development is subject. A very large proportion of total product costs is incurred during the design and debugging phases. These creates a number of issues. First, low barriers to product copying even in the presence of an adequate legal framework generate significant *free-rider problems* within the industry. New product development involves significant up-front investment in design, de-bugging, and programming. Once the product is marketed, it is easy for competing firms to duplicate the product with minor modifications, and to discount its price. Innovating firms may therefore find it hard to earn an adequate return on new product development. Second, there are substantial benefits to the economy as a whole (i.e., *externalities*) from the supply of software at marginal cost rather than at average cost (i.e., incorporating pre-production costs). Third, the time profile of costs generates substantial uncertainty for software producers. Frequently there is no guaranteed market. There are no salvage costs from product failures. And there is no collateral against which to secure external financing. *Information problems* in the product market coupled with *capital market imperfections* often combines to slow down product development.

3.31   To a certain extent, the market in the more advanced economies has responded to these problems through evolutions in industry structure. The industry is currently experiencing a period of rapid consolidation as companies become larger and multi-product (i.e., diversification and increased resources). This development provides the survivors with a larger capital base from which to finance development, a more stable revenue stream, and greater resources for information gathering. In addition, firms with market power are in a better position to address the free-rider problem through e.g., trade secrets, the delivery of superior after-sales service, and the threat of expensive legal action. In addition, growth of the software industry has been in parallel with the venture capital industry which is better geared to provide long-term risk capital than the banks. Nevertheless, these market-based responses only provide partial solutions to the underlying economic problems, and may even be counter-productive with respect to generation of externalities for the economy as a whole.

3.32   As a result, governments in many advanced economies have sought to provide additional support to the software industry (not least because of its perceived strategic importance). Governments have inevitably become involved in information technology in general and in software in particular as buyers and users, as commissioners of research, as setters of standards, and as negotiators of reciprocal access to other markets. Whether or not governments become involved directly with the sector (through subsidies, tariffs, start-up capital, and so forth), they are generally major customers of the software and computer services sector.

3.33   Various incentives to promote software industry development have been pursued by both OECD and newly-industrializing countries (Table 3.4 and Annex 4). Practically all the countries which have experienced sustained economic growth in the last decade, but most notably Japan, Korea, and Singapore have invested heavily in expansion of the software sector. These countries have all provided incentives to stimulate software firms to produce domestically, to export software, and to develop appropriately skilled and highly qualified manpower. Singapore, for example, gives developers of sophisticated software packages a ten-year tax holiday, and firms exporting software above $1 million (Singapore) receive a 20% concessionary tax rate. Japanese firms are eligible for a tax deduction amounting to 20% of all annual increases in training costs for software engineers.

3.34   In addition to these specific incentives, governments have typically sought to accelerate productivity growth in the software industry through: (a) procurement policies; (b) a strong legal framework for the protection of intellectual assets; (c) establishment of standards; and (d) financial sector policies conducive to venture capital financing. Each of these measures addressed different market problems faced by the industry. Procurement policies play a crucial role in reducing product development risks, in establishing technical standards for the industry, and in capturing the social benefits of software. A legal framework that protects software copyright and trade secrets corrects asymmetries that create resource misallocation between intangible and tangible assets (as well as strengthening returns to innovation). Standards close the productivity gap internal to the software industry (through diffusing best practice) and limit the destructive price competition caused by the entry of marginal firms (para. 3.23). A financial sector framework supportive of venture capital addresses capital market imperfections that would otherwise narrow the resource base available to a high-growth but high-risk industry.

Table 3.4: Incentives to Promote Software Industries in Selected Countries

	Tax Holidays	Preferential Credit	Hardware Investment Support	Export Assistance	Software Grant	Training Grant
United Kingdom					/	
Japan	/	/				/
France	Proposed		Proposed			
Taiwan	/			/		
Singapore	/			/		
Hungary	/		/			
Ireland	/		/	/	/	/

Note: / stands for yes. For further details see Annex III of this chapter.

3.35   In Turkey, the public sector also deploys a number of instruments to support software industry growth. Indeed, the software industry has been designated as a priority sector in the Sixth Five Year Plan (1990-94). First, the public sector is a major purchaser of software services and products; and accounts for approximately 40% of the total market. Second, limited research financing has been made available through the Council for Scientific and Technological Research (TÜBITAK). Four software development projects have been financed at a total cost of less than $1 million. Third, software imports have been almost completely liberalized[18]

---

[18] Software imports come under customs classification 85.24. They are exempt from customs duty and subject only to a fund levy of $5 per diskette- large or small.

with the aim to: (a) stimulate a competitive environment; and (b) reduce a major input cost for the software industry itself. Fourth, certain software development costs are subject to Research and Development Legislation (Law 3239), and therefore generate significant tax shields for software producers. In addition, software companies benefit from a lower investment floor (TL1 billion) in applying for the government's industrial incentive package.[19] Fifth, a number of small new companies have received benefits-in-kind from the Small Industries Development Agency (KOSGEB). Sixth, the government is developing a regulatory framework for the capital markets that should stimulate the venture capital industry.

3.36   Nevertheless, the overall framework for software industry development appears to be incomplete. Indeed, there are certain government policies that appear to be inconsistent with the objective of a dynamic software industry. First, public sector procurement practices are highly non-transparent and frequently create barriers to entry (into the government services market) for independent software houses. Second, the legal framework provides inadequate protection for software, and thereby discourages foreign investment in the industry. Third, there is a lack of standards for the software industry whose rate of investment is adversely affected by marginal firm entry. Fourth, the framework for human capital development attaches inadequate weight to the personnel needs of the software industry. Fifth, existing financial accounting standards create a protective barrier for the industry that may be inimical to its future growth.

3.37   *Public Sector Procurement Practices.* The software industry's development is retarded by procurement procedures and practices that are unnecessarily complex and could be simplified to the advantage of both government and industry. Moreover, it is seldom heard from interested bidders - hardware or software vendors - that public procurements under the existing system are carried out in an objective and impartial manner.

3.38   There are three problem areas. First, procurement in practice has a built-in tendency to favor the low bidder. In theory, electronic data processing tenders are freed from the requirement of Public Tender Law 2886 that the low bid wins the contract. However, structural problems in the technical committees (i.e., committee composition and terms of reference) prevent an adequate assessment of price/quality tradeoffs. The result is that the low bid normally prevails. This approach might be appropriate when buying commodity items like typewriters or personal computers (or an other standardized informatics product), assuming the functionality, reliability, and availability of parts and maintenance are all equivalent. However, the low bid model is far less appropriate when buying major computer systems with important applications, and systems integration services. These kinds of procurements are complex, and typically represent large investments. Factors other than purchase price become critical over time. Vendors who charge more but who provide a proven track record of performance, special expertise, reliability, and sufficient support can be well worth their price.

---

[19] In practical terms, this incentive has little value for the software industry, which is working not fixed capital-intensive.

3.39   Second, clear, detailed and unambiguous specification documents are not prepared for bidders.   Software specifications have been known to state simply "...and the related software required for the system described," or "...the required software for automating relevant departments."   This tendency leads many software firms not to even bid on contracts.   More hardware vendors that are in a position to offer the complete system tend to: (a) bundle the system price; (b) cross-subsidize the software bid (where separate pricing is required); and as a result (c) are given an unfair competitive advantage vis-a-vis the independent software houses.

3.40   Third, there is no standardized approach to evaluation and ranking of bids with significant components for information technology goods and services.   This is the stage of the procurement process that is most prone to differences of view and complaints, since matters of judgment inevitably are involved.   However, if evaluation criteria and procedures are adequately set out in the bidding documents, and properly applied, the award process would have stronger mechanisms for self-policing and transparency.

3.41   *Legal Defects*.[20]   The legal environment for software copyright protection in Turkey is today confused.   There are two possible sources of legal protection: (a) The *Intellectual and Artistic Works Law 5846* (1951); and (b) the *Cinema, Video and Musical Works Law 3257* (1986).   The 1986 law does not explicitly include software.   But as a product that can be electronically reproduced, it is possible that the courts might extend the protection offered under the Act to software.   The 1951 Law provides protection for "works which are interpreted as a language".   In addition, implementing legislation under the 1951 Law (enacted in 1986) explicitly extends the law's protection to disks and diskettes, but not to software.   As yet, no software company has been able to obtain (from the Ministry of Culture) the license that provides legal protection for their product.   A third possible source of legal redress for software companies is Penal Code Article 491 that covers theft.   However, prosecution under a criminal offence does not give rise (on an automatic basis) to civil damages, even where loss can be proved.   So far, 10 cases under different legal causes of action have been opened; but it is not expected that an unambiguous court ruling will be offered in the absence of supportive legislative initiatives.

3.42   This complex legal picture imposes three main costs for the software industry. First and at the margin, it discourages innovation and investment in the industry.   Although software users are beginning to recognize the benefits of a longer-term relationship with suppliers, copying is still rampant.   The magnitude of the unauthorized copying of software is illustrated by an estimate from Lotus Development Corporation that 90% of the copies of its flagship 1-2-3 spreadsheet program in Turkey have been pirated.[21]   Second, it increases the

---

[20] See Chapter 7, <u>The Legal Framework for an Information Economy</u> for latest developments in preparing draft legislation on software copyright.

[21] According to the U.S.-based Software Publishers Association, a rule of thumb in the software industry is that at least one unauthorized copy exists for every authorized sale of a computer program. See also Chapter 7.

difficulty software companies experience in obtaining external sources of finance. Third, it creates an additional disincentive to investment by foreign software houses. These companies already appear to be discouraged by the limited size of the domestic market, inadequate after-sales services, and uncertainty regarding the level of expertise and knowledge of relevant computing environments. However, the additional legal problems add to the business risk and, in certain cases, have prompted international software suppliers from refusing to market their products in Turkey.

3.43   *Lack of Standards*. User demand for "open systems" has been driving the computer market for the past few years. In essence, open systems mean the ability to run an application on a wide range of different hardware environments without rewriting; the ability to link together different types (and generations) of computers in a way most convenient to the user; and the ability to communicate between applications running on different environments across a network. By freeing users from technological dependence on the large computer manufacturers, open systems provide greater consumer choice and reduce barriers to entry in the hardware and software markets. As yet, Turkey has not developed (or adopted) standards for "open systems"; nor has public procurement of computer systems been used as an instrument to support user migration from proprietary to open standards.

3.44   To meet increasing demands for quality software in local and international markets, Turkish software firms will need to maintain standards and provide adequate software testing services. European firms, for instance, increasingly adhere to such standards; NATO's Allied Quality Assurance Program (AQAP, number 13) for software development and testing, and the British, European, and International standards (BS 5750, EN 29001, and the ISO 9000 series) for quality software development. In Singapore, a core function of the National Computer Board has been to establish and disseminate a set of standards for the software industry. These standards cover every stage in the software product life-cycle: from design through to documentation and after-sales service (including upgrade regulations). Very few software firms in Turkey develop software according to international standards. Nor do they have the mechanisms and arrangements to keep pace with the demand for standards in software development.[22] The lack of standards has a number of implications for the software industry. First, it is a major barrier to exports which increasingly need to meet international quality assurance standards. Second, it limits the extent to which independent software houses can take advantage of the shift from proprietary standards (which largely benefit the computer manufacturers) to open systems. Third, the standards vacuum lowers barriers to entry for more marginal companies which by providing e.g., lower quality after-sales service, are able to drive

---

[22] The Turkish Standards Institute (TSE) should play a more active role in promoting and diffusing standardization activities in both public sector IT departments (and ensuring compatibility) as well as the software industry. Special steps should be taken by the government to reinforce efforts towards "open" functional standards. For further discussion see B. Sarikaya and R. Yilmaz, "International and Turkish Information Technology Standardization," Working Paper, Bilkent University and TSE, February 1992.

down industry prices. While these companies may serve certain low value-added market niches, their overall impact may be to create excess price competition.[23]

3.45   *Human Resource Constraints.* The situation concerning manpower in the informatics field in Turkey is addressed in detail in Chapter V. Briefly, Turkey's ability to expand in all aspects of informatics is critically constrained by the shortage of adequately trained and experienced manpower. Very rough estimates place incremental demand for informatics professionals at around 21,000 over the next five years. The formal educational system provides less than a quarter of the personnel needs; and is not geared to the needs of a progressive software industry. The majority of its graduates either have a computer engineering background or, in the case of the vocational schools for higher education, basic computer programming. Few students emerge with the inter-disciplinary skills or advanced training in software engineering, project management or systems integration. Private sector training institutions have expanded rapidly to fill the supply gap, but are inappropriately regulated and provide sub-quality training.

3.46   *Limited Market Protection.* The domestic market for application packages in Turkey has enjoyed a sort of natural protection, mostly in accounting-related areas that have Turkish-specific characteristics, because of legal, tax, and other features. The need to adapt software to local accounting practices has dictated much of the growth in sales of application packages (e.g., general ledger, accounts payable and receivable, etc.). However, market pressure to change accounting practices of firms in the direction of Generally Applied Accounting Principles (GAAP) will (over time) eliminate this protection. It is far from certain that the protection currently enjoyed by Turkey's software industry is providing the learning curve essential for international competitiveness in this market.

Industry Prospects and Action Strategy

3.47   The software industry in Turkey will inevitably grow on the back of increased demand for information in the economy. Estimates of market growth over the next five years suggest a base case of approximately 30% per annum growth, resulting in a market of around $350 million by 1995. However, depending on the overall environment for the sector, there is also a low case and a high case (Figure 3.5). The trajectory that the industry follows will depend on two main factors: (a) the overall macroeconomic situation and annual growth rate; and (b) a set of specific factors that affect productivity growth in the software industry itself. The base case assumes unchanged sectoral policies and an average GNP growth rate of 5% per annum. The low case assumes ceteris paribus a deterioration in the macroeconomic situation, and an average GNP growth rate of 2% per annum. The high case assumes an average GNP growth rate of 5% per annum (as in the base case) *and* improved sectoral policies. This section identifies key elements in a policy framework that might support the high case trajectory.

---

[23] See also OECD, Information Technology Standards: The Economic Dimension, Information Computer Communications Policy No. 25, Paris, 1991.

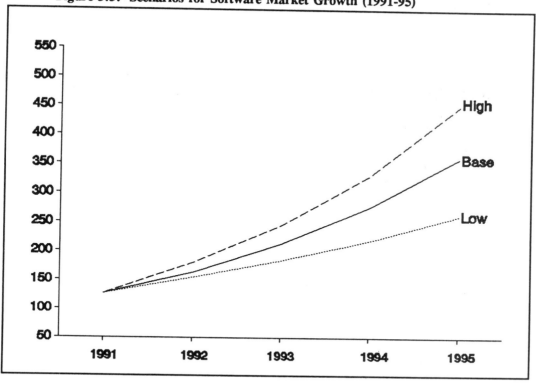

Figure 3.5: Scenarios for Software Market Growth (1991-95)

3.48   Even in the base case, continuous growth in hardware sales will result in a complementary demand for software. As noted elsewhere, investments in hardware and software are significantly behind both OECD and NIC countries. With customers' demands in Turkey for "total solutions," the informatics sector will face an increasing requirement for integration of hardware and software. Second, considerable demand for software has to date been hidden with hardware vendors still "bundling" their software. Separate pricing for software products will help establish software as a separate product in its own right. Third, Turkish software vendors are increasingly concerned about software piracy, and are seeking (with limited results) a software protection regime in Turkey comparable to that in most OECD countries. In the future, as users are increasingly able to count on support and maintenance, the high levels of piracy should decrease and sales of legitimate software increase. Finally, diffusion of information technology in small and medium-sized firms will no doubt play an important role in future growth of the domestic software industry as ever more specialized applications are required, and senior managers become more aware of the strategic role and importance of software and investments in information technology--investments too important to leave to "experts" such as Chief Information Officers (CIOs), Information Resources Managers (IRMs), and/or EDP staff.

3.49   However, if Turkey is to move to the high case, a more dedicated strategy will be required.   In the base case, software industry growth is essentially derivative and is driven by expansion in the domestic hardware market (accompanied by changes in observations not in activities i.e., unbundling of software services by hardware companies).   In the high case, software becomes a leading sector whose productivity (and hence value-added and employment) grows faster than the informatics sector, and much faster than the economy as a whole.   A number of key policies are available to affect the probability that Turkey shifts towards the high growth trajectory for its software industry.   These policy instruments include:

- measures to strengthen human capital formation;

- improved procurement practices and guidelines;

- changes to the legal framework;

- the introduction of software standards; and

- a stronger system for technology acquisition.[24]

The strategic thrust of policy should be to move Turkish software firms to era 4 (Box 3.3), where they can provide a full range of professional services including software development (according to international standards), functional management of large projects, maintenance, and training.

3.50   ***Expanding Human Resource Development in Software***.   Chapter V provides a detailed discussion of the composition and magnitude of demand for skills required by the software industry (and the informatics sector generally).   The Chapter analyzes the spectrum of programs and changes required in terms of institutional responsiveness, course structures, access and quality control.

3.51   ***Creating Demand Through Procurement***.   Due to the variety of missions of government agencies, its software needs span the gamut from small standard office automation packages (word processing, spreadsheets, statistics, and databases) to large, specialized systems (air traffic control, hospital information systems, military command and control) and much more.   In principle, the composition and size of public sector demand for software should create significant market (and learning) opportunities for qualified local suppliers, especially in light of the "launch" costs of packaged software.[25]

---

[24] See also OECD, Software Engineering: The Policy Challenge, Information Computer Communications Policy No. 26, Paris, 1991.

[25] It is estimated to cost between US$5-10 million to "launch" a PC software product--for advertising, public relations, packaging, and collateral material.

3.52   A key element, and first objective, to expanding Turkey's informatics sector depends on treating investments in information systems, technology, and new applications like investments in other essential systems. Government managers should view these as investments in a trajectory of development that will take the government in a specific direction, rather than as discrete purchases of devices or services--computers, software packages, training, etc. The greater the investment, the more committed to the direction Government becomes, and the more costly it is to divert to a different course. This makes thorough planning and coherent specifications crucial to the process of competitive procurement.

3.53   To address the issue of improving the quality of informatics-related tenders to the advantage of both Government and industry, key actions are likely to include:

- establishing a detailed set of procurement guidelines for informatics-related acquisitions including: (a) pre-qualifying firms and institutions; (b) explanation of the proposed investment's relationship to the agency mission; and (c) explicit evaluation criteria and weighting;

- training for key staff in each of the Ministries in technical and specialized issues related to the new procurement guidelines;

- specification of minimum procurement guidelines for the software components of any informatics investment;

- designation of centers of expertise within the public sector together with certified private firms to provide technical assistance on informatics procurement specifications;

- requiring that all tenders have an unbundled pricing structure so that software bids (including maintenance and training) can be separately evaluated;[26]

- specification of regulations regarding: (a) the composition of external technical committees appointed to assist in bids evaluation; (b) formal evaluation criteria and weighting; and (c) information pro-formas to be provided to the committees;

- a requirement that all qualifying firms should be certified in line with international standards for software quality assurance (para. 3.43); and,

---

[26] This may require an amendment to the Budget Law (Schedule R, Title 390) that restricts government procurement of training services from private companies.

- explicit reservation of a percentage (e.g., 10% to 20%) of large-scale informatics procurements for independent local software suppliers.

These procedures for government procurement of software logically complement the guidelines and approach suggested in Chapter 2 for system procurement (para. 2.30).

3.54   *Setting Standards*. Widespread adoption of internationally recognized software standards are essential if Turkey is to take advantage of rapid growth in international software markets. Turkish firms that are certified according to these standards will be better able to exploit their labor cost advantages in supplying quality software engineering or design capabilities. They will also be better placed to enter into strategic alliances with developed-country firms both for large-scale domestic projects and for exports to the international market. The Turkish Standards Institute (TSE) in collaboration with other members of the National Quality Council, software user community and the software industry should therefore:

- accelerate preparation of key technical and quality assurance standards for the software industry;

- actively promote standards, especially "open" functional standards, in government procurement activities;

- provide training courses (for a fee) for software companies in the new standards;

- strengthen certification resources within TSE and in the private sector;

- accelerate the work of the National Quality Council in establishing accreditation procedures for private firms and the Software Industry Association;

- provide certification services to independent software houses, as well as to internal EDP departments (both public and private sector);

- increase public awareness of software quality assurance standards through e.g., the proposed revisions to procurement guidelines, and a media campaign;[27]

---

[27] for which the Technology Development Project (Loan 3296-TU) already provides resources.

- promote competence in standardization in University computer engineering programs;

- launch a Software Quality Initiative aimed at significantly increasing the number of software companies and employees attaining ISO 9000 series certification. This Initiative should have monitorable benchmarks: i.e., that half the companies with 10 or more professionals should be certified by the end of 1996; and,

- enhance the role of the software industry association as a source of technical information, as a conduit for training, and as a mechanism for industry self-policing.

3.55   *Protecting Intellectual Property*. Legal protection for software is increasing rapidly around the world. However, the scope and effectiveness of that protection varies significantly from country to country, as illustrated in Annex 3. The trend is toward statutory protection--at least in theory by copyright law--of software programs (in both human readable and machine executable form) and the related manuals.[28/] At an earlier stage in the development of the Turkish software market, there were a number of arguments against legal protection of software copyright. Low-cost copying accelerated diffusion of software packages, and reduced the foreign exchange costs associated with software imports. Today, it is probable that the benefit/cost ratio of inadequate legal protection for software is less than unity (para. 7.10). Within the context of Uruguay Round GATT negotiations, the Government should take steps to provide and enforce explicit protection for software assets.

3.56   *Ensuring Access to Technology and Information*. Government, in association with industry associations and organizations, has a role to play in identifying and monitoring key software engineering programs and products early in their development. This includes technologies that are likely to have a major impact on existing businesses, and those capable of creating new commercial opportunities that firms in Turkey may be well positioned to exploit. Various software technology centers have been established in countries with vigorous software industries. They perform a number of vital functions including: (a) systematic evaluation and improvement of software engineering processes; (b) technology transfer to industry; and (c) initiatives to upgrade software quality and productivity through proper use of tools, methods, and integrated environments.

3.57   In Turkey, there has been very little firm-sponsored R&D-- despite the relatively attractive incentives for investments-- and Government sponsored R&D in informatics has only

---

[28/] For further discussion, see the U.S. Office of Technology Assessment on <u>Computer Software and Intellectual Property</u>, Washington, D.C., 1992.

recently begun.[29]   In 1991, TÜBITAK established a Software Research and Development Center (SRDC) at METU, and an Informatics Group at Marmara Research Center. However, both the Center and the Group lack broad industry support and appear to be motivated principally by academic interests. In software (as in other fields of technology development), Turkey will need to mobilize additional resources for investment in research and development; and to ensure that they are spent efficiently. Measures that might contribute to this objective include:

- targeting the software industry as a potential recipient of matching Challenge Grants from the Technology Development Foundation;[30]

- re-establishment of the SRDC and the Informatics Group as limited companies with 50% ownership by the Software Industry Association; and,

- implementation of research proposal guidelines requiring commercial pre-feasibility study for all software projects.

3.58   *Conclusions*. The Turkish software industry is still in an early phases of development, and suffers from low international competitiveness of its software products and related support services. Investments in software in Turkey are equivalent to less than 20% of total demand for computer systems and services; compared to an average of approximately 40% in OECD and NICs. In the future, Turkish firms will find themselves competing against leading international software companies that are heavily export-oriented--including many hardware manufacturers and vertical market firms moving into software, as well as other multinationals. These companies have a number of key strategic assets. These include:

- resources to effectively deliver products and support end users;

- commitment to continuously upgrade and enhance products;

- dedicated channels through which to market products and services;

- teams of skilled software engineers;

- global systems for monitoring and sourcing software techniques;

---

[29] For more details on specific R&D projects currently in progress by these organizations, see TÜBITAK, "Research and Development of Information Technology in Turkey," Working Paper, Ankara, February 1992.

[30] This Foundation was established in 1991 with the support of the Bank. Its primary role is to provide grants to private firms that are making matched investments in research and development.

- adaptive skills to localize international products; and

- increasingly, well-defined and predictable procedures.

3.59   Given these competitive assets of leading international software firms, Turkey faces a special challenge as it determines how best to keep pace with changes in the software industry and how best to acquire similar assets. Specific measures within a coherent policy framework will be required to accelerate the development of the software industry. A central implication of this study is that entry into sophisticated European and world markets requires a long-term commitment to: training and education in software engineering; quality assurance; standards development; interoperability; project management; the presence of international software houses; and intellectual property rights. From the perspective of this report, a "business as usual" approach will not be sufficient for the 1990s.

CHAPTER 4

HUMAN CAPITAL FOR AN INFORMATION ECONOMY

Introduction

4.01   Structural transformation of the Turkish economy over the past decade shifted resources from agriculture towards industry and services, and realigned the labor markets. Since 1980, urban white collar jobs, driven by private investment, have dominated employment creation in the formal sector. This is the mirror image of employment creation in earlier decades when most jobs were generated either in agriculture or in the public sector.

4.02   As the economy became more information-based, this transformation translated into exceptionally high rates of growth in demand for informatics specialists: people to run the mainframes, develop the communications services, and write the software. At the beginning of the 1980s, demand for these skills was concentrated in the public sector where the majority of informatics investments took place (see Chapters 1 and 2). However, market liberalization and the emphasis on private sector development has resulted in more widespread pressure on the labor markets to supply informatics specialists. In Turkey (as in other OECD and NIC economies), this demand pressure has translated into a combination of skills shortages and high relative wages for individuals with appropriate experience/training mix.

4.03   Further development of an information-based economy (IBE) during the 1990s will be progressively human capital-intensive. The essence of an IBE is a diffused application of informatics throughout an economy; and the substitution of knowledge and information (embodied in informatics) for both low-skill labor and other inputs. In the future, it will be people rather than technology deficits that constrain further structural transformation of the Turkish economy. The technology is internationally available. Provided that Turkey can become a highly sophisticated consumer (see Chapter 2), there is no technological barrier to progress. However, people with appropriate skills for an information-based economy are in very short supply. First, there is only a limited cadre of informatics professionals with the *specific skills* to develop new applications, and to overcome the "technology fear" experienced by an increasingly diversified user community. Second, the rapid development of the profession (and unforeseeable technological changes) challenges the responsiveness and efficiency of systems for training informatics specialists. Within an environment of sustained market-based change, new methods of labor market analysis and system feedback need to be developed that can substitute for conventional tools of manpower planning. Third, continued economic modernization and related informatics diffusion will create growing demand for labor with *general skills*: as information processors, and informatics user. Fourth, creating a workforce with both general and specific skills requires sustained public and private investment; and institutional reforms to increase the efficiency and flexibility of Turkey's training system.

4.04   The challenges that Turkey faces in this field are not unique. Rather, they are common to all economies that are negotiating the transition to an information-based economy.

The experience of more advanced economies is that the very fast evolution of informatics has created severe (but temporary) skills shortages. These shortages have a significant and adverse impact on the process of informatics diffusion. They create a labor market culture of job-hopping and employee-poaching, which in turn creates a strong disincentive to employer-financed investment in specific training. They generate high relative wages for key skill categories, which discourages smaller enterprises from informatics investment. Even in larger enterprises, recruitment problems in these occupational categories may cause economically inefficient capital-labor substitution in informatics applications (again stifling development of informatics-specific skills). The response of other OECD countries has been an array of programs, many of which are based on public-private cofinancing and organization. These range from upgrading universities (e.g., through company-endowed professorial chairs), through the development of cross-over training programs especially for graduates in non-technical fields, to vigorous tax incentives for industry training. The main lesson appears to be one of a division of labor between public and private institutions. In informatics (as in other professions), public institutions are better equipped to provide training for: (a) development of general skills in informatics literacy; and (b) a few highly specialized fields which anticipate future market demand or the research needs of the economy. Private institutions (including in-house company training) are more efficient and flexible in responding to the demand for specific skill development, especially when the returns on that skill can largely be captured by employer/ee.

4.05   In certain respects, Turkey has a natural advantage over other OECD economies in the development of a productive information workforce geared to the latest technologies. The age structure of Turkey's population is significantly lower than that of other OECD countries (25.5 compared to 38.5). This difference is likely to expand over the next two decades as the OECD population (except for Turkey) continues to grow older. Especially at a time of technological and occupational discontinuity, a young population confers a potential competitive advantage for countries that can mobilize adequate resources for human capital development. Informatics provide such a technological window of opportunity through its impact on market conduct, institutional structures, and the organization of work. In an information-based economy, workers are more likely to be: (a) retrained frequently over the employment lifecycle; (b) dependent on information technology; (c) evaluated through new performance measurement techniques; and (d) organized in more decentralized units. The characteristics of productive work - albeit related to today's work environment - will change significantly, disrupting traditional patterns of institutional development and learning. Skills and behavior that generate successful career paths in the public and private bureaucracies of advanced OECD economies have (in many cases) become sources of institutional inertia and inappropriate role models for younger employees. Turkey's status as a late modernizer means that she does not have to correct adverse demonstration effect that backward-looking corporate structures inevitably generate. Rather, the opportunity for Turkey is to leverage its younger population and its less ossified private organizations; and to make the youth factor a springboard for a more rapid transition towards an information-based economy.

4.06   This Chapter has four main sections.   Section one reviews labor market developments during the 1980s, and in particular analyzes demand growth for informatics-specific skills. Section two assesses the response of public and private mechanisms to meet the demand for these specific skills. As the economic modernization continues through the 1990s, section three evaluates probable changes in the composition of labor market demand for general and specific information-intensive skills. Section four assesses the adequacy of the existing institutional and policy framework to meet future demand requirements; and develops a preliminary set of recommendations.

Developing an Information Workforce: 1980s

4.07   The 1980s were a period of massive change in the occupational structure of the Turkish population. Perhaps the most pronounced development has been the large-scale transfer of workers (and households) from rural to urban areas. During the past decade, over 10 million people have migrated from the rural areas. The consequences of this migration for the information economy are as profound as they are hard to predict. Essentially, the experience of all advanced economies is the close correlation between urbanization, the spread of literacy and knowledge, and economic development. While many of the new migrants have found their first jobs in the informal and low-skill sector, the implications for economic transformation are more likely to be found in the next generation. For new urbanites, the relative complexity and information-intensity of urban (compared to rural) life increase incentives for investment in human capital formation, and also provide greater informal and formal learning opportunities. Spatial transformation of the Turkish economy therefore forms a virtuous circle with the development of an information workforce.   One early sign of this process has been the continuing growth in workforce literacy: from an estimated 70% in 1980 to almost 85% in 1989.

4.08   Accompanying this geographic shift has been a change in the occupational structure of the workforce. In 1980, 60% of the workforce were in the agricultural sector; by 1989, this had declined to less than 50% (though it appears that the rate of change is slowing as macro-instability affects modern sector performance). Employment growth has occurred largely in those sectors that are intrinsically more skill and information-intensive: manufacturing (11% to 14%); trade (6% to 10%); transport and communication (3% to 5%); and finance (1% to 3%). The share of public service employment remained constant (13% of total workforce) over the decade; and therefore did not add to social overhead costs imposed on productive sectors of the economy.

4.09   Within non-agricultural (formal) employment, there has been a dramatic increase in the number and share of white-collar workers, increasing from 3.3 million (44% of non-agricultural workers) in 1980 to 5.1 million (54% share) by 1989. This increase in white-collar workers is particular striking for two reasons. First, it accounts for 86% of total formal sector employment growth over the period. Unlike earlier industrializers which experienced a shift from agricultural to factory employment (during initial structural transformation era), expansion of white collar employment in Turkey appears to be leading traditional job creation in the manufacturing sector.[1] While white-collar jobs vary substantially in their information content, the broad picture is one of a market economy in which growing specialization and complexity require increased resource allocation to information-intensive coordination, marketing and monitoring activities. Second, most white-collar job creation appears to be market driven. Although there was some expansion in civil service and social sector employment during the 1980s, over 80% of the white-collar jobs were created in the private sector (mainly in the manufacturing, trade and tourism, and finance sectors). In the 1980s, Turkey avoided the experience (of many other developing economies) in which expansion of the information workforce is largely associated with public sector employment growth. Even within the white-collar class, the share of management, professional and technical staff has increased from 13% to 15% of non-agricultural workers over the decade.[2]

Table 4.1: Composition of Non-Agricultural Workforce 1980-89

Millions of Employees	1980	1985	1989
Non-Agricultural	7.4	8.5	9.5
White Collar	3.3	4.0	5.1
% of non-Agri.	44	47	54
Professional/Managerial	1.0	1.2	1.4
% of non-Agri.	13	14	15

Note: Definitional changes in 1988 affect totals, but not percentages

Source: SIS/World Bank Estimates.

---

[1] One possible interpretation is that Turkish industrialists are able to access the international technology set; and that therefore incremental capital/labor ratios in manufacturing are in a range similar to those in other OECD economies. Modern sector employment creation has therefore leap-frogged the era of factory-work; and is based on more information-intensive jobs.

[2] Indeed, Turkey experienced faster growth in white-collar employment creation (54%) during the 1980s than Portugal (26%), Korea (51%) or Japan (20%).

4.10   Development of an information-based economy and workforce has disproportionately increased demand for informatics specific skills. At the beginning of the 1980s, there was only a small market for computer operators, programmers, systems analyst/engineers, or data/information specialists.[3] Indeed, in 1978 there were only 345 computers in Turkey; and growth of the hardware park (and hence the derived demand for informatics skills) remained sluggish through 1984 (by which time there were 1331 computers). Much of the demand emanated from the public sector, which was the main source of investment in information technology (and also of in-house training). Public sector demand was also concentrated in mainframe facilities (in line with informatics configurations at that time); and the result was formation of a narrow base of informatics specialists who occupied a work environment entirely isolated from the mainstream of public administration. Neither public sector managers nor professional staff had direct access to computing facilities. Rather, information users were kept at arms-length from the data (and the technology) by the organization of separate data-processing centers in which programmers performed batch processing of information requests.

4.11   As the process of market liberalization took hold and private sector demand for information increased, the market for specific informatics skills widened. Between 1985 and 1990, the total value of Turkey's hardware park (for larger installations) increased from $200 million to over $1 billion, implying a very substantial increase in the demand for complementary labor input. Estimates suggest that a derived increase in demand (between 1985 and 1990) for almost 15,000 informatics specialists merely to manage this investment. In addition, demand for complementary software and computer services inputs grew even faster, creating a market for new kinds of informatics skills. Table 4.2 provides an estimate of growth and changing composition of demand for specialist informatics skills during this period.

4.12   Over the same period, the composition of informatics investment also shifted towards the purchase of newly available smaller systems and personal computers. Between 1985 and 1990, almost $850 million was invested in over 225,000 personal computers (in addition to continuing investment in the larger system hardware park). As in other economies, this shift towards more decentralized informatics systems was accompanied by changes in the demand for informatics specialists. First, the composition of specialist labor demand began to change. There was (relatively) less demand for programmers and mainframe systems analysts; and relatively faster demand growth for those categories of informatics skills that are necessary complements to investments in a PC environment: networking specialists, end-user support technicians, system analysts and integration experts, etc. Second, growth in the PC market has provided new market opportunities for the independent software houses - especially those specializing in packaged software. However, growth of a complementary software industry appears to have been hampered (inter alia) by a lack of appropriately trained software engineers and program development managers. Third, the PC investments have and created a market for user training: i.e., for general (e.g., keyboarding, DOS) software package-oriented skills

---

[3] See Annex 5 for a more complete classification of informatics occupational streams.

development by professional and administrative staff (who are not and should not be informatics specialists).

Table 4.2 Demand for Informatics Specific Skills
1985-90

	Mainframe Computer Staff	Software & Computer Services	TOTAL
1985	6,800	400	7,200
1986	7,800	800	8,600
1987	11,600	1,200	12,800
1988	14,900	1,500	16,400
1989	16,800	1,800	18,600
1990	20,500	2,800	23,300

Note: (1) Mainframe computer staff estimated from value of large system computer park. Labor productivity assumed to rise by 50% over period.

(2) Software and computer services staff estimated from industry sales.

Source: World Bank Estimates.

4.13   The sectoral composition of demand for informatics specialist skills is largely a function of each sector's relative information-intensity. Based on a sample of the leading 120 Users (See Table 4.3), labor demand appears to be concentrated in the finance and public administration sectors, which are also centers of: (a) informatics investment; and (b) white collar employment. These two sectors appear to account for approximately 70% of the demand for informatics specialists (excluding independent consultants and software houses).   The manufacturing sector employs a further 13% of informatics personnel; while the education sector accounts for approximately 8%. Given its focus on data-processing centers (i.e, mainframe facilities), the sample finds that the public sector still accounts for over 60% of informatics specialist demand.   However, it is likely that a broader sample of informatics users and employers would reverse the relative share of public and private sectors.

Table 4.3: Sectoral Composition of Demand for Informatics Professionals - 1990-91

	Public	Private	Total	White Collar(%)
Banking	23	47	22	15
Education	12	-	8	-
Services	53	14	38	55
Manufacturing	1	35	13	13
Mining	1	1	1	2
Agriculture	3	1	2	1
Transportation	5	-	4	6
Other	3	2	2	9
Total	100	100	100	100

Note: White Collar % is based on 1989 data

Source: IBS/Bilgisayar/SIS.

Systemic Response to Market Pressure

4.14   The speed with which the Turkish economy became more information-intensive during the 1980s presented enormous challenges to the system of formal education and training. These challenges are not unique to Turkey; but have also affected other OECD/NIC economies in which: (a) education systems are under less demographic pressure; and (b) the transition towards an information-based economy has been more gradual. Across the OECD and NIC economies, rapid growth and diversification of the informatics industry has been constrained by skills shortages and by institutional rigidities in the higher education system. These common difficulties imply a high payoff for those countries (Box 4.1) that systematically foster a dynamic informatics profession. This implies development of a training system that responds not only quantitatively to market signals, but also qualitatively. In the future, the key to sustained competitive advantage will be a nation's endowment of highly-skilled informatics professionals. Already, software production is becoming more automated due to the introduction of productivity tools and packaged solutions, reducing the business significance of low-wages. Similar trends are taking place in computer mainframe management in which demand for low-level operators is continuing to decline (with each new generation of hardware and software). Given these trends, Turkey must position herself for an international informatics market in which high skill rather than low wages are central to competitive strategies for product differentiation.

4.15   *Framework for Informatics Supply*. Informatics training in Turkey is provided by public universities, vocational schools of higher education (VSHEs), vocational schools, and by the private sector. The public education system is only able to supply a small fraction of the informatics skills required by the market. Indeed, the proportion of Turkey's estimated demand for informatics specialists that is met by the public education system has declined since 1985 (from one-third in 1985 to approximately one-fifth in 1990). However, this relative decline in public sector provision has been (in part) offset by a rapid but largely unrecorded growth in private mechanisms for informatics skills development. These mechanisms include: (a) vendor-supplied training ; (b) private training institutions; and (c) informal training that takes place within companies and data-processing centers.

Box 4.1: Singapore - Building an Informatics Workforce

Between 1980 and 1988, Singapore increased its human capital endowment of informatics professionals from 850 to 8,300. By 2000, Singapore expects to increase this workforce to increase to 30,000. There have been 5 main initiatives:

- rapid growth of informatics degree programs in the higher education system, which today supplies almost two-thirds of market requirements;

- a sustained program of sending students overseas to the US, Japan and UK for post-graduate training;

- a program of continuing education for informatics professionals under which the Government subsidizes 70% of the total (including payroll) costs of skills upgrading and refresher courses;

- a broad initiative to raise informatics literacy throughout the workforce through: (a) incorporating information technology into all university disciplines; (b) upgrading the computing resources of the universities; and (c) a special program for office workers;

- constant monitoring of labor market trends, future requirements, employer preferences, and wage structure.

The Government is now switching its focus from the quantity to the quality of informatics professionals. The latest initiatives aim to increase specialization through the establishment of advanced training institutes - in collaboration with leading computer and communications companies - in telecom software, computer-integrated manufacturing, and artificial intelligence.

4.16   In certain respects, the role played by the private sector in meeting the demand for informatics skills is similar to the experience of more advanced economies. It is clear that public institutions in many countries are not geared to anticipate (nor respond to) rapid changes in labor demand that informatics has generated. Nor is it appropriate for the public sector to be financing investments in the formation of specific informatics skills, since the return on this investment is easily captured by the private sector in terms of increased wages or profits (para. 4.04). A more appropriate role for the public sector is to provide: (a) general informatics training; (b) specialized training in fields subject to high externalities i.e., informatics research; (c) information that corrects problems in the labor market and support efficiency of privately supplied training.

Table 4.4: Sources of Informatics Skills
1985-90

		Public Sector Supply				Private Supply	
	Annual Demand	UNI A.S.	VSHE A.S.	VHS A.S.	Total A.S.	Total A.S.	%
1986	1,400	149	62	230	445	955	68%
1987	4,200	237	62	230	529	3,671	87%
1988	3,800	270	148	240	658	3,142	83%
1989	2,200	203	154	240	597	1,603	72%
1990	4,700	233	216	240	689	4,011	85%
1991	6,500	260	221	335	816	5,684	87%

Notes (1) For estimated of annual demand, see Table 4.2.
       (2) Private Supply is an estimated residual; and assumes that forces respond to supply/demand gap.
       (3) A.S. equals annual supply.

Source: IBS/SPO.

4.17   Nevertheless, public universities and vocational schools play a crucial role in a market-oriented training system. First, they supply a core of professionals with a more formal intuition and understanding of informatics (than is supplied by market-based training). Second, university graduates are likely to occupy positions where they exercise a disproportionate influence over the skills development of other informatics personnel. Whether as professors, private sector trainers, or as managers of information technology, these graduates provide substantial knowledge transfer to the rest of the profession. Third, universities play an important role in complementing private training resources through e.g., the provision of specialized courses and staff. Fourth, the relationship between academia and the international informatics community provides an essential gateway for tracking global scientific and technological developments. Hence, the emphasis placed by most OECD economies in ensuring the parallel development of university resources in informatics with a market-based system for less academic skills formation (e.g., keyboard and software program use), refresher courses, and development of a cross-disciplinary informatics profession. As demand for informatics skills becomes more specialized and quality sensitive, a key issue is therefore the efficiency and flexibility with which universities in Turkey can respond to the informatics challenge.

4.18   *Role of Universities*. There are currently ten universities offering four-year computer engineering programs with an enrollment of about 2,700 undergraduates and graduates (Table 4.5). The first Departments of Computer Engineering - at the Middle Eastern Technical University (METU) and at Hacattepe - were formally established in 1977 with responsibilities for the education of undergraduate and graduate engineers, and for research in various aspects of computer engineering. Similar Departments were established at Istanbul Technical University, Bosphorus, Ege and Yildiz Universities between 1980 and 1983. Bilkent's program began in 1986, the first year of the University's operations. Departments within Istanbul, Marmara, and Trakya Universities were more recently established (1990-91).

Table 4.5: University Role in Informatics Training

University	Start	Teaching Staff/RAs (1)	Total Graduates	Annual Intake	Program Focus
Hacettepe	1977	9/17	290	50	Software
METU	1977	16/24	504	60	Software
ITU	1980	12/25	300	60	Hardware
Bosphorus	1982	11/13	215	50	General
Ege	1982	21/17	200	60	O.S. (2)
Yildiz	1982	8/10	200	41	General
Bilkent	1986	9/28	33	50	General
Istanbul	1990	4/10	-	40	Software
Marmara	1990	6/4	-	30	Software
Trakya	1990	4/5	-	30	Software
TOTAL		253	1742	471	

Notes: (1) Teaching Staff includes Professors (Full, Associate, Assistant)   instructors; RAs = research assistants; (2) Operation Systems.

Source: SPO/IBS (1991 data).

4.19   In computer engineering, undergraduate enrollments have increased significantly since the mid-1980s. Between 1984-1991, undergraduate computer engineering enrollments increased by 7.1% per annum, compared with an average undergraduate expansion of 2.4% per annum. However, this growth rate lags behind growth in the national market for informatics goods and services (Figure 4.1). The computer engineering programs attract the brightest applicants, many of whom score in the top 2% of the national university entrance exams. It is therefore particularly discouraging that the average success rates for computer engineering undergraduates is less than 70%, implying significant efficiency losses in the system. At the graduate level, the situation is also not encouraging. Only 18 out of 151 students graduated from post-graduate programs between 1984-91; most of those who did not complete their programs left to take up immediate employment.

Figure 4.1: Relative Growth Rates within Informatics Sectors

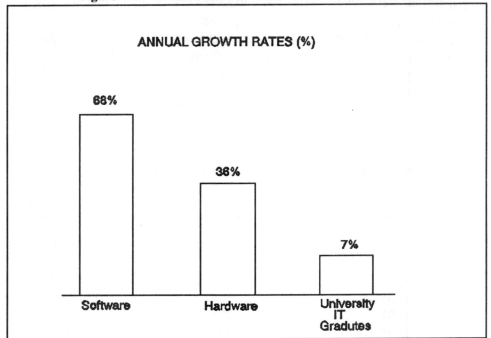

4.20   Expansion of the university system for supplying informatics professionals is principally hampered by salary-based difficulties in attracting teaching staff from what is in any event a limited pool of qualified potential manpower. Already, the salary differentials between university and private employment have created recruitment problems for the newly established computer engineering faculties at Marmaris and Trakya. The current student-professor ratio in computer engineering is 24:1.[4] With a constant teacher:student ratio, a more rapid expansion in the university system (e.g., at 10% per annum) would need approximately 150 professors and instructors over the next five years. This figure exceeds by more than eight times the number of students who have completed informatics graduate degree programs in Turkish universities since 1985. The "pipeline problem" is not simply related to a legacy of inadequate early expansion of the university system for informatics training. Rather, it is an inevitable consequence of wage differentials between private sector employers of informatics staff and the universities. These salary differentials (para. 4.35), act as disincentives to potential applicants for entry-level university positions (and also for tenured staff). Despite the opportunities (via Revolving Funds) for contract work by university staff, the combination of heavy teaching loads and inadequate compensation undermines the quantity and quality of university human resources.

4.21   The curricula and pedagogical focus in all ten Departments are similar, and aim to provide sound technical skills in utilizing computer hardware and software in a range of applications. The quality and content of the curricula (see Annex 6 for METU example) appear comparable to those provided in various OECD/NIC countries. However, there are two key differences which fundamentally affect (and limit) the value of training provided in Turkish universities. *First*, computer departments overseas are much less likely to be connected to engineering faculties. They have often evolved as independent departments, and as a result have a more inter-disciplinary approach which draws on analytic resources across the university community. The development of separate computing departments has been essential for the discipline's graduation away from a preoccupation with the technology per se towards a broader approach: (a) geared at solving social and economic problems through informatics applications; (b) more integrated with related disciplines, such as information science and communications theory; and (c) able to adjust curriculum content more rapidly. *Second*, in other countries there appears to be a greater emphasis on courses oriented toward computer applications, problem-solving techniques, computer networking, and software engineering. This development is a natural response both to market pressures, and to the institutional separation of computing from engineering departments, resulting in a proliferation of sub-disciplines more uniquely relevant to informatics applications.

4.22   The provision of hardware at the main universities is generally not adequate (with the exception of Bilkent) to satisfy student and staff aspirations. Additionally the rapid rate of technological change in informatics poses significant problems for the delivery of undergraduate and graduate training programs that are relevant to the market. While certain elements of technical training in informatics are non-equipment intensive, much of the applied training requires exposure to state-of-the-art computing facilities. In addition, research work (in both informatics and most other scientific fields) increasingly requires access to workstations and high-performance computing facilities. In time, these problems may be addressed through the (proposed) implementation of university data transmission networks that would allow remote

---

[4] A ratio which is significantly better than the university average of 36:1 in Turkey. However, the ratio is still inferior to those in Spain (19:1), Italy (22:1) and Greece (16:1).

access to computing facilities. However, in the interim, most universities appear to suffer from facilities that are out-of-date, in very short supply, and nonviable as platforms for programs in software engineering. This infrastructural problem affects not only the training of informatics specialists, but more generally precludes exposure to informatics and advanced techniques in information-retrieval, processing and analysis across all the university disciplines.

4.23   The high rate of technological change in informatics makes research activity (and participation in international conventions) a necessary condition for effective teaching. However, university research on informatics appears to be very limited. Less than 40% of informatics researchers are located in the universities (Table 2.7), which are the source of only 1% of informatics research expenditure.[5/] In sharp contrast with other fields, the majority of informatics research appears to be based in the enterprise sector (especially communications equipment companies). The two principal centers of university research in informatics appear to be at Istanbul Technical University (the Electronics Industry Foundation, mainly financed by the large electronics companies (para. 2.44)) and at METU (the Software Research and Development Center, partly financed by TÜBITAK (para. 3.57)). University staff have little time to devote to research, given heavy teaching loads (staff/student ratio of 1:24 in informatics) and the need to supplement salaries through problem-solving contract work. The close link between research and effective teaching in the informatics field suggests a need to: (a) reconsider the work-program of teaching staff; and (b) attract additional resources into university-based research.

4.24   Universities are also the home for Turkey's *Vocational Schools of Higher Education* (VSHEs). Sixteen universities offer two year vocational programs to train students basically as programmers. Admissions to these programs have increased by 33% per annum, increasing from 143 enrollments (i.e., first and second year students) in 1984 to 1452 in 1990. The average success rate of these students is approximately 55%, resulting in approximately 300 graduates per annum. However, the constraints that have limited expansion of university informatics resources are also present in the VSHEs. The shortage of teaching staff is particularly damaging, and is only partially resolved through cross-support from the university faculties. Moreover, funds available for equipment and training materials are even more limited than in the universities. One exception to this is an interesting pilot scheme in selected VSHEs where the PTT has installed computer terminals connected to the telecommunications system for use by the students to gain practical experience of the operation and maintenance of such systems.

4.25   One activity in which certain universities have enjoyed success has been in the provision of short continuing or adult education courses. Three universities - Bosphorus, Marmara and Istanbul - offer training programs in computer programming and systems analysis (Table 4.6). The trainees are usually university students or high school graduates seeking to

---

[5/] For further information, see Research and Development on Information Technology in Turkey (TÜBITAK, 1992 Working Paper).

acquire basic informatics skills and thereby improve employment prospects. By 1991, there were a total of 9,000 graduates from these programs, representing almost 20% of the total supply of the informatics workforce. In addition to these programs, almost half of the computer engineering departments have provided special once-off courses, geared to provide computer literacy (largely to public sector organizations).

Table 4.6: Continuing Education at Universities

University	Duration	Focus	Total Graduates
Bosphorus	48 hours	Programming	2500
Marmara	One year	Systems Analysis	3000
Istanbul	60-100 hrs.	Computer Literacy	3500

Source: IBS.

4.26   Despite gains made by the higher education system with regard to informatics skills formation, there remain serious deficiencies. These include: (a) constraints on system expansion; (b) quality problems; (c) inefficiencies even within existing mechanisms for resource allocation; and (d) failure to systematically integrate informatics into other disciplines. Together, these problems prevent the higher education system from fully playing its role in the development of a competitive informatics profession.

4.27   The constraint on system expansion is largely a product of the overall incentive systems within the public universities. As explained above (para. 4.20), the main bottleneck is the difficulty that universities face in recruiting new staff (and retaining old staff) in the computer engineering departments. In part, the source of the problem is an inherited one: delayed expansion of the system in the mid-1980s created a buoyant job market for informatics professionals, thereby reducing the potential pool of graduates and university staff in this field. However, the problem also lies in the systemic rigidities that prevent university salary structures from responding to market forces. University pay-scales are independent of discipline (and are largely a function of tenure). Similarly, stipends and scholarships for graduate students do not appear to be based on any relationship to market-based comparators. The only exception to this situation is the private university - Bilkent - in which market forces have a more direct bearing on tenure, salaries and stipends. For the other universities, the result is dynamic inefficiency.

Recruitment and retention problems among computer engineering faculty result in slow system expansion, which in turn generates high relative wages for informatics professionals, feeding back into further leakages from the higher education system.

4.28   The problems relate not only to quantity; but also to the quality and content of the training.   The computer engineering faculties recruit the brightest undergraduates in Turkey;[6] and yet appear to experience difficulty in producing the junior informatics professional demanded by the market.   First, almost 1/3 of undergraduates in computer engineering fail to finish their degree, resulting in significant efficiency and financial losses for the system.   Second, the universities appear to produce informatics graduates whose skill-base is out-of-line with market requirements.   Many employers of informatics professionals (especially the hardware vendors with extensive training programs) regard the training of engineering graduates as too technical and theoretical.   The course requirement of only 60 days of summer training in industry means that graduates emerge from their degrees lacking both practical and business experience.   As a result, major employers of informatics professionals: (a) retrain their new hires even in basic computing concepts; (b) hire a large proportion of their intake from departments[7] other than computer engineering; and (c) regard a degree in computer engineering as a signalling device of basic intellect and motivation rather than as a guarantee of acquired skills.   To some extent, this friction between the output of computer engineering departments and market requirements is inevitable; and the complaints are not unique to Turkey. Nevertheless, the problems appear to be particularly severe,[8] and imposes an additional tax on an already strained system for supplying informatics professionals.   Moreover, the incorporation of computing within the engineering faculties (in Turkey) creates a structural obstacle to closing the university-business gap on informatics training.

4.29   The (public) higher education suffers from both dynamic (para. 4.26) and static (para. 4.27) inefficiencies with regard to system expansion, drop-out rates and retraining.   In addition, it appears that the system does not generate its existing output at minimum resource cost.   Figure 4.2 illustrates the problem.   In 1991, approximately 50% of computer engineering graduates became programmers; a job with relatively low skill content that two year diploma holders appear equally able to perform.   The average cost of training a computer engineering graduate is estimated at $10,800 (over the 4 years), compared to $3,600 (over 2 years) for diploma holders.   Given the final job profile of computer engineering graduates (half of whom appear to leak into relatively low productivity informatics occupations), resource reallocation towards the two year diploma courses would enable the system to provide an

---

[6] Potentially, these top undergraduates represent members of the future business and government elite in Turkey. Education of this group is therefore likely to have significant externalities for the society.

[7] Hardware vendors recruit almost exclusively from Turkey's first-tier universities (where the medium of instruction is English).

[8] For example, computer vendors in Turkey report that retraining of new recruits takes an average of 1 year, compared with 6 months in the US.

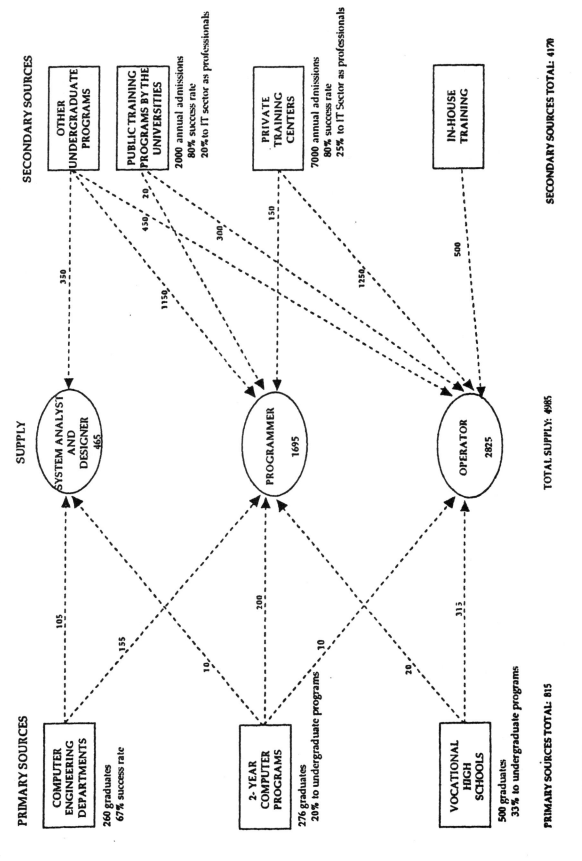

Figure 4.2: Supply of Informatics Professionals: Flow Design 1991

PRIMARY SOURCES

SECONDARY SOURCES

SUPPLY

COMPUTER ENGINEERING DEPARTMENTS

260 graduates
67% success rate

2-YEAR COMPUTER PROGRAMS

276 graduates
20% to undergraduate programs

VOCATIONAL HIGH SCHOOLS

500 graduates
33% to undergraduate programs

OTHER UNDERGRADUATE PROGRAMS

PUBLIC TRAINING PROGRAMS BY THE UNIVERSITIES

2000 annual admissions
80% success rate
20% to IT sector as professionals

PRIVATE TRAINING CENTERS

7000 annual admissions
80% success rate
25% to IT Sector as professionals

IN-HOUSE TRAINING

SYSTEM ANALYST AND DESIGNER
465

PROGRAMMER
1695

OPERATOR
2825

350
450
20
300
150
1150
1250
500
105
155
10
200
10
315
20

PRIMARY SOURCES TOTAL: 815

SECONDARY SOURCES TOTAL: 4170

TOTAL SUPPLY: 4985

SOURCE: IBS Estimates.

equivalent supply of programmers at a significantly reduced overall cost. Given the shortage of informatics professionals in Turkey, it is particularly disturbing that such a high proportion of computer engineering graduates should become programmers rather than e.g., systems analysts and software engineers.

4.30   Universities have also experienced only limited success in integrating informatics into disciplines other than computer science and engineering. In other countries, market demand for computer-literate graduates across the range of arts and science discipline has required: (a) substantial curriculum revision; (b) retraining of existing university staff; (c) expansion of computer facilities; and (d) financial programming of university-wide informatics requirements by higher education agencies (Box 4.2). In Turkey, this work is being carried out in certain universities; but there has been no broader policy initiative to tackle the general impact of informatics on university productivity or output. As a result, graduates - especially outside the core science and engineering fields - tend to have limited practical exposure to computer-based quantitative methods of analysis. In addition, universities have yet to take advantage of informatics to raise the productivity of information services (e.g., libraries, journals and periodicals), administration or financial management.

Box 4.2: Computer Requirements of Undergraduates
Middle-Income and Upper-Income Country Examples

Discipline	Connect Time p.a./ Student (Hours)	Workstation/ Student Upper Income	Middle Income
IT, Computing, Maths	300	1:2	1:3 1:1 (Final yr)
Engineering, Tech.	180	1:2	1:5 1:2 (Final yr)
Science, Business, Management	120	1:3	1:5 1:3 (Final yr)
Humanities, Education, Social Science	90	1:8	1:8
Medicine, Arts	60	1:8	1:8

In the case of the middle income country, planning was based on two types of workstation: (a) an equivalent to IBM XT (with 286 processor, 1 megabyte RAM), and (b) an equivalent to Sun Workstation with high resolution graphics, 4-10 megabyte RAM. All students would use XT equivalent; but IT, computing, maths, engineering and technology students would use Sun equivalent during the latter part of their studies.

4.31   The problems in the university system have generated a compensating response from the private sector. First, there has been a rapid increase in the number of private training establishments for informatics. Second, there is a significant role played by the major hardware vendors in providing both internal and external training. Third, in-house training offers an additional channel for informatics skills acquisition and experience-based learning.

4.32   *Private Training Industry*. The first private computer training center was established in Istanbul in 1975; and other major institutes were established in the first half of the 1980s. As the skills shortage become more pronounced, the 1985-90 period witnessed rapid entry of smaller training companies into the sector and also the expansion of conventional vocational training centers to cover computer training. By 1991, there were a total of 500 institutes providing computer training, including 10 major centers (all of which are concentrated in the Istanbul, Ankara, and Izmir). Training focuses on software and programming. The major centers offer training in computer languages such as BASIC, COBOL, FORTRAN, PASCAL and also in universal software packages (i.e., LOTUS 123, DBASE IV, WORD). Smaller centers focus on user training in software applications. Fees range from $1000 for programming courses to $100 for training in software packages. Approximately 50% - 60% of the course participant are employed individuals who self-finance their training. In total, the private training industry supplies almost 5,000 computer literate workers to the market per annum.[9] Other participants (given facilities shortages on campus) are university students seeking additional 'hands on' computer experience prior to graduation.

4.33   The private training industry has played an important role in responding to labor market pressures. Indeed, the rapid expansion has taken place despite a number of institutional barriers to entry and growth.[10] Government regulations requires that the private training schools: (a) navigate a cumbersome licensing process in which the MOE General Directorate for Private Education is only one of a number of agencies whose approval must be obtained to create the school; (b) get government approval for appointment of the principal; (c) hire only certified teachers; (d) provide scholarships to low-income participants; (e) teach the centrally agreed curriculum; and (f) prepare students for centrally set and marked exams. These rules impose significant costs on the industry; and at times have the effect of lowering quality. They prevent private schools from making "industry hires" to provide applied training courses, where these staff do not have the necessary academic certification. The curriculum approval procedures discourage the introduction of new courses; and at times disrupt existing training schedules. While the regulatory framework may provide certain safeguards for trainees, ironically they do not help in the dimension that matters most: the market value of the training diploma. There is little in the existing regulations that ensures that diplomas (provided by

---

[9] Only 25% of these trainees become informatics professionals. The rest are office workers, who are computer users.

[10] Indeed, private training schools in Turkey are by and large restricted to computer skills, foreign languages, and driving.

private training institutes) are in line with market demand, and therefore have a direct impact on the trainees' employment prospects. If anything, the regulations on curricula and hiring of non-certified instructors from industry may actually discourage the private training industry from tailoring its courses to employer demand.

4.34   The result is somewhat paradoxical. On the one hand, the industry has expanded very fast and is responsible for the formal training of over 50% of Turkey's informatics workforce. On the other hand, informatics industry representatives (i.e., the large hardware and software companies) are uniformly emphatic about not hiring programmers from the private training institutes because of quality and reliability problems. It appears therefore that growth of the private training schools is largely a response to the needs of second-tier informatics users: employees that are seeking greater job mobility and medium-scale (and a few large) businesses that: (a) cannot afford the overhead of in-house training programs; and (b) are recognizing the benefits of increased investment in information. One result of this (unsophisticated) customer base is that the private training industry has little incentive to upgrade skills, innovate and diversify into more advanced training products. At present, potential trainees experience significant information problems in assessing course quality, and in determining which courses actually meet their training objectives. The lack of a formal certification system means that apparently identical courses may be significantly different in terms of both content and quality. In addition, there is no or little post-training employment services or information regarding the job destinations of previous trainees. Given these large information gaps and the pace of technological and occupational change, competition between the training schools may not generate expected efficiency gains and may even be counter-productive! With a price-sensitive and information-constrained client base, a proliferation of small private training institutions may in fact be able to win a market share without making necessary investments in curriculum and staff development. The consequence is to reduce the returns for the industry as a whole on investment in staff, curriculum development and reputation.

4.35   *Vendor Training*. A second source of informatics training in the private sector are the hardware vendors (and, to a lesser extent, a few more established software companies). Their role has been crucial in the development of an informatics profession. First, they provide the most rigorous training in applied informatics to new hires and also (on a refresher basis) to existing staff. The major hardware vendors recruit a total of 200 to 300 new staff per annum; and provide a home (or initial training) for the elite of the informatics profession in Turkey. Second, the hardware vendors also provide training services to all purchasers of major systems. However, in the case of government procurement (and to a less extent in the private sector), training services are not purchased on a separate contractual basis from the hardware vendors. It is simply bundled into the system installation and commissioning contract. As a result, vendors often provide minimal training in systems operation, contributing to the low productivity of many public investments in informatics.

4.36   *In-house Skills Development*. Larger companies in Turkey all provide some in-house training for informatics staff. With certain exceptions, the training is not structured or formal. Rather, it comprises experience-sharing and informal knowledge transfer from more senior staff. A small number of companies have contracted private and university trainers to strengthen skills formation in informatics. In an equally limited number of cases, companies have provided financial support for employees that are attending private training institutes. However, the corporate environment for in-house training for informatics appears fragmentary and relatively under-developed. Few companies have human resource strategies with accompanying professional resources. And there appears to be a marked reluctance to provide training in skills including informatics that enhance the inter-firm mobility of technical staff.

4.37　　　During the second half of the 1980s, rapid increases in demand for informatics skills accompanied by problems in the overall training system generated both: (a) real wage growth throughout the profession; and (b) specific skill shortages. Informatics personnel are among the best paid in the Turkish business market. The level of wages paid to informatics personnel is so much above that for other skills that major groups (e.g., Sabanci, Cukurova) have chosen to separate out these activities in the form of an independent subsidiary. This was the only way in which large companies could provide market-based salaries to informatics personnel without disrupting existing corporate pay-scales.

4.38　　　Surveys of informatics wages carried out in 1990 and 1991 reveal 4 main findings (Table 4.7). First, there is a striking difference between public and private salaries for informatics personnel. This pay differential: (a) increases with seniority; and (b) appear to have widened between 1990 and 1991 as a result of public sector wage restraints. Second, there is a relatively gradual wage slope within the profession. Even in the private sector, EDP managers are paid less than two times the salary of computer engineers, and less than four times the salary of computer operators. This salary structure appears to be the result of the relative youth of the profession, and also its isolation from the overall management hierarchy. Third, comparison of 1990 and 1991 salaries shows a substantial tightening in the labor market for programmers. This is due to the fact that a shortage of two year VSHE graduates (para. 4.28) resulted in market pressure to hire computer and other engineering graduates for lower-productivity programming jobs. Finally, there are significant salary differentials within the private sector. Rewards are not surprisingly highest in those sectors (e.g., banking) in which information is most valued, and the cost of system failure is high.

4.39　　　Given the supply lag to wage signals in the informatics labor market, there is still an acute skills shortage in three main fields. First, there is a lack of professional expertise in software engineering and projects management, primarily in large systems development and systems integration projects. Second, Turkey suffers from a skills deficit in the "hard part" of building software: the specification, design and testing of the data set, data relationships, algorithms etc. Third, all industry representatives expressed a problem in recruiting staff with the communications and marketing skills that permit clear analysis of end-user requirements and efficient development of customized software.

Table 4.7: Informatics Salaries (1990-91)

Average Net Monthly Wages, TL millions

| | 1990 | | 1991 | | November 1991 | |
	Public	Private	Public	Private	Finance	Manufact.
EDP Manager	2.8	5.2	3.2	7.6	9.8	7.3
Computer Engr.	2.3	3.5	2.4	4.8	5.8	4.5
Programmer	1.6	2.7	2.2	4.2	4.3	2.8
Operator	1.2	1.8	1.4	2.2	3.3	2.3

Source: IBS/Bilgisayar.

4.40   While high real wages for informatics personnel have a positive effect on incentives for employee-financed informatics training, the immediate consequences of an excessively tight informatics skills market are less favorable. First, the high real wages of informatics professionals[11] have slowed down the diffusion of informatics. Smaller companies that cannot afford the recurrent costs of high-cost informatics personnel instead are forced to delay introduction of more information-intensive business practices. Second, the shortages of specific informatics skills (para. 4.37) have resulted in the sub-optimal utilization of informatics investments, and even in larger companies, have discouraged the introduction of new applications that are essential for international competitiveness. Third, persistent employee-poaching (despite gentlemen's agreements to the contrary) create free-rider problems and a severe disincentive to employer investment in skills formation for their informatics staff. In addition, market demand is siphoning off potential graduate students and academic staff (para. 4.26). Although this provides a temporary palliative to existing skill shortages, it prevents efficient expansion of the formal training system and constrains more advanced informatics skills formation. In effect, the current (inadequate) supply situation is sewing the seeds of future supply shortages.

4.41   Problems in the informatics specialist market are compounded by the limited availability of *general* informatics skills i.e., computer literacy. In light of the technological shift towards personal computer and distributed application, the Government has recognized the need for a strategy to broaden the diffusion of computer literacy. As a result, the Ministry of Education has initiated computer-assisted education (CAE) programs in the vocational high schools and also in the secondary education system. As is shown by Table 4.8, computer

---

[11] Although they have also provided a powerful signal to the labor market, encouraging entry into the profession and private investment in informatics skills.

penetration in these schools remains extremely low; and computer:pupil ratios are discouragingly high. In this respect, Turkey lags significantly behind comparator and OECD countries.

Table 4.8: Computer Park in Vocational and Secondary Schools 1991

	# of Students	# of Computers	Ratio
Vocational Schools for boys	1,245,000	2,294	1:304
Vocational Schools for Girls	240,000	690	1:105
Commerce and Tourism Educ.	47,000	1,362	1:68
Secondary Education	106,000	4,092	1:78
Theological Education	92,000	460	1:200
Apprenticeship	250,000	710	1:352
TOTAL	1,980,000	9,068	1:218

Source: Ministry of Education.

4.42   The adoption of computer-aided education (CAE) programs was initially considered in 1984. Over the next two years, a CAE project took shape. The initial aim was to spread computer literacy. In addition, computers were seen as one tool to compensate for the poor quality and persistent deficiencies of suitable teachers. Project phases included: (a) preparation of the curriculum; (b) software design; (c) training the teachers; and (d) incentives for local hardware and components production. Various pilot projects were initiated, and vendors selected to supply test equipment and programs. During 1985-90, 48 training programs were organized and 2240 teachers trained in computer literacy and programming. The plans for 1991 were to train a further 5,300 teachers. However, the CAE Project appears to have run into certain implementation obstacles. First, the available software has not been integrated with curriculum developments. Second, there is a severe shortage of suitably trained teachers. As a result of these constraints, the hardware could not be used in the originally intended manner. Third, a number of the potential vendors dropped out complaining of excessive bureaucracy and inadequate terms of reference and project definition. Although program implementation is continuing, it is at a reduced growth rate (less than 40% of target) and with significantly reduced expectations.

Restructuring the Informatics Profession

4.43   As the information economy continues to grow, there will be sustained demand for both specific and general informatics skills. These are crucial resources for organizations that seek to implement a technological environment consistent with a more information-intensive way of doing business. Over the next five years, Turkey will need almost to double its workforce of informatics specialists (Figure 4.3) in addition to diffusing general computer literacy throughout the workforce.[12] However, supply growth cannot be at the expense of efforts to deepen the skill-base. If anything, the market tradeoff is likely to favor quality over quantity of informatics personnel.

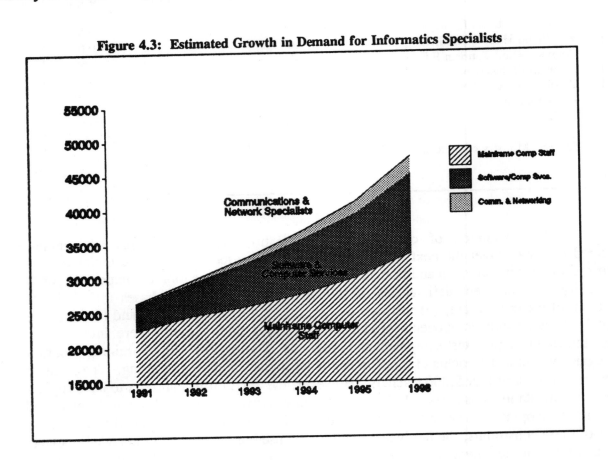

Figure 4.3: Estimated Growth in Demand for Informatics Specialists

4.44   Demand for informatics professionals will also become more diversified and specialized. Within each of the existing occupational categories (see Annex 5), skill intensity will need to deepen; and there is likely to be a significant increase in a range of more specialized

---

[12] Existing methodologies do not permit accurate forecasting of demand trends for informatics professionals. Estimates should therefore be treated as orders of magnitude.

sub-professions. In particular, international trends suggest rapid growth in the numbers (and sub-disciplines) of systems analysis, software engineering, object-oriented programming, communications and network design, project management and techniques in total quality assurance for mainframe installations. A critical area for skills development will be that of information technology management.

4.45   Transformation of the informatics profession is likely to involve both a proliferation of new specialties, and the obsolescence (or down-grading) of existing occupations. For example, there is likely to be a decrease in the demand for low-skill programming, as software productivity tools (e.g., Computer Assisted Software Engineering: CASE) substitute for manual coding. Similarly, computer mainframe facilities are likely to require diminishing numbers of low-level operators and technicians. The training and curriculum currently offered in the vocational schools for higher education (para. 4.23) will need to be substantially revamped in line with evolving market-requirements for end-user support staff, and higher level programming.

4.46   A third human capital requirement for an information economy is the diffusion of computer literacy throughout the workforce. Turkey has already experienced a rapid growth in its white-collar (i.e., information) workforce (para. 4.09). Nevertheless, the proportion of information workers (in the total labor force) remains significantly below that of other OECD and NIC economies. As the structural transformation of the Turkish economies continues during the 1990s, information-oriented jobs are likely to be a leading source of employment creation. This development will be accentuated by two other factors. First, a number of occupations that today have limited information content are likely to become more information-intensive; and will therefore require basic informatics skills. Second, growing applications of informatics outside the workplace - in the home and across the spectrum of social transactions - will make general informatics skills a requirement for full participation in society. From an equity as well as an efficiency perspective, informatics literacy can play a pivotal role in Turkey's modernization.

4.47   Given systemic problems that today prevent the adequate supply of informatics professionals, it is clear that significant reforms will be required to meet the challenge of the next decade's demand for informatics skills. At present, there are three main issues. First, the public sector system of higher education in informatics appears to be lacking both the resources and direction essential for its central role in training provision. Second, private sector mechanisms for informatics training are not yet equal to the tasks of: (a) augmenting the supply of qualified informatics professionals; (b) providing the highly diversified job-specific skills that are consistent with evolving market demand; and (c) continuous skills upgrading in the face of rapid technological change in informatics. Third, general informatics skills are not as yet widely diffused throughout the workforce. As personal computer and distributed informatics applications become the dominant technology for information processing, there is a need to create a much broader class of computer-literate information workers. This is essentially the task of training the next generation.

Creating an Information Workforce for 2000

4.48   A strategy to build an information workforce responsive to the needs of the Turkish economy should be based on three main elements:

   a.   *universities* have a pivotal position within the overall system for the development of a high-skill informatics profession. As centers of knowledge and learning, they provide linkages with international developments in informatics and are a crucial source of high calibre professionals for industry and also for future academic requirements. They must also respond creatively to the challenge of converting graduates from many disciplines into competent informatics specialists through postgraduate programs.

   b.   the *private sector* is best-equipped to provide job-specific training in informatics. A high proportion of investment in specific informatics skills is captured by employers/employees; and should therefore be privately financed. Public sector efforts in job-specific training should therefore be limited to initiatives that increase private resource mobilization, and correct existing information problems.

   c.   the *public sector* can play a crucial transformative role in diffusing general informatics skills throughout the economy. These are skills which generate broad social benefits; and which will permit equitable participation of Turkish society in the opportunities created by an information-based economy.

The high rate of change in the informatics profession (and skills market) requires a training system that: (a) is based on a deep understanding of labor market information; (b) has flexibility to reallocate resources in line with the market; (c) supports continuous skills upgrading; and (d) provides access to a growing community of informatics users. This implies a shift away from structures built around manpower planning models, slow (and predictable) rates of demographic and institutional change, and the rationing of publicly financed educational resources.

4.49   *Universities*. Universities currently experience 3 main problems in fulfilling their role for informatics skills formation. First, structural and organizational problems prevent the development of intellectual and pedagogical resources in line with needs of the Turkish economy. Second, incentives for the recruitment and retention of qualified staff are inadequate to permit expansion of the system in line with market demand. Third, the physical infrastructure in most universities cannot support a state-of-the-art learning experience for the students.

4.50   The computer engineering departments of Turkish universities have (despite hiring constraints) grown significantly over the past decade. Initially, the departments were small and relatively weak. To minimize overheads associated with establishing a new discipline and to accelerate its growth, a logical "foster home" was the engineering faculties. Today however, there is a strong case for creating - at least in the leading Universities - separate Informatics Faculties. Two major benefits would result from this restructuring. First, the new Informatics Faculties would be liberated from an engineering culture, and would thereby be better positioned to develop an independent identity and focus on Turkey's needs.[13/] Technology (in the sense of computer hardware) is a diminishing constraint on the spread of informatics. Rather, the constraints lie more in software, integration of informatics with organizational strategies, and data/information management. This is especially true in Turkey which is not (and should not expect to become) a major hardware supplier. Informatics Faculties that were independent from Engineering would more naturally reorient activities towards these market and technological developments. Second, informatics training has become progressively multi-disciplinary. Engineering is only one of the relevant disciplines required either for student teaching or for research. Many of the growth fields (both in industry and in academia) involve a combination of information science, management theory, and concepts of cognitive perception, occupational psychology and abstract mathematics. The development of inter-disciplinary Informatics Faculties would exert a strong influence over future professionals, and might be more successful in attracting both academic and business support.

4.51   Physical and human capital constraints are endemic at Turkish universities. Almost all university department suffer from problems in: (a) recruitment and retention of staff; and (b) the supply of teaching materials, textbooks and facilities. In certain respects, it could be argued that computer engineering departments have fared relatively well during a decade of overall budgetary restraint in the universities. The departments have expanded significantly faster than the university system as a whole; and indeed teacher: student ratios have marginally improved. Nevertheless, the situation remains unsatisfactory. Demand for places far outstrips supply; and the quantity and composition of the departments' output is equivalent to less than 20% of market requirements (compared to over 60% in Singapore).

4.52   The Government already recognizes that computer engineering (and more generally informatics training) deserves special treatment. Nevertheless, institutional barriers to the rapid reallocation of resources towards informatics is leaving universities behind the market, and is translating into a constraint on the overall process of economic transformation. Additional measures are therefore required to address this situation. In particular, approaches that have been implemented successfully in other countries (that face similar problems) aim to correct these problems through:

- *improved incentives*: if a more general reform of university salary structures cannot be envisaged, more limited options for reform might include: (a) to remove the Revolving Fund restriction that

---

[13/] In the US, there is now a trend towards establishment of multi-disciplinary Information Centres, which provide a meeting point for computer science, information management, journalism, library science, and communications.

limits contract-based income to 200% of university salary; (b) industry hires on a term basis that would be based on non-university salaries and could be financed jointly by universities, TÜBITAK, and the Technology Development Foundation; (c) special chairs and non-tenured positions that would be endowed by business (especially the hardware vendors);

- *stronger business-university linkages*: that might include: (a) the sponsorship of informatics graduates by industry in a way that supplements (or substitutes for) publicly-financed stipends; (b) initiatives to encourage competition among vendors to provide equipment grants, and endowed computer labs for a range of university disciplines; (c) a much stronger program of work-experience for informatics students; and most importantly (d) establishment of industry-university advisory committees to improve curriculum design and strengthen feedback from the market to the universities; and

- *university computing network*: that would enable universities, TÜBITAK and advanced computer users in the private sector to share scarce computing resources (especially more expensive high-performance computing facilities), to build a public domain software resource for students and staff, and share information and ideas through electronic mail systems. Initiatives that are already under way in this area should be accelerated, and broadened to include access for non-university individuals and organizations.

In addition, the Council for Higher Education (YöK) should initiate a broader project to: (a) review the appropriate use of informatics in non-engineering disciplines; (b) assess priorities for curriculum change; (c) determine investment and recurrent resource implications of a more systematic integration of informatics into university education; and (d) identify major opportunities to raise university productivity (e.g., administrative, information services) through informatics applications.

4.53   In general, Turkey will realize substantial gains through measures to improve the institutional responsiveness of the universities. While it may be difficult to effect systemic changes throughout the universities, informatics training may provide an appropriate pilot vehicle for innovation, and a catalyst for academic entrepreneurialism. It is clear that market pressure already exists for reform; and that these pressures are already being communicated through the Turkish Informatics Association (which represents major informatics suppliers, users and universities). If these pressures can be converted into action, then universities will become better positioned to resume their leadership role in informatics skills development.

4.54   To accelerate reform in the university system, one instrument might be establishment of a private *Institute for Informatics*. Such an Institute would have three main functions:

- to provide post-graduate training for top students in the informatics field;

- to become a center of research excellence for industry, and a source of curriculum innovation for the universities; and

- to diffuse more general computer skills through development of e.g., television courses, course materials for secondary schools, and educational software.

The Institute should aim to become a magnet for the informatics profession; recruiting high-performance teaching staff, providing refresher courses to practitioners, bringing together industry and academia, and reversing the brain-drain from Turkey. If successful, the Institute could become a catalyst for informatics sector development, and foreign direct investment in informatics research, design and manufacturing. To meet these goals, development of such an Institute will require: (a) substantial private involvement in financing and governance; (b) cooperative arrangements with leading universities; (c) detailed business plan; (d) up-front investment in curriculum development and programming; and (e) political support to acquire necessary approvals and funding.

4.55   *Private Sector Role*. Accompanying improvements in the university system, the private sector must also increase (and improve the efficiency of investments) in informatics training. There are 3 key areas in which institutional strengthening and additional resource allocation are necessary: (a) occupational standards and certification, (b) the provision of labor market information, and (c) protection of employer investments in job-specific training.

4.56   An obstacle to the growth of the informatics profession in Turkey is the lack of accreditation and certification standards. This is a fundamental problem throughout the economy, but is particularly important in informatics given the rapidly changing nature of job requirements (see Annex 5) and technologies, and the growth in private training organizations offering computer programming courses. By law, the Ministry of Education (MOE) manages the certification process for skilled occupations; and the Council for Higher Education (YöK) the certification of technicians and professional occupations. But the certification dispensed by these agencies: (a) reflects academic views of the preparation necessary for a given occupation; (b) does not include demonstrated proficiency by applicants to perform the tasks required in an actual job; and (c) covers only a small proportion of occupations - especially in those categories which are fast-growing; and (d) is frequently out-of-line with international occupational standards.

4.57   The Government is already planning (with Bank support[14/]) to establish an Occupational Standards Commission, which would include representatives from key public sector agencies, employers' associations, and trade unions. The Commission (through its Secretariat in IIBK) would: (a) support the development of employer-relevant occupational standards; (b) establishment of a documentation center; (c) define procedures for carrying out occupational

---

Box 4.3: Creating an Information Workforce in the UK

The British Government has implemented an aggressive program to ensure that the workforce acquires informatics skills. Initiatives are focussed on all levels and types of education - schools, further, higher and continuing education. Special funds have been made available through several ministries. Some of these were and are available only to the public sector (schools, colleges, polytechnics and universities); others through the Training Agency,1/ to both private and public sector institutions. In all cases funding is not automatic; proposals have to be prepared so that they conform to published guidelines and eligibility criteria.   Selection is on a competitive basis and monitoring of implementation is subject to public scrutiny. Successful projects may receive funding for a few months or several years.

In higher education, funding has been earmarked by both the Department of Education and Science (DES)2/ and Department of Trade and Industry (DTI)3/ to support the creation of informatics centers of excellence. The Universities Grants Commission and the Polytechnics and Colleges Funding Council have also had programs of special funding for this area. These have proved very successful in promoting advanced developments in informatics software and hardware applications. Projects supported have included fundamental research, pre-developmental work and applied research of direct interest to industry and commerce. The last category has also benefited from private sector funding. In addition to research project funding, there has also been earmarked support for Masters programs and Doctorates, including conversion of arts and humanities graduates to informatics professionals.

Special funds have also been available to Universities and Polytechnics to bring Computing to a wide range of programs. These funds have provided equipment and software so that students can have hands-on computing experience no as an optimal extra but as an integral part of their course. Thus, for example, students on all types of programs that include design (whether engineering, architecture or art) will have some experience of CAD. All higher education students are expected to acquire keyboarding skills early in their studies.

Notes: 1/   The Training Agency reports to, and receives its funding
                   from, the Department of Employment (Employment
                   Ministry).
           2/   DES = Ministry of Education and Science.
           3/   DTI = Ministry of Trade and Industry.

14/ Employment and Training Project: Republic of Turkey (Report No 10331-TU).

analysis; and (d) accredit and certify training agencies. However, it is not clear whether this Commission will have the specialized resources (or mandate) to focus on the requirements of informatics employees and employers.

4.58   As Turkey develops the overall framework for occupational standards and training certification, progress in the field of informatics could be accelerated by transferring international know-how. A number of other economies have already improved the quality of their informatics profession through accreditation and certification schemes. In particular, the British Computer Society (BCS) and the US Institute for Certification of Computer Professionals (ICCP) have already developed extensive definitions of occupational standards and corresponding test procedures. Formal certification schemes adopted by these bodies already include assessments in the following general areas: procedural programming, systems development, management, communications, software engineering, systems programming, scientific programming, and systems security. To accelerate progress in this field, Turkey might (through its Informatics Association) follow the example of Singapore which has formal agreements with BCS and ICCP for annual certification examinations for informatics personnel. This transfer of "training technology" would significantly improve the quality of computer programmers graduating from private training organizations; and would enhance professionalism of the informatics occupation in Turkey.

4.59   An area which demands particular attention is the availability of labor market information: employers' current and future needs, job placement of graduates and diploma-holders, real wage trends by occupational category, etc. Initiatives are already being developed by the Government that would provide a more coherent set of labor market information (Footnote 7). However, it is not clear whether this information would provide adequately detailed content for the informatics profession. To complement the approach developed in the proposed *Enterprise and Training Project*, key steps include:

- support for a regular and comprehensive informatics market survey to be carried out in collaboration with the Turkish Informatics Association, the private training schools, and the State Institute of Statistics; and

- a periodic review for the informatics sector of: (a) employer needs; and (b) job placements of diploma-holders from the private training schools.

This information should be made widely available through specialized computer periodicals, the private training schools' publicity material, proposed vehicles for career guidance, and through more general media.

4.60   In addition, there are a number of further measures that might significantly enhance the role played by the private training industry. First, the existing administrative requirements for establishment of centers, and for curriculum development should be streamlined. Second, private training centers in informatics should be given greater freedom with regard to industry hires. Third, (as in the case of universities), the larger training centers should be encouraged to establish industry-advisory boards that would provide support on curriculum design and on job placement. Fourth, catalytic funds could be provided (potentially through the Technology Development Foundation) to catalyze development of a Computer Training School Association that could strengthen self-regulation of standards and address the information problems of potential trainees. Fifth, the Small and Medium Business Agency (KOSGEB) should consider establishment of a training fund to subsidize small and medium enterprises that sent employees to courses at certified training institutes. Together, these measures would overcome free-rider problems faced by the private training industry, correct information gaps, improve output quality and reliability, and improve industry responsiveness to the market.

4.61   Turkish companies are already providing significant formal and informal training for their informatics staff (para. 4.34). But the tight labor market creates strong incentives for job-hopping and employee-poaching, thereby discouraging this employer investment. To some extent, it is possible for companies to limit this problem through labor contracts and (more fundamentally) reputation-building as an outstanding employer. For example, Turkish hardware vendors have an agreement among themselves not to "poach" staff. However, this agreement is honored more in the breach than in its observance. The experience of other countries suggests that these market-based practices need to complemented through additional measures that enable employers to protect their human capital investments, and that encourage employer-financed training where social benefits exceed private returns. In particular, there might be significant gains from:

- the introduction and enforcement of *trade secrets legislation* that would protect confidential information held by an employee hired by a competitor;

- a more systematic approach to existing subsidies (provided through the tax code) for employer-financed training that would restrict tax exemptions to *certified training and refresher courses*;

- the development of a competitive *award scheme* (or other form of national recognition) for those companies with outstanding training programs for their informatics staff. This might be accompanied by a joint business-government evaluation of Turkey's "top employers" that would publicly recognize those companies with the strongest corporate commitment to training in different fields;

- exemption from *minimum wage legislation* in the case of low-skill employees that are receiving systematic training in informatics skills. This would allow employee self-financing of skills that provide a high degree of inter-firm mobility;

- support for the establishment of *non-profit training consortia* that would enable (in particular) small and medium enterprises to strengthen human resources in the informatics field.

4.62   *General Skills Building*. A computer literate workforce will be central to the future competitiveness of the Turkish economy. A key issue therefore for the Government is to design an instrument that will efficiently accelerate the diffusion of these skills throughout the next generation workforce. The current strategy has been to utilize the secondary schools as intermediaries for this program (para. 4.40); however, it appears that progress has been slower than expected, and the results below expectations. What may be required is a more direct approach to the issue: one that both complements the CAE initiative in the schools, and also bypasses its administrative difficulties.

4.63   Most learning and habit formation takes place in the home; not at school. While schools can reinforce behavioral patterns and provide access to information, current theories of developmental psychology suggest that the domestic environment is central to children's learning experience and opportunity set. If children can be exposed to computers not only in the formal learning environments that school provides but also at home, it is likely that they will overcome computer fear, acquire core skills and cognitive processes, and experiment with informatics at much earlier stage. Middle-class parents throughout the OECD (and the computer and software industry) have already acknowledged this learning pattern, and have purchased home computers for their children (and to some extent their own use). In certain countries, the national public library service or local community center has become the access point to computers and information networks (offering one way to take advantage of Turkey's investment in a rural telecom network).

4.64   If Turkey is to take advantage of its relatively young demographic structure, it is essential that there is rapid growth in the market for home-computer purchases. Today, that market is relatively small; and is restricted to more affluent groups within the population. These parents are thereby able to provide their children with a head-start, and to prepare them for future employment opportunities. From both equity and efficiency perspectives, there would be tremendous social benefits if: (a) access to home computers could be significantly broadened; and (b) these computers could be inter-connected through the digital telecom network (see Chapter 5). Children could then be exposed to the world of computers, and to a vast range of educational software, computer games, knowledge-bases, and electronic mail contacts through the network. In addition, the development of this home-computer network could create the basis for welfare gains through: (a) electronic banking; (b) a host of private electronic information services; and (c) significant increases in the efficiency of public administration (e.g., tax collection, social security, health services, etc.). The creation of such a network would in effect generate substantial learning externalities, and would pave the way for development of an information market-place.

Box 4.4: French Minitel Experience

In the early 1980s, the French Government decided that an initiative was needed to: (a) create broad-based informatics literacy in the population; (b) support rapid improvement in the telecom network; and (c) build a private information industry providing electronic data-services. The strategy adopted was the free distribution of 5 million minitel terminals - all of which are connected through the (progressively digital) telecom network. The terminals can support a mixture of text, and low-level graphics. The system us currently used for a number of different applications such as messaging, database inquiry, electronic bulletin boards, reservation systems, home banking, advertizing, "personal services" and electronic mail integrated with the postal system. A further enhancement of the system is the link established between television and Minitel services whereby audiences participate in TV programmes and are able to respond to advertisements. The system as a whole continues to grow at over 15% per annum; and the number of private information services is over 13,000. While the system now lags far behind PC-based networks in terms of speed, video, interactive and data-processing capabilities, it has been a crucial mechanism for educating the public on the potential and the pitfalls of an information based economy.

4.65   One possible approach to the development of an information market-place which offers both economies of scope and substantial learning externalities would be the creation of a nationwide network of inexpensive terminals that builds on the experience of the French MINITEL and other "information utilities" (many with substantial public funding) in OECD countries. The proposed "BILGITEL" program would have the following functions:

- to support the design of low-cost intelligent computer terminals with standardized communications software through a process of competitive tendering with the major hardware vendors;

- to select a number of companies that would compete to manufacture the terminals that meet the requisite technical specifications;

- to provide partial financing to households (possibly with the level of grant inversely related to household income) that purchase computers within the program;

- to provide grants on a competitive basis for software and information companies to produce public domain educational software; and

- to work with the telecom authority on interconnection, tariffing and one-stop billing issues.

BILGITEL would be established as an independent company, associated with the PTT. Initiatives to develop applications could initially be supported by both TÜBITAK and the Technology Development Foundation, with close interaction with the software and information industries. Success of the BILGITEL concept will be dependent on:

- establishment of a private profit-oriented company (possibly with PTT as the main public shareholder) to implement the project;

- design and systematic evaluation of a pilot project in one of the major urban areas;

- lowest possible terminal costs through appropriate design, competitive bidding practices, financial leasing arrangements and economies of scale in procurement and manufacturing;

- a critical mass of applications on the system that meet genuine communications (e.g., E-Mail) and information needs;

- easy-to-use terminals with direct system access;

- a billing system that effectively meters usage and ensures payment to service providers; and

- a trigger service (e.g., in the case of the French Minitel, the electronic directory was the first significant service, which was also significant in reducing fears among end-users of using "high-technology").

4.66   BILGITEL would simultaneously accomplish a number of key policy objectives. First, it would radically accelerate the diffusion of general computer literacy among future entrants to the workforce. Second, it would substantially lower future costs of specific informatics training (for the specialized informatics profession). Third, it would provide a significant stimulus for the local software and information industries. Fourth, it would expand utilization of PTT's advanced network, increase its return on assets, and support its transition towards a suppler of data transmission services. Fifth, it would offer the Government new opportunities to improve public administration and the delivery of social services. Sixth, it would help to stimulate behavioral changes in the next generation, consistent with an evolving culture of open access to information.

CHAPTER 5

THE COMMUNICATIONS NETWORK

Introduction

5.01   Telecommunications provides the infrastructure for an information economy. It is an integral part of financial services, commodities markets, media, transportation and tourism, and provides vital links between manufacturers, wholesalers, and retailers. As economies become more information-intensive, over 70% of employment will be telephone-dependent.[1] Moreover, industrial and commercial competitive advantage is now influenced not only by availability of telecommunications facilities, but also by choice of network alternatives and control to reconfigure and manage network in line with corporate objectives. Countries and firms that lack access to modern telecommunications systems cannot participate effectively in the global economy.

5.02   The perception of telecommunications as a strategic investment - one that influences national growth and competitiveness potential - is relatively new. Only a few years ago, telecom was viewed as a traditional utility with stable technology, substantial economies of scale, and returns that appeared uninviting to private capital. In almost every country, telecom services were provided by a state monopoly (many of which still exist) and were combined with other low-growth services, such as telegraph and the mail. In the 1980s however, driven by rapid changes in informatics technology and demand, telecom has become a high-performance sector of the economy. On the one hand, informatics has radically transformed telecom technology: reducing unit costs, improving the rate of productivity growth, and generating a proliferation of new multi-media services over digital(ized) networks. On the other, informatics is changing the structure of demand for telecom services. In more advanced economies, the voice telephony service is experiencing slow rates of growth (especially in local market segment). Growth is concentrated in data-transmission and in a host of value-added services that depend on the interconnection of intelligent terminals (computers, private exchanges, fourth-generation faxes, telemetering devices, and ultimately interactive TV) with the network. The result is a pervasive role for communications in society.

5.03   One consequence of this paradigmatic shift is that many countries have been forced to reform their framework for telecom. In most OECD and developing countries as recently as 1980, the basic framework for telecom was one of an unregulated public monopoly. System expansion was slow, service was poor, the tariff structure generated massive cross-subsidies (largely in favor of residential users), and the telecom operator owned the telephones and had absolute control over network access. However, the last decade has witnessed a wave of liberalization, regulatory reform and privatization in both developed and developing countries. These reforms have increased supplier responsiveness to user requirements, greatly broadened

---

[1] See Frederick Williams The New Telecommunications (1991).

choice, increased the underlying rate of telecom productivity growth, and reduced prices and cross-subsidies. At the same time, the reforms have enable telecom companies to mobilize capital for network modernization and have spawned a new industry, providing value-added information services across the network.

5.04   Turkey has followed a number of these global trends, and in certain respects has taken advantage of its status as a telecom latecomer. Since 1985, Turkey has invested almost 1% of GNP per annum to develop an advanced telecom network that would support a market-based economy. The network has expanded to a point where there is universal geographic coverage. Over 50% of the network is now digital, exceeding ratios achieved in most OECD countries. The terminal equipment market has been substantially liberalized; and local industry supplies almost 90% of the public network's investment requirements. Telecom revenues have increased from under 1% of GNP (1980) to over 2% in 1990, a further indication of the information intensification experienced by the economy during the 1980s. Perhaps the most striking aspect of this success story is that it has been achieved with almost no public sector borrowing. The Turkish PTT has mobilized 90% of the necessary investment resources from a combination of growing revenues and declining costs.

5.05   The Government is now looking for ways to capitalize on these substantial communications assets. As the period of *rapid* infrastructure accumulation draws to a close, the question is how to reorient the system to meet the next set of objectives: those of network intensification, increased consumer choice, energizing the private information industry, and development of PTT as a world-class telecom business. According to newspaper reports, the Government has already prepared a draft bill that would significantly open up the markets for mobile telephony, data-transmission and cable TV services. As the Government shifts its policy focus to the next strategic era for telecom, it will face a number of complex issues with regard to optimizing the sector's performance. In particular, developments in other OECD and NIC economies raise fundamental questions about: (a) the role of the public sector in communications; and (b) the need to promote competition and to establish an independent regulatory framework.

5.06   This Chapter is organized in three main sections. Section one reviews the successful strategy and structure of the communications sector in the 1980s. Section two assesses sector performance, and considers its consistency with future sectoral objectives. Section three outlines a set of actions that would support transition to the next strategic era of the communications sector.

Strategy and Structure

5.07   *Strategy*. In the early 1980s, the Government recognized that world-class communications were essential for a market-based economy. Policy reforms in the product and financial markets generated a parallel increase in demand for information and efficient communication services. In addition, there was an increased awareness of the role that communications could play in the broader structural transformation of the economy. First, a telecom and television system that could reach out into the countryside would have a substantial impact on agricultural productivity, and on the cognitive horizons and information resources for rural modernization. Second, investment in the communications infrastructure could provide a potent instrument for technology development. From the late 1970s, commercial application of informatics in the communications sector was transforming the process of storing, switching, and transmitting information. Investment in the network would therefore provide Turkey with an opportunity to "take advantage of being a technology latecomer", and to provide sustained support for local informatics suppliers.

Box. 5.1: Technological Change in Communications Sector

The Communications sector has been an arena for sustained technological change over the past two decades. The days are almost over for the telephone operator, limited international services, electro-mechanical switches and rotary phones. In their place is a dazzling array of new technologies that are principally a product of the informatics revolution. Advanced telecom networks are being built around.

- *digital switches - essentially computers -* that by replacing electro-mechanical switches provide the platform for a range of enhanced services (e.g., call forwarding, voice mail, caller I.D.) and are central to proposed integrated services digital network (ISDN) that will allow transmission of voice, data and images (in digital format);

- *fibre-optic and satellite transmission systems* that provide high quality/speed band-width necessary for much greater volumes of voice and data transmission;

- *data-processing terminals* such as modems, video-phones, computers, telemetering devices, and third generation fax machines that distribute intelligence onto the periphery of the telecom network;

- *data-compression techniques* that permit greater functionality to be squeezed out of existing copper-based networks; and

- *mobile communications devices* including cellular radio systems, and before the end of the decade, voice-mobile satellite networks.

Technological progress in the communications sector has brought about: (a) an explosion of new services; (b) rapid declines in real prices; and (c) a systematic convergence between previously separate domains for telecom, broadcasting and information services. The era of information and communications overload is upon us.

5.08   The Government had three options to finance and implement network modernization: (a) public sector debt or tax-based financing; (b) mobilization of private sector resources; or (c) increasing the financial and managerial autonomy of PTT. However, the first two options presented a number of problems. First, public sector tax/debt financing of network investment were difficult to justify in light of overall budget constraints. Moreover, public sector financing could not be guaranteed on a medium term basis since Parliament approves budgetary allocations year-by-year. Network investments would therefore not be protected; and would be subject to the same across-the-board budget cuts inflicted on the public investment program. Second, privatization of the network presented even more complex issues. At the time, there was no social consensus on the merits of privatization. Telecom would have been a particularly difficult candidate for privatization given its reputation[2/] as a natural monopoly. Moreover, the only viable operators and investors would have been foreign; and network privatization would have required establishment of a sophisticated regulatory framework. The Government therefore set out to mobilize private resources for that part of the network where competition would ensure efficiency: the highly diversified terminal equipment market for telephones, faxes, modems, etc. In 1988, the terminal equipment market was liberalized - an initiative that preempted developments in most other European countries. In light of these concerns, the Government chose the third option: to provide PTT with increased autonomy in exchange for realization of ambitious investment targets. High income and low price elasticity of demand for telecom services would provide a unique opportunity for cash-flow financing of infrastructure development.[3/]

5.09   *Structure*. The communications system in Turkey is owned, managed, planned and regulated by the public sector.[4/] PTT owns and operates the telecom network and the (legal) broadcast transmitters. PTT enjoys a legal monopoly over the basic network, and therefore faces no private sector competition. Shares in PTT are owned by the State (through the agency of Treasury). Sector policy and regulation is vested with the Ministry of Transportation (in particular the General Directorate for Radio Communications (TGM)). Investment review is carried out by the State Planning Organization (SPO). However in practice, this separation of powers among various agencies has left PTT with a high degree of operational and financial autonomy.

[2/] Informatics has significantly reduced minimum efficient scale for telecom. Natural monopoly arguments are today reserved for the local loop; and even there mobile communications and cable TV create the basis for a contestable market structure.

[3/] Given other tax distortions, monopolistic price-setting for telecom services could be regarded as a second-best tax instrument (i.e., Ramsey rule).

[4/] A number of other studies including The Telecommunications Sector: Republic of Turkey: 1985 (5691-TU) provide more detailed description of the main sectoral institutions. With the exception of terminal equipment liberalization (1988), the institutional framework has not changed since 1985.

5.10   Since the early 1980s, PTT has been protected from any source of external discipline that might limit its resources to finance rapid network expansion. First, PTT's shareholder has provided the institution with a ten year tax and dividend holiday: (a) permitting a higher reinvestment ratio; and (b) implicitly subsidizing network development. Second, PTT has been free to set prices at or near monopoly levels. With no competitive threat from the private sector and a passive regulator (in the Ministry of Transportation), PTT has been able to set prices to meet investment financing requirements, except in price-sensitive election years. Third, PTT's investment program is largely insulated from critical evaluation. Poor investment decisions are not reflected in e.g., a fall in PTT's share price, or in reduced bonus packages for senior management. Nor does SPO have adequate power to influence PTT's internally financed investment program. Finally, there is no organization representing consumer interests that might provide a forum for complaints about pricing, service quality, arbitrary regulations, etc.

5.11   *Investment and Financing.* The results of this approach have been dramatic (Table 5.1). Investments increased from $290 million in 1983 to $815 million in 1990 (with a peak of $875 million in 1987). PTT has consistently implemented over 100% of the original investment targets (and 100% of mid-year revised targets). The telecom/GNP investment ratio has averaged 0.86%, higher than any other OECD country (and surpassed only by 1.07% in Brazil). Over 85% of the investment program was financed from internally generated funds. The self-financing proportion has risen over time (as PTT cash-flow benefits an expansion in the revenue base). And suppliers credits have covered the financing gap. The telecom business of PTT has also strengthened its capital structure: interest coverage increasing from 3.5 in 1981 to 7.8 in 1990.

Table 5.1: PTT Investment and Financing
1983-90

Year	Investment ($ million)	Self-Financing Ratio (%)	Investment/GNP %
1983	288.8	65.5	0.56
1984	341.2	60.1	0.70
1985	459.4	78.1	0.85
1986	677.2	70.6	1.16
1987	876.5	74.5	1.28
1988	634.2	72.0	0.91
1989	402.4	90.8	0.50
1990	815.7	97.8	0.77

Source: PTT.

Performance

5.12   *Benefits*. The structure of the communications sector has therefore been highly supportive of the Government's strategy during the latter half of the 1980s. In the absence of either private competition or serious regulatory oversight, PTT has been able to: (a) triple network size over 6 years; (b) extend network coverage to reach every village and provide universal access to a telephone; (c) incorporate the latest informatics technology in an advanced digital network, thereby increasing productivity; (d) diversify service range; (e) stimulate the local telecom equipment industry; (f) substantially deepen organization skills and improve customer service; and (g) finance investments in broadcasting equipment (terrestrial and satellite) that are required to provide national high-quality television signals.

5.13   *Network Expansion*. The network has expanded rapidly during the 1980s. Until 1983, the total number of telephone subscribers was less than 1.5 million. More than 70% of villages had no access to a telephone; the penetration rate of less than 3.5 per 100 population; and the waiting list was higher than the total number of subscribers. By the end of 1990, the system had expanded dramatically (Table 5.2):

**Table 5.2: Network Expansion
1983-90**

Year	Subscribers (000s)	Public Telephones	Villages No Access
1983	1,666.5	6,718	25,883
1984	1,933.1	8,018	23,989
1985	2,222.8	11,379	20,022
1986	2,765.2	14,391	11,847
1987	3.676.6	20,298	448
1988	4,881.9	29,030	33
1989	5,721.0	35,550	-
1990	6,822.1	39,384	-

Source: PTT.

● there were over 6.8 million subscribers, a compound annual growth rate (CAGR) of almost 20%;

● the number of public telephone (mainly installed in densely populated regions, tourist resorts, and at service stations on major highways) increased from 7,000 to 40,000 (25% CAGR);

- the number of villages *without* telephones had decreased from 26,000 (i.e., 2/3 of total villages) to zero; and

- 2/3 of subscribers are residential; 1/3 are business users.

Although the penetration rate in Turkey continues to lag behind that of other OECD and (some) NIC economies (Figure 5.1), the speed with which PTT has been able to expand the network is almost without parallel. Turkey today enjoys universal telecom service albeit in the restricted sense that everyone has access to either a public or private telephone within an immediate geographic vicinity.[5]

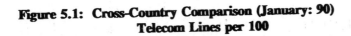

Figure 5.1: Cross-Country Comparison (January: 90)
Telecom Lines per 100

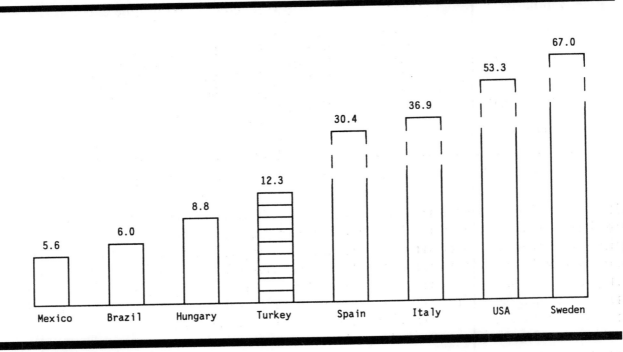

5.14   *Technological Change*. At the same time, PTT has been able to incorporate the latest digital switching and fibre-optic technology into the network (Table 5.3). As the network has expanded, the *digital switching* capacity has increased from zero to almost 50% (1990) of total lines; while the proportion of automatic analog switched lines has decreased from 80% to 46% (with manual switches for rural connections constituting the balance).   The two

---

[5] Telecom lines per 100 reached over 14 by March, 1992.

international gateway switches (in Ankara and Istanbul) are new digital exchanges (type DMS 300) with a 7,500 trunk capacity per switch. These switches, in addition to handling international traffic to and from Turkey, are also able to provide switched transit facilities. In addition, the network is interconnected with a large number of private automatic branch exchanges (PABX) that are financed by private investment and provide further system capability for more than 1 million users.[6]

Table 5.3: Switching and Transmission Technology 1985-90

Year	Switching Digital	Capacity Analog	(000 Lines) Manual	Transmission Fibre-Optic KM.	Capacity Equipt. Number
1985	78.0	2,088.0	400.9	102	36
1986	414.0	2,503.7	430.5	224	102
1987	1,459.0	2,912.4	470.1	535	270
1988	2,142.5	3,159.3	515.8	1,036	430
1989	2,693.2	3,289.4	505.4	1,546	574
1990	3,532.2	3,461.8	472.6	3,438	886

Source: PTT.

5.15   Prior to 1985, the main *transmission* media for long distance services were open-wire lines, (more recently) coaxial cables and analog radio-link systems. Since 1985, fibre-optics cables with complementary line equipment and digital radio-relay systems have been introduced as the main medium for long distance transmission. As a result of investments in multiplex and PCM systems (see Annex One for terminology), by 1990 about 85% of the long distance transmission systems employed digital technics. Additional investments in transmission include: (a) three major underground cable projects;[7] and (b) three satellite earth stations, each of which serves a different satellite. These international satellite links provide direct telephone, telex, and data communications connections, equivalent to 4,800 telephone channels.

---

[6] PABX subscriber rate in Turkey is above that in Spain (0.4 million) and Greece (0.1 million); but below that in Italy (1.7 million) and Germany (over 2 million).

[7] The three projects are: (a) Western Anatolia Underground Coaxial Cable System (BAKOK) completed in 1989; (b) the Thrace Underground Optical Fibre Cable System (TRAYFOK); and (c) the Eastern Mediterranean Submarine Fibre Optic Cable System (EMOS) connecting Turkey, Israel, Greece and Italy. PTT is also co-owner of TAT-8, TAT-9, MAT-2, SEA-ME-WE 2, and TSL cables.

5.16   *Productivity Growth*.   The consequence of these investments has been a tremendous increase in PTT's efficiency. Between 1981 and 1990, the per unit cost (to PTT) of a telephone call declined from TL360 in 1981 (in 1990 constant TL) to TL110 in 1990.[8] It is also striking to note that the rate of productivity growth has been declining since 1986! Per unit costs halved from 1981 through 1985 (from TL360 to TL180 per unit), a compound rate of productivity growth (CRPG) equivalent to 17% per annum. Since 1986, the CRPG has been equivalent to 10% per annum, a rate which however remains significantly higher than that of e.g., British Telecom (6.5% per annum). A high proportion of the benefits from productivity growth have been passed onto consumers in the form of significant real price reductions since 1981. Real per unit prices have fallen almost as rapidly as unit costs: from TL540 per unit in 1981 to TL190 in 1990. The rate of price reductions is almost the mirror image of the cost time-series: real prices declined by only one-third from 1981 to 1985 but then halved between 1986 and 1990 (as PTT began to realize the extent of its productivity gains over the decade).

Figure 5.2: Price and Cost Declines Per Unit

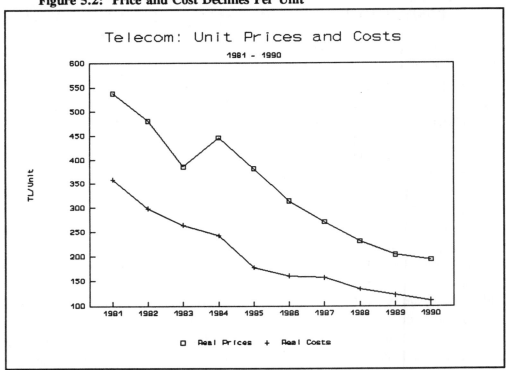

Source: World Bank.

---

[8] Unit cost is estimated before telecom contribution to general overhead expenses of PTT, and excluding the cost of equity finance (but including the cost of debt finance). The estimated costs in Figure 5.2 are therefore a slight understatement.

5.17   *Service Diversification*. The range of products and services provided by PTT has increased significantly over the past decade. First, the basic voice telephone service has been upgraded. There is direct dialing to over 200 countries. The digital systems also permit upgrading of the basic service range, including itemized billing, abbreviated dialing, last-number redial, transfer calls, conference calls, 1-800 and 1-900 numbers, etc. Apart from itemized billing (which is used by 250,000 subscribers), the use of other upgraded services remains low. Second, PTT has implemented systems for:

- *Mobile Communications*: Introduced in 1986, the system now covers Western, Central, Southern Anatolia, interconnecting highways, as well as the coastal strip in these regions. Total subscribers equalled 32,000 by 1990.[9/] PTT also operates a radio-paging service (installed in 1986) that today has 24,000 subscribers and covers the 24 major cities.

- *Data Communications*: As long as the demand for datacom was small, leased lines and dial-up slow speed lines with appropriate modems could serve the market. With increasing demand for high quality and speed data transmission services, PTT systematically upgraded facilities from a circuit switched data network (DATEX-1 in 1986) to a packet switched data network (TURPAK in 1990). TURPAK is a joint venture between PTT and Northern Telecom, and is able to serve up to 4,000 subscribers. The number of subscribers has increased from 155 in 1989 to 1500 in 1990. In addition, PTT has established a joint venture with COMSAT to provide 64 kilobit international data-transmission services to the large corporate sector.

- *Value-Added Services*: Most value-added services are still in the programming stage. Services at various stages of implementation include: (a) teletex (initiated in 1986); (b) videotext; (c) electronic mail, electronic post boxes and electronic data interchange; (d) telemetering and teleshopping. The value-added services are to be provided through the TURPAK network, and should operate independently of terminal type. Among the services that are already in commercial operation are: (a) TELEBILGI which

---

[9/] The mobile communications system in Turkey was supplied by Nokia who proposed a unique system (the Nordic Mobile Telephone System 900) operating in a non-standard 410-450 MHZ band. This system is incompatible with the proposed Pan-European digital cellular service system (Groupe Speciale Mobile - GSM) that will cover main roads in 18 European countries by 2000, and to which PTT is a co-signatory. Penetration rate for mobile communications in Turkey is 0.8 per 1000 compared to European average of 10.75. Rates for Sweden, Spain and Portugal are 64.1, 2, and 0.9 respectively.

provides information about radio/TV programs, weather, plane and train schedules, financial information, horse racing results, etc; and (b) a computerized enquiry service for telephone numbers and postal codes. A number of value-added services are being provided by the private sector, mainly in financial services market.

Despite this proliferation of services, PTT still earns over 98% of its revenues from basic voice telephony (para. 5.23).

5.18   *Industrial Development*. One major consequence of PTT's program has been a strengthening in local capability to supply public network telecom equipment. In the early 1980s, PTT manufactured most equipment in-house through its joint venture operations with ITT-Alcatel (TELETAS) and with Northern Telecom (NETAS). In 1987, PTT divested control of these companies[10] in order to focus on its main functions (of network investment and management), and to create a more competitive market for supplying its investment needs. The benefits of this more liberal framework for procurement have been very substantial. First, PTT was freed from investment requirements in its manufacturing operations. Both NETAS and TELETAS have been able to mobilize domestic and foreign capital for investments in plant and personnel development (especially software engineers) to meet PTT's demand for advanced digital switches. Second, additional suppliers have entered the market (in particular, a Siemens subsidiary) generating additional competition and technological choice. Third, the combination of a sophisticated monopsonist (PTT) and supplier competition has encouraged the industry to invest heavily in research and development. The telecom equipment industry invests approximately 5% of sales revenue in R&D; and is by far the main source of applied informatics competence in the Turkish economy.

5.19   Today, the local industry supplies more than 90% of the telecom equipment required by PTT (though local value added is significantly lower). In addition to the supply of public switches, there is a vibrant industry supplying all kinds of cables and transmission systems, a range of end-user terminals, and a number of vital components including printed circuits boards, and thin/thick film hybrid circuits. As PTT rate of investment declines, Turkish telecom suppliers have begun to move into export markets especially the C.I.S. (to which a $200 million line of export credit for telecom equipment has been granted).

5.20   *Service Quality*. PTT has significantly upgraded the quality of its *service* and of its *personnel*. On key service indicators (i.e., number and duration of faults), increased attention to maintenance and repair operations (together with higher reliability of digital compared to electro-mechanical switches) reduced total network faults to 2 per 1,000 lines by 1990; and the average duration of faults declined steeply to less than eight hours. Service has also improved as a result of significant upgrading in personnel quality. The proportion of PTT staff with university degrees almost doubled during the 1980s; and human capital was strengthened at all

---

[10] though in both cases, the Government retains a substantial minority shareholding.

levels of the organization. In 1989, PTT had 14,600 technical staff. This represents 1 for each 460 subscribers, a ratio similar to that of France (395) but above that of Italy (340). A decline in staff turnover (from 4.8% in 1981 to 1.9% in 1990) has reinforced PTT's incentive to invest in training and developing its workforce.

**Table 5.4: Telecom Equipment Production
Turkey 1990, $ millions**

Products	Production
Public Exchanges	198
Telecommunications cable (including Fiber-Optic)	156
Transmission Systems	66
User End Apparatus	28
Others	14
TOTAL	462

Source: Electronics Association.

5.21   *TV Broadcasting*. PTT is currently responsible for the transmission of TV and radio programs (the content of which is supplied by Turkish Radio and Television). PTT is fulfilling this through investments in three complementary but at times overlapping systems. First, PTT is upgrading the existing system of terrestrial transmitters to increase geographic coverage and signal quality. Second, PTT has leased transponders from an Intelsat satellite, which bounces signals to about 100 television receive only (TVRO) systems installed across Turkey. To meet expected growth in demand for high quality communications, PTT has also commissioned from Aerospatiale a national satellite system - TURKSAT. The TURKSAT project comprises two communications satellites. The first is to be launched towards the end of 1993, while the second (a back-up satellite) is due to be launched in 1994. The expected life-time of these satellites is 10-15 years. TURKSAT will be equipped with 19 transponders that will enable: (a) TV broadcasting to remote regions of Turkey and the Turkish Republics where reception is otherwise inadequate; (b) transmission of TV programs to Turkish populations living in other European countries and in the former Soviet Union; and (c) additional Very Small Aperture (VSAT) systems for in-house corporate voice and data networks. However, as a result of the satellites' relatively low transmission power, direct satellite broadcasting will not be possible in the absence of expensive antennae and satellite dishes. Third, PTT has begun investment in Cable TV networks in the major urban centers. The first stage is to connect 3 million households by mid-1992; however the program has been subject to certain delays and, at present less than 100,000 households have been connected.

5.22   *Costs*. A structure that was geared towards self-financing of network expansion inevitably generated a number of less desirable side-effects. Over the past decade, PTT has been virtually a law unto itself; and has been in a position to set the rules for the whole communications sector. At the same time as PTT has invested heavily in the network, the organization has also: (a) engaged in massive cross-subsidization of money-losing postal, telex, telegraph, and broadcasting businesses; (b) developed a high overhead cost structure; (c) been able to extract excessive consumer surplus through maintaining high price-cost margins; (d) create significant barriers to entry for private sector service providers; ((e) avoid pressure to develop a more commercial orientation; and (f) create planning uncertainty for its suppliers. The result has been substantial network expansion without the necessary accompanying network intensification. These adverse side-effects, while not hindering the primary objective of network expansion, need to be corrected to maximize the potential benefits of PTT's investment for Turkey's information-based economy. Unless corrected through policy and institutional reform, they are likely to prove an obstacle to Turkey's ambition to be truly competitive in the next communications era.

5.23   *Cross-Subsidization*. The sharp increase in the profits of the telecom business have enable PTT to mask a corresponding decline in the performance of all other business units. Over the decade, the contribution of telecom profits to PPT pre-overhead gross income[11] has increased from 78% to 116%. Over the same period, the other businesses - mail, telegraph/telex, and broadcasting - have deteriorated from a rough breakeven position to severe losses. The inefficiencies associated with the cross-subsidies are considerable. First, they are based on PTT's ability to tax telecom users to subsidize the true costs of e.g., postal services, and therefore result in a sub-optimal utilization of the network. Second, they delay the necessary improvements in business performance (or in the case of telex/telegraph, speed of business exit) that would be required to make the postal service a viable stand-alone operation.[12] Third, the cross-subsidies (together with regulatory barriers) discourage private sector entry into potentially profitable services. Fourth, they distract scarce management resources from PTT's main function: the operation of a highly efficient telecom network. While the cross-subsidies and multi-business strategy of PTT may be a necessary short-term social measure, experience of many OECD countries suggests that they inconsistent with the goal of an internationally competitive telecom operator. At present, PTT cannot compete on an equal basis with e.g., British Telecom, ATT or Cable & Wireless, leading telecom companies that do not have the burden of non-commercial mail and telegraph operations.[13]

---

[11] The variable is measured by business unit as (operating income) - (proceeds from asset disposals and other exceptional items) - (allocated contribution to central PTT overheads). The measure provides the most accurate indicator of the relative performance of PTT's business units.

[12] possibly with explicit subsidies for perceived social objectives of the mail service.

[13] The various cross-subsidies within PTT's telecom business cannot be estimated (due to data deficiencies). In a more liberal policy framework for telecom, these cross-subsidies would generate high barriers to entry for potential private suppliers of value-added services.

Year	Post	Telegraph Telex	Broad- Casting	Exceptional Items	Telecom	Total
1981	0	-0.3	0	3.9	13.1	3.9
1982	-0.3	-3.3	0	5.4	20.8	22.6
1983	1.6	-4.3	0	8.5	27.2	33.0
1984	1.5	-0.2	0	18.6	82.7	102.6
1985	0.6	5.9	0	23.1	154.9	184.5
1986	-4.9	3.2	0	37.6	222.1	258.0
1987	3.6	-3.6	0	68.9	349.6	418.5
1988	-9.2	4.2	0	275.6	640.7	911.3
1989	-128.6	-40.3	-81.2	369.4	1162.8	1282.1
1990	-325.6	-148.1	-191.4	359.7	2210.2	1904.8

Table 5.5: Business Unit Contribution to PTT Income 1981-90; TL billions

Source: World Bank Estimates.

5.24   *Excessive Overhead Costs*. The lack of market or regulatory discipline on PTT has also had the effect of permitting operational inefficiencies within PTT. In particular, it appears that the 1980s have seen a substantial increase in PTT overhead expenses: i.e., those expenses that

Figure 5.3: PTT Overhead Cost Ratios

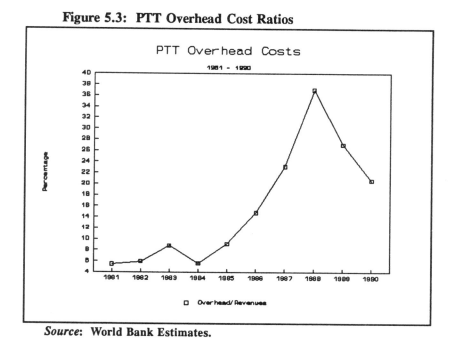

Source: World Bank Estimates.

cannot be *directly* attributed to the business unit operations. Overhead expenses increased from 5.5% of total PTT revenues in 1981 (7.3% of total PTT expenses) to a peak of 37% of revenues in 1988 before declining again to 20% in 1990.[14] These overhead expense ratios are significantly out-of-line with international comparators,[15] and suggest the scope for large efficiency gains within PTT. Significant improvements in operating efficiency are essential if PTT is to become an internationally competitive telecom company.

5.25   *Price-Cost Margins*. PTT has been able to sustain (and indeed increase) its gross margins[16] for telecom services during the 1980s. Although real prices have declined significantly (para. 5.15), the rate of price decline has not been in line with that for telecom costs. As a result, gross margins increased from 50% in 1981 to a peak of 115% in 1985 before

Figure 5.4: PTT Price Cost Margins

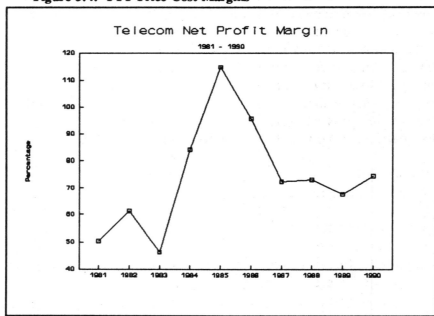

Source: World Bank Data.

---

[14] Overhead estimates have been derived from the "other" category in PTT published accounts, and appear to cover a range of non-attributable items.

[15] US telecom companies (both RBOCs and ATT) typically experience 1-2% overhead expenses plus 15% non-attributable commercial expenses for marketing and advertizing service. These commercial expenses are not a major cost category for PTT given its monopoly status.

[16] Gross margin is estimated in constant 1990 TL on a per unit basis as (telecom revenues net of asset disposals) - (telecom expenses net of contribution to overhead).

declining to 74% in 1990. To a large extent, gross margins and telecom prices are endogenous variables, driven by PTT's annual investment program and targeted self-financing ratio. Hence, the sharp increase in margins between 1984 and 1986 when subscriber base was too small to generate revenue growth without margin increases. However, less positive results of PTT's freedom to raise prices at will include: (a) the inflationary impact of telecom nominal price increases;[17] (b) significant welfare losses as a result of non-competitive pricing; and (c) the disincentive to efficiency that a soft budget constraint generates (para. 5.23). If PTT can raise prices to cover expenses, there is less reason to improve management practices or to strengthen the underlying quality of earnings.

5.26   *Barriers to Entry*. PTT is in a position to regulate: (a) the entry of private value-added service providers; (b) the type of value-added service provided; (c) the price charged to the provider for network access; and (d) the type of terminal equipment to be connected to the network. In certain cases, this regulatory power has been used to permit private entry, and therefore network utilization. First, PTT's stated policy is to encourage the private supply of electronic information services; and today there are a range of financial information services and 1-900 numbers. Second, leased circuits have been provided to public and private organizations (especially in the financial sector) that require data transmission with high speed, quality and security characteristics. Third, PTT has formed a number of joint (or revenue-sharing) ventures to deliver value-added services (e.g., TURPAK, COMSAT, cable TV). While this approach has supported introduction of advanced services, it has also permitted PTT to establish barriers to competition - by coopting potential rivals under its monopolistic umbrella.[18]

5.27   Nevertheless, private sector value-added service (VAS) providers and terminal equipment suppliers face a number of entry barriers. First, PTT protects its legal monopoly and will not interconnect any private common carrier of basic telecom services. This legal monopoly extends to all international telecom links in, out and through Turkey (contrary to the practice in certain other countries). Second, although PTT leases lines, simple resale of capacity is not permitted. This restriction prevents private entrepreneurs from constructing (albeit limited) networks, and arbitrating away PTT's large price-cost margins[19] (para. 5.24). Third, private VAS are not provided access if the service is/might be in direct competition with an information

---

[17] This inflationary impact is non-trivial. PTT revenues are now equivalent to approximately 2% of GNP (increasing from less than 1% in 1980). PTT nominal price increases either: (a) directly affect residential consumers; or (b) are passed onto final consumers by businesses with an additional margin. Telecom forms part of the basket underlying the Istanbul Chamber of Commerce Cost of Living Index.

[18] Higher prices and the absence of customer choice are the consequence of this coopting monopolistic behavior. In one case (the joint venture with COMSAT), the basic service package costs $7,000 compared with $1,200 for the equivalent in US (and $5,000 in less competitive EC countries).

[19] The concern (in Turkey and many EC countries) is that private resalers will indulge in "cream-skimming" practices: i.e., resaling capacity to the highly profitable corporate sector.

service provided by PTT. In other economies (especially following the European Community Green Paper of Telecommunications (1987)), telecom sector liberalization has been initiated in VAS, especially in data transmission and mobile telecommunications. In Turkey, these fast growing VAS businesses are the preserve of PTT - effectively locking the private sector out of contestable (and highly attractive) markets. Fourth, PTT has increasing control over the distribution channels for broadcasting, given its ownership and control of terrestrial transmitters, the cable TV system and (after 1993) TURKSAT. This control raises significant questions about the framework for the media industry which (even if private TV channels are legalized) will be dependent on PTT as a monopoly supplier of entertainment and information transmission services (see Chapter 6). Fifth, even the supply of terminal equipment that private vendors are allowed to supply is confronted with many obstacles. Type approval of all equipment connected to the network is required and the testing is performed by PTT. The result is significant and unnecessary bureaucratic delays in type approval; and the duplication of testing procedures often already carried out in other OECD countries.

5.28   The only field in which PTT is subject to effective (albeit cooperative) regulation is in the allocation of the radio spectrum, which with the proliferation of radio-communication systems, is becoming an increasingly valuable (and crowded) resource. In Turkey, regulation of the spectrum is carried out by Telsiz Genel Mudurlugu (TGM), a regulatory General Directorate established under the Ministry of Transportation. TGM is responsible for the national planning of the radio frequency spectrum and the allocation of the frequency bands to various services;[20] domestic frequency management, assignment and registration of frequencies for the users, and international frequency coordination. TGM is authorized to determine national standards for radio communications systems and to issue licenses for the use of radio-communications equipment and systems. As the operator of all radio and television transmitters, and the provider of all wireless systems and services (including mobile communications), PTT is the dominant user of the radio frequency spectrum in the civilian sector. The current system of radio spectrum allocation is largely driven by PTT technical requirements. Economic considerations are secondary, and the needs of private sector radio-spectrum users are met only on a residual basis (i.e., after PTT needs are fulfilled). One result has been an increase in unauthorized uses of the spectrum (especially by local municipalities for retransmission of television broadcasts), and growing signal interference.

5.29   *Commercial Orientation.* PTT has a captive market for its telecom services, and therefore has little incentive to develop its marketing function. There is no independent marketing unit; and even where consumer research activity has been carried out, it is sporadic and not systematic. The costs of this marketing failure are significant especially with regard to the development of PTT's enhanced services (para. 5.16). Many of these services have been introduced without prior market analysis or research; there is no or little information on the target customer base; there is no assessment of price elasticities of demand (and therefore

---

[20] including potentially to private sector TV and radio broadcasters (Box 6.1).

Table 5.6: Regulatory Framework for Competition and Entry
Cross-Country Comparison

	Private Telecom	Simple Line Resale	Private VAS	Terminal Equipment	Private Television
Turkey	3	3	2	2	3
U.K.	1	1	1	1	2
Japan	1	1	1	1	2
Spain	2	3	1	2	2
France	2	2	1	2	2

Key: 1 = Allowed with minimal restrictions
2 = Allowed but restricted
3 = Not Allowed

Source: OECD.

maximum revenue yield); nor is there an examination of the optimal time or location to introduce new services. The result is that the customer base for many of PTT's enhanced services (para. 5.16) has failed to develop; and that on a fully costed basis, many of these services would fail to pass rate of return criteria that would be standard in more market-driven telecom companies. Although PTT can afford (given its monopoly status) to cross-subsidize these activities, a more disciplined approach will be essential in a more competitive environment.

5.30   *Planning Uncertainty.* The PTT investment program has been instrumental in the development of a local industry to supply public network telecom equipment (para. 5.17). However, its growth might have occurred in a more efficient manner had the PTT investment program been: (a) prepared on a medium term basis; and (b) subject to less variance on a year-to-year basis. The investment program was largely prepared on an annual basis with little PTT-industry coordination or information-sharing. Investments swung from $876 million in 1987 to $402 million by 1989 back to $815 million by 1990. These changing investment requirements map into significant uncertainty for the local industry, and may have also created false signals to potential entrants. The result is that today Turkey has significant over-capacity in the supply of public network equipment, and the local industry is struggling to gain share in highly politicized export markets. Telecom equipment exports remain low, and it is not clear whether Turkish suppliers will in practice preferential treatment in e.g., the Turkic Republics of the former Soviet Union.

5.31   *Conclusions.* In many respects, communications sector strategy has successfully met its objectives over the past decade. A structure that provided PTT with significant managerial and financial autonomy has enabled unprecedented network expansion without imposing any burden on public sector finances. Turkey now enjoys universal service in the sense that everyone has relatively easy access to either a public or private telephone. At the same time, the network has been modernized, productivity has increased at over 13% per annum, and a range of enhanced and value added services are now available. However, it appears that *network expansion* has come at the expense of *network intensification*. The substantial investments in the network are generating a high rate of financial return only because of PTT's monopoly pricing power and the low price elasticity of demand. The economic benefits associated with the network have been significantly reduced because of pricing well above marginal costs, and because barriers to private sector entry have constrained consumer choice and service innovation.

5.32   This failure to maximize the economic benefits associated with the network can be seen in the apparent absence of network externalities. One justification for public provision of telecom services is that of "natural monopoly" i.e., that there are significant economies of scale related to the marginal subscriber. In principle, this implies that network expansion (i.e., an increase in the subscriber base) should be accompanied by network intensification (i.e., an increase in call units per subscriber). However in Turkey, this intensification has not occurred.

5.33   Prima facie, it appears that units per subscriber have increased from 1,798 in 1981 to 3,915 in 1990 (line A in Figure 5.4). However, this increase can be largely attributed not to network expansion but instead to GNP growth. Since the demand for telecom services is highly sensitive to changes in income, the rapid increase in Turkey's GNP over the same period emerges as a major determinant of network utilization. Indeed, based on unitary income elasticity of demand for telecom services,[21] it appears that GNP growth rather than network expansion has been the main source of the increase in units per subscriber. As shown in line B (Figure 5.5), if GNP had remained constant over the decade, it is estimated that units per subscriber would have increased from 1,798 in 1981 to a peak of 2,773 in 1985 before declining again to 1,747 by 1990. These estimates appear to show that: (a) PTT has generated limited and then negative externalities; and (b) that there are diminishing returns to further network expansion. The key to increased productivity in the future is no longer a structure and strategy geared towards network expansion. Rather, it is one dedicated to network intensification through reducing prices to more competitive levels, increasing operating efficiency, and eliminating barriers to a diversified private supply of value-added and other electronic information services. Today, a structural change needs to take place. As the policy objective shifts towards network intensification, organization of the communications sector based on PTT autonomy and self-regulation may no longer be optimal, and may instead become an obstacle to the next stage of sectoral development.

---

[21] which is in line with estimates for other OECD countries.

Figure 5.5: Network Externalities

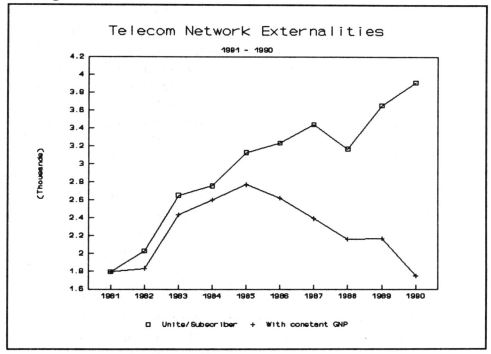

Objectives and Strategy

5.34   Substantial achievement of the network expansion policy objective has laid the foundation for the next strategic era of communications sector development. This era is likely to be characterized by four main policy objectives:

- *network intensification*: to generate maximum economic benefits from network (and radio spectrum) resources through greater competition in telecom service provision and a cost-based pricing structure;

- *private information industry development*: to increase the range and quality of network-based information services through fostering growth of a competitive private information industry;

- *universal access*: to ensure wide distribution of network benefits, and to improve information flows to geographically dispersed locations; and

- *PTT as a world-class telecom company*: to separate telecom from the mail, and to accelerate PTT's entry into the international telecom services market.

5.35   These objectives imply the need for significant change in the communications sector. The structure and strategy that succeeded in the network expansion era may no longer be optimal with respect to a different set of objectives. Indeed, the specific factors which have been the basis for Turkey's success in the 1980s may (in the absence of reform) prove to be the obstacles to further progress in the 1990s. *First*, PTT's autonomy with respect to pricing has resulted in high price-cost margins, cross-subsidization within telecom (and between telecom and other business units), a reduced rate of network intensification, and diminished incentives for PTT to be a dynamic learning organization. *Second*, PTT's mixed role as a basic *and* value-added telecom services provider is stifling potential competition and choice, and adding to the market uncertainty faced by potential private value-added (i.e., electronic information) suppliers. Even if a private value-added service is created, the absence of transparent rules regarding PTT pricing, billing services and access distorts the market.   And when a private service is successful, there is the underlying threat that PTT may enter the market (with an unfair competitive advantage). *Third*, PTT's resource base to invest in increased universal service provision has been: (a) a function of its non-competitive pricing practices; and (b) diminished by organizational inefficiencies and massive cross-subsidies to loss-making mail and telegraph/ telex businesses. In a more competitive pricing environment, PTT would no longer be able both to expand universal access and to cross-subsidize other businesses. *Fourth*, PTT lack of exposure to the market has enabled the organization to deliver a supply-driven investment strategy, and to build strong engineering assets. However, if PTT is to become internationally competitive, then it will need to give greater emphasis to development of its non-engineering skills. The current lack of market discipline and performance incentives is reflected in under-investment in core marketing, finance, and planning functions.

5.36   There are therefore two major structural changes that will be required to achieve policy objectives geared to the 1990s. The *first* is an explicit separation of the regulatory functions from the operational responsibilities of PTT. These regulatory functions which today are largely performed by PTT itself include: (a) determination and enforcement of pricing policy, including a clear formula for updating; (b) open network provision (i.e., terms of access) rules for private value-added service providers;[22] (c) explicit cross-subsidization to increase universal service provision; (d) type approval rules for terminal equipment; and (e) efficient allocation of the radio spectrum. The benefits of this separation will accrue to three groups of stakeholders in the system. First, consumers will benefit through lower prices and increased choice. Second, the private information and value-added services industry will be provided with a new set of market opportunities.   Third, PTT will itself benefit both through network

---

[22] Ultimately, the access rules may be broadened to include competition in the provision of a broader range of telecom services as technological change creates the potential for efficient market conditions (and therefore market-based price determination) in all telecom services.

intensification (i.e., higher revenue generation) and through the impact of external discipline on internal learning processes. The *second* change would be steps that strengthen PTT's core competences, thereby increasing competitiveness on the international market for telecom services. Potential areas for institutional reform include: (a) separation of the telecom from mail businesses into independent enterprises; and (b) progressive privatization of PTT businesses that are not part of the basic telephone service.

5.37   These measures are fully consistent with developments that have already taken place in the USA, UK, Japan, a number of NICs (including Mexico, Philippines and Portugal), and at a slower pace in the European Community. In the European Community, the leadership role has been played by Directorate General XIII of the Commission. In its Green Paper of 1987, DGXIII set down the basic elements of the Community's telecom policy in "ten commandments", the most important of which are that:

- the regulatory and operational functions of PTTs should be separated through establishment of independent regulatory bodies;

- PTTs can retain a monopoly over the basic network, and for voice telephony over than network;

- common technical standards should be adopted to allow for network interconnection;

- Open network provisions (ONP), allowing third party access to PTT operated networks, should be made possible by adopting clear rules on items such as tariff structure and technical standards;

- EC competition law should be applied to both PTTs and private operators, as an additional tool for pricing open markets; and

- the terminal equipment market should be opened up for competition (as has already largely been achieved in Turkey).

In addition, DGXIII has issued a range of further directives (approved by the Council of Ministers) that: (a) liberalize public procurement practices; and (b) harmonize technical standards for satellite communications. In general, it appears that EC policy has evolved away from permitting cross-subsidies (to finance infrastructure building) towards the provision of a direct subsidy (i.e., Regional Development Grants) that will facilitate an evening out of the EC telecom infrastructure. In particular, the Southern European countries can expect significant financial support for network expansion and modernization. An important benefit of the proposed realignment of the communications sector in Turkey will be harmonization with developments in major trading partners.

5.38   *Independent Regulatory Agency*. An independent regulatory agency would have five main functions. First, it would aim to set prices in a way that reduce price-cost margins, encourages network intensification and provides an incentive for PTT to increase efficiency. Second, the agency would reduce barriers to entry faced by private sector value-added and information service providers. Third, the agency would help to eliminate residual bureaucratic obstacles experienced by providers and users of advanced terminal equipment. Fourth, it would define clear and monitorable quality of service indicators for PTT, together with sanctions for non-compliance. Fifth, the agency would be responsible for radio spectrum allocation. The main rationale for an independent regulatory agency is to overcome the imperfection created by the absence of a competitive market in many telecom services and facilities provision. As such, the agency is a "second best" solution to the actual development of a competitive market.[23] As pace of technological change in communications continues unabated, it might be expected that the role of the agency will change and possibly diminish over time.

5.39   The agency would be responsible for establishing *pricing* rules for the telecom network. The principles that determine these pricing rules normally include: (a) a progressive elimination of cross-subsidization; (b) non-discrimination between different users of the same service; (c) a reduction in price-cost margins; and (d) an incentive for PTT to increase efficiency. The practical application of these principles is however quite complex, and is typically based on gradualism. The objective *over time* is that PTTs should price in line with the conjectured market price for a basket of services. However, the determination of the basket, the disaggregation of price-setting, and the permitted degree of cross-subsidization appears to vary from country to country. One attractive pricing formula is that applied by the Office of Telecom Regulation (OFTEL) in the UK (Box 5.2).

5.40   The second responsibility of an independent regulatory agency would be to establish *interconnection* and *market access* rules. There are three main aspects to this function. The first is to implement objectives with regard to open network provision. This would require PTT to abolish monopolies over value-added service such as data transfer, or message storing. It would establish a clear set of rules regarding the right of private value-added service providers to: (a) obtain interconnection from PTT on an automatic basis; (b) be charged for their use of the network on a non-discriminatory basis; and (c) have certain access rights to PTT billing procedures and customer databases. The second aspect relates to line resale rights, which would enable private operators to construct networks out of leased circuits, and provide lower cost telecom services to major corporate clients. The third responsibility would be to determine PTT's right to enter the market for value-added and information services. Given PTT's dominant market position, it enjoys a competitive advantage vis-a-vis most private suppliers of value-added services (except where there is a high and specialized information content). A key issue therefore is whether and how PTT should be eligible to deliver value-added services.

---

[23] Regulatory agencies are unlikely to be a first best solution given information asymmetries between the agency and the PTT (which typically benefit the PTT).

> **Box 5.2: International Pricing Models**
>
> Two main pricing models have been developed since the establishment of independent regulatory agencies. In the US, the model is largely based on rate of return criteria. In an aggregate sense, prices should be set to permit a rate of return on capital in line with the market-determined riskiness of telecom stocks. Since the beta on telecom stocks is low, prices are set to generate relatively low rates of return. In addition, there are a variety of individual price-caps and taxes to achieve other social objectives that include: (a) relatively low residential rates; (b) relatively low rural interconnection rates; and (c) a fund to subsidize telecom service provision to low income households.
>
> In the UK, OFTEL established a pricing rule of "Retail Price Index minus X" (RPI-X), where X is a target rate of productivity growth established by OFTEL. Until 1991, X was set at 4%; subsequently, X has been increased to 6.5% because of continued excess profits earned by British Telecom. British Telecom has to meet the RPI-X rule for a weighted basket of residential and business telecom services. The rule has the dual merits of simplicity, low information costs, and (unlike rate of return rules) a strong incentive for British Telecom to increase efficiency.

5.41   The third function of the proposed regulatory agency would be to provide further impetus to liberalization of the *terminal equipment* market (para. 5.16). The agency should be empowered to accredit private sector (and other public sector) organizations that would carry out equipment testing, and could issue type approvals. In addition, type testing carried out by accredited foreign organizations should also be accepted on an automatic basis, thereby accelerating the transfer of state-of-the-art terminal equipment market to Turkey.

5.42   The agency would also be responsible for setting *quality of service* targets for PTT (and in the long run for other suppliers of basic telephone services). These targets are essential for three reasons. First, they serve to safeguard consumer interests against PTT's incentive to trade reduced price-cost margins (para. 5.39) against a lower quality of service. Second, they will help to strengthen a consumer-oriented culture in PTT, and thereby support this aspect of organizational learning. Third, since PTT is not legally liable for the economic consequences of system failure or poor service, these targets substitute for the ex post legal incentive to maintain high performance standards (para. 7.35). Internationally recognized quality of service indicators[24] cover six generic areas that would provide a useful starting point for the agency:

---

[24] These have been formally adopted by the European Conference of Postal and Telecommunications Administrations (1987 Copenhagen meeting).

- provision, alteration, cessation and recovery of service;

- loss of service (fault reports);

- call set-up time;

- call failure rates, transmission quality and privacy;

- call release time; and

- billing integrity (account queries).

An additional target that might be emphasized in Turkey is proportion of public telephones in working order.

5.43   The fifth major regulatory issue is the allocation of the *radio spectrum*, and more generally the *integration of a regulatory framework for telecom and for television* (whether satellite, terrestrial or cable broadcasting systems).   Traditionally, broadcast and telecom regulation has occupied separate worlds.   Telecom regulation has concerned itself with pricing, access, and terminal equipment issues; and has been based on common carriage principles in which the system is content-neutral.   On the other hand, broadcast regulation has largely been concerned with issues of content and cross-media ownership.   With the proliferation of electronic information services, narrowcasting techniques (e.g., cable TV), and competing demands for scarce radio spectrum (from additional television channels and mobile communications services), many countries have recognized that the easy distinctions between broadcast and telecom regulation are breaking down.   These same countries are however trapped by existing regulatory structures that frequently create arbitrary distinctions between different forms of information service.   In the US (for example), cable TV is regulated according to different principles from either TV or broadcasting.[25]   As Turkey moves towards a more liberal regime for private TV and radio broadcasting, there exists a unique opportunity to develop a regulatory framework that integrates across the communications sector.   This is especially true in the case of regulating information content, for which there is no a priori reason to distinguish between various electronic media (para. 6.44).

5.44   There is no international best practice as to the optimal model, organization or powers for a regulatory agency.   In each country, the regulatory framework for the communications sector has evolved along distinctive lines as a consequence of unique cultural, geographic or technological circumstances.   In the US, the Federal Communications Commission (FCC) arrangement is largely a product of the federal nature of the country's political structure.

---

[25] These distinctions are however likely to prove increasingly untenable in light of the new ruling that the Baby Bells can enter (under a range of restrictions) the information services market. USA v. Western Electric Company (Civil Action 82-0192, 1991).

In the UK, the development of private broadcasting, telecom and now cable services all evolved at different times; and are subject to separate (though coordinated) regimes. In continental Europe, broadcasting and telecom is still under greater state control; and the regulatory regimes are correspondingly less developed. In certain cases, regulatory functions are carried out by the

---

Box 5.3: Latest Developments in the Radio Spectrum

At the 1992 International Telecommunications Union Conference, representatives of 124 countries (including Turkey) cleared the way for a new multi-billion communications system that would use dozens of low-orbiting satellites to relay calls to and from people carrying pocket-size phones anywhere on Earth. The Conference set aside a portion of the world's increasingly crowded radio spectrum for the new system, which still faces a number of regulatory, technological and commercial uncertainties. The leader to provide the system is a multi-national partnership put together by a subsidiary of Motorola Inc (Iridium), which has proposed a $3.5 billion system using 77 satellite circling the earth in low orbit. Plans call for it to be fully operational in 1997. Due to the satellite's low orbit, phones would be small. Satellites would receive a call from the ground, route it from satellite to satellite, and then drop it down to earth, either to another pocket phone or a conventional desktop phone. The service would initially cost $3 per minute; and therefore would not replace regular cellular service. However, it would be used in areas where cellular service - which requires users to be near ground-based relay stations - is not available. For Turkey, the proposed system offers the opportunity to increase communication links with the rural areas, but without the high fixed costs associated with further expansion of the land-based network. Implementation of the system in Turkey inevitably raises the regulatory issues of pricing, interconnection, and radio spectrum allocation.

Ministries for Communications (e.g., Germany, France). In other cases, there has been a transition to an independent regulatory agency (e.g., UK, Spain). In either case, the key success factors appear to be: (a) rapid development of competition to PTT especially in value-added services; (b) personnel quality; (c) PTT reporting requirements; and (d) political support for the regulatory functions.

5.45   Nor is there an optimal speed at which a regulatory agency should reduce prices, increase competition, and restrict PTT lines of business. The agency would be responsible for broad implementation of government policy, which is likely to include a mix of purely commercial and more social objectives. PTT has achieved geographic coverage for the network, but not yet universal service provision. PTT investment requirements (as a percentage of revenue) will continue to be higher than that of the more advanced OECD countries; and therefore need to be balanced against short-run consumer welfare gains. Similarly, it is not clear that Turkey would benefit immediately from a more competitive market in basic telecom services or through simple line resale provisions. Premature liberalization of the entire telecom services market is likely to result in "cream-skimming" activities by the private sector, and the loss to PTT of major revenue-generating corporate clients. Regulation therefore needs to be phased in according to a transparent pre-announced schedule.

5.46   Turkey already possesses two regulatory agencies with jurisdiction in the communications sector. First, TGM already performs one of the key regulatory functions (i.e., radio spectrum allocation); and appears to have developed an understanding of the key policy and regulatory issues. TGM was established in 1983 under the Ministry of Transportation in order to implement the Radio Code 2813 (subsequently amended by Code 3293, issued in 1986). The main function of TGM is regulation of land-based radio-communications systems. Second, the Supreme Council for Radio and Television Broadcasting (RTYK) is responsible for policy formulation and supervision of TRT, and is about to assume expanded jurisdiction over: (a) licensing of private TV and radio broadcasting stations; (b) information content of TV and radio; and (c) cross-media ownership issues (Box 6.1). Neither agency however, has yet developed the technical skills to deal with complex pricing, barriers to entry, terminal equipment and service quality issues that are central to telecom sector regulation. Turkey today therefore faces a choice: either to merge TGM and RTYK into a single regulatory agency for the communications sector (following the FCC model but with more unified jurisdiction over electronic media), or to retain a more decentralized regulatory framework with three agencies - TGM, RTYK and a telecom authority. Key factors in making that choice should be: (a) the ease with which overlapping issues (e.g., on radio spectrum allocation, information content) can be handled; (b) speed of institutional development; and (c) robustness of institutional design against regulatory capture.

5.47   *PTT Development.* The second major structural reform would be steps to increase the competitiveness of PTT. Two key issues need to be addressed. The first is the separation of mail and telecom businesses into independent enterprises; and the second (in the future) is the progressive privatization of the telecom business. The main benefits that such an enterprise reform program would generate are: (a) an elimination of cross-subsidies that reduce PTT's resources for investment in universal telecom service provision; (b) greater commercial orientation and management focus on the core telecom business; and (c) a strengthening in PTT's competitive position in the international telecom services market.

5.48   In an increasing range of countries, governments are *separating the delivery of mail from telecom services.* The principle driving this development is the lack of business logic behind joint production and delivery of mail and telecom. The organizational skills required in the two businesses are quite distinct; the technology set is unrelated; and the underlying economics are incompatible. Mail is a high variable cost business which is: (a) labor intensive; (b) facing low growth in demand; and (c) threatened by a range of substitutes including electronic mail and fax technologies. By contrast, telecom is capital-intensive, high fixed cost, and facing an era of unprecedented expansion. In Turkey, the numbers paint a stark picture of two increasingly divergent businesses. The mail business is experiencing less than 4% real growth per annum in revenues; its labor expenses are 140% of primary revenues;[26] and operating losses have increased from zero in 1980 to TL350 billion in 1990 (Figure 5.6). The telecom business is a mirror image: experiencing 16% real revenue growth per annum; with labor expenses approximately 20% of primary revenues; and generating an operating profit of TL2210 billion in 1990. The main consequences of an integrated mail-telecom PTT are: (a) sustained but hidden cross-subsidization, implying a large transfer from telecom users to mail users; (b) higher than necessary telecom prices, reducing consumer benefits and network intensification; (c) an increase in the telecom business's implicit cost of capital which adversely affects both PTT's competitiveness and its capability to increase universal telecom access; and (d) a diversion of scarce managerial resources.

5.49   If an independent regulatory framework is established (paras. 5.35-5.42), it will become progressively more difficult to avoid a complementary initiative to separate mail and telecom. As price regulation begins to curb excess telecom profits, PTT will no longer be in a position to provide growing cross-subsidies for mail as well as to meet legitimate telecom investment targets. In effect, separation of the mail business (especially given its growing operating deficit) is a pre-condition for appropriate regulatory development in the telecom sector. The present combined operation is a recipe for inertia in improving mail performance and is an obstacle to the new structures required for progress in the communications field. Key steps in the establishment of a separate mail enterprise are likely to include: (a) design of a clear and

Figure 5.6: Telecom versus Mail (1990)

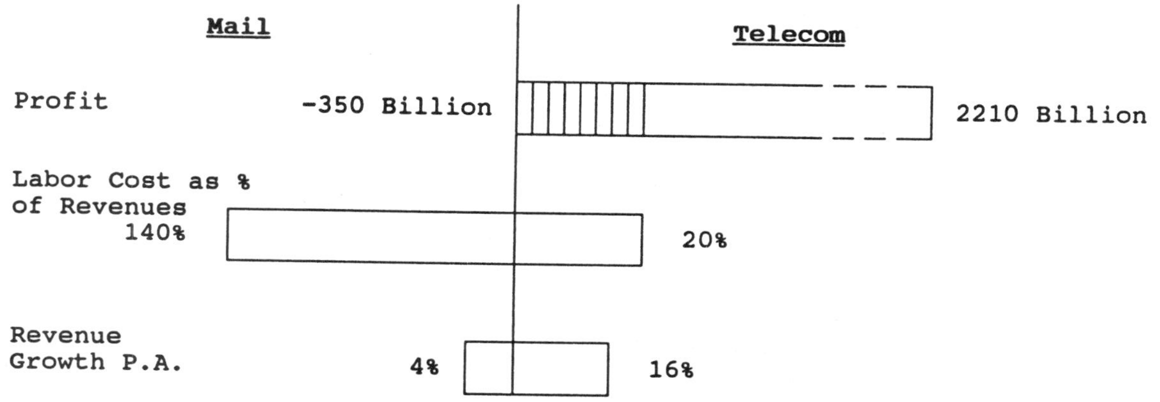

Source: World Bank Data.

[26] Primary revenues are defined as revenues before exceptional items, transfers and asset disposals.

liberal policy framework for postal services that clearly defines entry opportunities for the private sector; (b) development of separate financial accounts for PTT's mail operations; (c) separation of jointly owned facilities; (d) financial restructuring of the mail operations to improve commercial viability, including a phased reduction in telecom transfers to mail; (e) legal change to remove civil servant status of majority of PTT workers;[27/] (f) operational restructuring to reduce over-staffing; and (g) new investments to increase productivity and to develop new business services.

5.50   Over the next decade, Turkish Telecom (TT) should accelerate its transition from the role of public utility to that of an internationally competitive business, supplying a range of telecom services. By 2000, network coverage (both fixed and mobile) will be on a par with other OECD countries. Given an appropriate regulatory framework, the range/volume of value-added services delivered over the network will be growing at 20%-30% per annum. Continued convergence between communication systems will result in the delivery of multi-media services, utilizing a combination of transmission and switching technologies. And in more and more business segments, new technologies will increase market contestability and reduce minimum efficient scale of operation. Even in the local loop, natural monopoly arguments will be challenged by a range of radio-communication devices. As a result, the economic rationale for public provision of telecom services (i.e., network investment requirements, natural monopoly) is likely to diminish.

5.51   As Turkish Telecom negotiates its changing environment, there may be substantial benefits from a policy of progressive privatization, starting with data transmission and mobile communications operations, and (possibly) ending with the network itself. This process of commercialization and then privatization would require three preliminary steps:

- establishment of Turkish Telecom as a legal entity;

- separation of non-core businesses (e.g., TURPAK, the mobile telephone operations, cable TV) into independent subsidiaries of TT i.e., as enterprises under private commercial law; and

- placing TT under private commercial law through changing its legal structure (under Law 406) from that of a public economic institution to joint stock company (that would initially be 100% owned by the Government).

Following the introduction of a corporate legal structure, privatization itself would: (a) provide access to private investment resources; (b) increase the commercial orientation of TT's culture and business systems; (c) provide a transparent indicator of performance (through the share

---

[27/] 88,000 PTT employees (out of 110,000 total) currently enjoy civil servant status, and therefore have protected tenure.

price); (d) allow for personnel hiring at market rates; and (e) place Turkish Telecom on an equal competitive footing with other international telecom businesses. The benefits would accrue not only to Turkish Telecom (and to Treasury through privatization proceeds). Rather, the main beneficiaries will be the consumers who will enjoy increased choice, a more innovative range of services, and lower prices.

5.52   *Conclusions.* There is a substantial temptation for policy-makers to avoid reform of the communications sector. During the 1980s, Turkey has developed a successful formula for network expansion and productivity growth. PTT has over-achieved many of its targets, and also most neutral observers' expectations. There is a high level of public satisfaction with PTT services; and indeed it is regarded as a role model for the public enterprise sector. PTT staff have a strong sense of institutional pride and, in many cases, have accepted below-market wages to participate in PTT's mission. Already, an implicit coalition of PTT and equipment suppliers is arguing the case for further network expansion and modernization, based on local loop fibre-optics and Broadband-ISDN technology. This advanced network would permit simultaneous voice, data, and image transmission to households in the major metropolitan areas. However, the investment costs are enormous (estimated at over $30 billion over the 15 years), there are significant technological risks, and the economics of the system appear very uncertain.[28] Rather than additional supply-driven investment, what is required is a systemic shift that achieves a better balance between the technologically feasible and the commercially viable.

5.53   Reform is therefore essential if the communications sector is to realize its full potential and to build upon the foundations that PTT has laid in the 1980s. The benefits of policy and institutional reform are substantial: increased services and choice, lower prices, a vibrant private information industry, an explicit strategy for universal service provision, and an internationally competitive PTT able to serve the needs of the business community. The potential costs of policy and institutional inertia are equally severe: restricted choice, monopolistic pricing, and an insular PTT whose institutional imperative is to protect a growing empire. That today Turkey enjoys this choice is a tribute to the wise decisions and sustained commitment characteristic of sectoral development in the 1980s.

---

[28] A recent OECD report <u>Convergence between Communications Technologies: A Policy Review</u> (1992) argues that "fibre to the desktop/home is a technological solution to a problem that does not yet exist. Almost all future communications needs can be met by a hybrid network of fibre close the home with a copper (coaxial cable or twisted pair) feed in the local loop". (p.21).

CHAPTER 6

REDUCING UNCERTAINTY - THE ROLE OF INFORMATION

Introduction

6.01   Efficiency in a competitive economy depends on the free flow of information. Reliable and timely information provides the basis for good decision-making. It creates new market opportunities, is central to the learning process (at all levels of society), affects the quality of public policy, and reduces response time with which resources can be shifted to higher productivity activities.   A competitive market in information lies at the heart of a well-functioning democracy, and fosters development of an open, pluralistic society. By contrast, information problems and defects generate significant losses for the economy, and undermine the potential for participation in the political process. Information reduces uncertainty; and when information is not readily available, the result surfaces in failures in the principal factor and product markets, aggravating problems of unemployment and capital shortage. Information scarcity also translates into policy mistakes, educational disparities, slower productivity growth (through barriers to technology diffusion), and into additional time-related costs. In societies where information is provided by public or private monopolies, the democratic safeguards cannot work.

6.02   Information possesses a unique set of economic characteristics. First, information frequently has the attributes of a public good. This means that there are significant economic benefits from its widespread dissemination at zero or marginal cost. Examples of public good information are news about the weather (that might affect the whole agricultural sector), the location of traffic jams in Istanbul (allowing drivers to optimize their route), national announcements about computer viruses (Michelangelo: March 6, 1992) or share prices on the Istanbul Stock Exchange (and prices in general). Second, other types of information bear a much stronger resemblance to private goods.   In these cases, information is proprietary, confidential and has a direct influence on corporate competitiveness (and policy effectiveness). Examples of this type of information might include share-price sensitive information on corporate strategy, changes in tax or monetary policy, or customer databases.   Third (and complicating the story), much information has both public and private good attributes. For example, most market research processes publicly available data (on e.g., demographic trends and structure) to tailor information for the needs of a specific client. Similarly, there is a new information industry specialized in interpreting public data from remote-sensing satellites, and selling the information to e.g., resource-extraction companies.   Essentially, data without customized content usually has public good attributes.   But as data is transformed into information (whose value can be captured by a small number of private agents), it becomes more and more a private good. This generates a strong interdependence between public and private information activities; one in which the *public sector* has a lead in *data collection and dissemination*, and the *private sector* is responsible for *supplying information*.

6.03   The economics of the information industry has been recast by informatics. First, informatics has radically increased the availability of data by bringing down the costs of data-collection and storage. Data is collected (in digital format) through an increasing number of devices: satellites, transactions-generated databases, digital measurement instruments, telemetering, etc. As the data storage media also improve in terms of capacity and reliability, governments (and other large organizations) are confronted with an ever-increasing data management task. Second, the technology for data-processing has also become much more powerful, increasing productivity at the stage of translating data into information. Anyone with a personal computer and a modem can become an information-supplier. Third, informatics has transformed communications technology (which is today part of the informatics paradigm). Informatics is overcoming the earlier limitations of bandwidth, a limited radio spectrum, and distance-sensitive data transmission costs. As a result, information can be disseminated on a global basis; and a proliferation of media distribution channels is providing increased consumer choice (even if the relationship between competition and quality is less pronounced).

6.04   The result of this technological change (and increased demand for information in advanced economies) has been sustained growth in the private information industry. The industry comprises 3 main segments: the print and broadcast media, specialized information houses, and the consulting profession. All three main industry segments have grown at rates exceeding 8% per annum during the 1980s. Films are now the US's second largest export (after airplanes). In Europe, there has been an explosion of media outlets over the last 20 years. In 1980 there were no satellite television channels; in 1990 there were 82. The number of radio stations has more than doubled (to 5,820); consumer magazine titles have increased from 5,400 to 8,240; terrestrial television channels have grown from 15 to 38. Across the OECD, the market for specialized information services delivered through on-line databases is expanding at 25% per annum - from $4.2 billion in 1984 to a projected $48 billion in 1994. At the same time, demand for consulting services in finance, management, engineering, and informatics has taken off as firms find that internal information resources are inadequate to compete successfully in a global technology-driven marketplace.

6.05   While changing market conditions have fuelled growth of the private information industry, this development could not have taken place without complementary government action and policy reform. Traditionally, governments have been the largest producers and consumers of information in an economy. Government is by its very nature highly information-intensive. In addition, governments in all countries have carved out a significant role in: (a) data collection; (b) data archiving; (c) data dissemination; and (d) control over communications sector. Over the past decade, governments across the OECD and NICs have looked for ways to increase the productivity of the private information industry as a source of national competitive advantage. The public sector has intensified its data collection efforts; new (more liberal) rules are governing public data dissemination to maximize its economic value; reforms are removing restrictions on private media; and telecom investments and regulatory change are creating new market opportunities for private value-added service providers (see Chapter 5). As governments move out of the direct role of information supplier, they are assuming a stronger regulatory function: setting standards for financial, technical and consumer information; protecting confidentiality and privacy; and strengthening competition in the information marketplace.

6.06   The private information industry in Turkey is still in its infancy; and is dominated by the newspaper industry (which itself is highly fragmented and faces low readership rates). Total industry revenues are less than 2% of GNP - significantly lower than the ratio in most other OECD countries.   Television and Radio broadcasting is still (legally) a public sector monopoly, though liberalization measures are expected before the end of 1992. The specialized information industry is concentrated in the financial markets; and there are only a small number of on-line database services.   And in general, market demand for information and external consulting is growing only slowly.   Larger corporations typically internalize information activities, and do not yet display much confidence in local management or technical consultants. And the residential market for consumer information (e.g., product comparisons) has been slow to develop.   While the industry has invested heavily in informatics (especially newspaper publishers), growth rates are low, specialization is limited, and the process of horizontal integration across the industry is just beginning.

6.07   The Government strategy for economic modernization explicitly recognizes the value of a vibrant private information industry.   Massive investment in telecommunications, proposed reform of the television broadcast and PTT laws, and increased dissemination of public sector data are all measures designed to increase industry productivity. Progressive liberalization of the economy and accompanying reduction in government-directed investments will over time increase market demand for accurate and timely information.   Nevertheless, the Government in Turkey still appears to have a larger direct and smaller regulatory role in the information industry than is the case in many other OECD economies. A reformulation of this role can be the catalyst for a more dynamic private information industry.

6.08   The Chapter is organized in three main sections.   Section two reviews major trends affecting the international market for information services.   Section three assesses recent developments in the Turkish private information industry. Section four examines the role played by government policy and institutions, and proposes certain initiatives that might increase dynamism and investment in the private information industry.

Global Market Trends

6.09   The global information industry has experienced an era of rapid growth, driven by technological and policy change.   As informatics has increased data supply, lowered the cost of data-processing, and generated new media for data transmission, the demand and supply of information continues to experience high rates of growth.   In 1990, it is estimated that the combined media, telecom and computer (global) market was worth $1.3 trillion. By 2000 it may reach $3 trillion - or roughly $1 out of every $6 of global GNP. Information services (excluding consulting[1]) accounts for approximately 20% of the total information market. Within the information services industry, the fastest growing segments appear to be: (a) cable TV (36% per annum growth since 1988); and (b) value-added network services (33% per annum growth, with total market revenues estimated at $39 billion by 1995).

Table 6.1: Composition and Growth of Global Information Market

$ Billions	1985	1990	1995	CAGR
IT Hardware[1]	200	380	730	12.8%
Software & Svcs.[2]	70	175	400	18.4%
Telecom Eqpt.[3]	80	108	145	6.0%
Telecom Svcs.[4]	225	310	410	6.2%
Information Svcs.[5]	170	290	380	8.2%
TOTAL	745	1263	2065	9.5%

1. IT hardware includes electronics, computers, private telecom equipment, and user expenditures for IT introduction.
2. Includes value-added networks, services and maintenance.
3. Public switched telecom network (PSTN) investments only.
4. PSTN revenues.
5. Revenues from film, television, publishing, and specialized information services. Excluding consulting services.

Source: World Bank Estimates adapted from OECD.

6.10   The information services segment of the market has experienced a number of significant developments over the past decade. In particular, technological change has begun the process of creating an integrated information industry. In the past, broadcasting, print media, telecom, and information services have been quite separate industries with distinctive business cultures, revenue structures, and regulatory regimes. With the exception of the US film industry and the international news agencies (Reuters, Associated Press), the information sector was organized largely national lines. Moreover, there were clear distinctions between the information and other sectors (e.g., retailing, manufacturing). Now that informatics has created a unified technological paradigm for data processing and distribution, information can flow seamlessly from print, to broadcast material, and then into specialized teletext information

---

[1] No good estimates are available for the size of the consulting industry. The top 10 financial and management consultants have revenues of approximately $15b, which may equal one-third of the total market.

service. Similarly, visual information (i.e., films) can be distributed as films, rebroadcast through cable TV, sold as videos, and ultimately stored in digital format for retransmission (in the future) through Broadband-ISDN networks (see Chapter 5). Informatics has lowered barriers to:

- *horizontal integration* spawning a number of multi-media companies which attempt to generate "synergies" across television, publishing, on-line databases, and other information services;

- *geographic diversification* resulting in a spate of cross-border investments, and the interpenetration of news and information services across national boundaries;

- *vertical integration* between the manufacturers of informatics hardware and the suppliers of information services; and

- *cross-industry entry* encouraging (inter alia) retailers of consumer products to move into the information distribution services.

The result has been an era of rapid if somewhat convulsive growth for the information industry (Figure 6.1).

Figure 6.1: Information Industry Dynamics

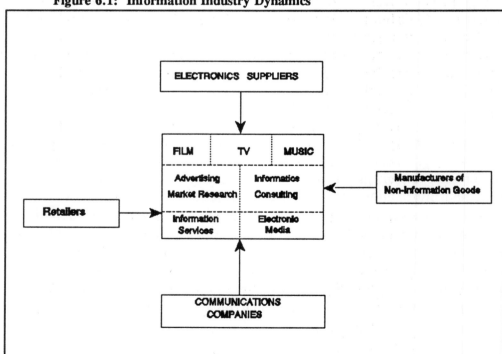

6.11   *Horizontal Integration*. The information industry has experienced significant consolidation over the past decade with the formation of large media conglomerates, spanning publishing and broadcast activities. By 1990, the top ten international media companies were responsible for over 15% of total industry sales, led by the Time/Warner conglomerate (almost 4% of the global market). The rationale behind this consolidation has been alleged economies of scope i.e., cost savings and revenue enhancements through a multi-media product range. While merger activity has been particularly pronounced in the USA, the 1992 phenomenon has also fuelled cross-border acquisitions within Europe as media companies position themselves for a single European information market. Today however, there are signs that the process of industry consolidation is slowing down. It is not always the case that print journalists translate easily into other media; record artists usually fail in their attempts to become film stars; the economics of book publishing bear little relationship to that of magazines. Moreover, few of the expected cost savings have materialized, and indeed certain costs (e.g., book advances, royalty fees, film star contracts) have risen in oligopsonistic price wars. In short, the diversified media conglomerates of the 1980s now face the task of controlling costs and designing institutional arrangements that stimulate creativity and capture the returns from flexible specialization.

6.12   *Geographic Diversification*. The 1990s is likely to witness further globalization of the information industry. During the past decade, there has been a spate of cross-border acquisitions and a growth of transnational communication systems. Telecom, broadcasting and the music industry provide compelling examples of the trend. In telecom, the value of cross-border acquisitions increased from $399 million in 1985 to $16.5 billion in 1990 as the major telecom companies (ATT, Cable and Wireless, BT, US Sprint) position themselves for future business as suppliers of integrated communication services for multinational corporations. In broadcasting, the development of cable and satellite TV networks has alleviated constraints of the radio spectrum, and paved the way for global information services. Examples include the Cable News Network (CNN) and the News Corporation, which owns interests in: (a) newspaper and magazine publishing in Australia, UK, US, and Hong Kong (40% of revenues); (b) TV stations in the US (Fox Broadcasting) and Europe (British Sky Broadcasting) (12%); (c) the 20th Century Fox film studio (20%); and (d) commercial printing and publishing holdings throughout the world (28%). 1990-911 revenues equalled $8.6 billion. In the music industry (CDs, tapes and records), 6 companies now control over 97% of the global market (Figure 6.2).

6.13   *Vertical Integration*. The information services industry has also been subject to both up- and downstream integration pressures. Upstream, a number of consumer electronics companies are seeking to control media channels in order to strengthen the competitive position of their hardware products. This trend in effects parallels evolution in the computer industry, where hardware and software companies are today forming strategic alliances. The best known examples of upstream vertical integration involve two Japanese consumer electronics firms: Sony (which acquired CBS and Columbia Pictures) and Matsushita, a consumer electronics conglomerate that recently acquired MCA. At present, it seems that the main beneficiary appears to be Hollywood, which has received an infusion of fresh capital while retaining

Figure 6.2: Structure of International Music Market

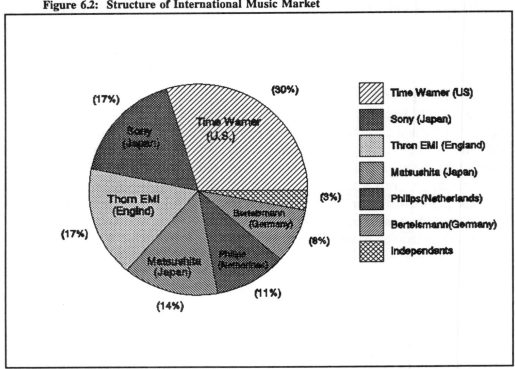

maximum management autonomy (allegedly the key to creativity). Downstream, the telecom companies are moving aggressively into cable TV and other value-added services. In the US, the regional telecom companies (the "RBOCs") have succeeded in overturning the ruling[2] that prevented their entry into the information services market, and are currently developing their services through test marketing in the UK cable TV market. Perhaps the most telling example of the economics driving downstream integration was the response of ATT to the anti-trust suit (brought by the Department of Justice in the early 1980s). Recognizing that growth would largely come in software and in the selling of value-added information services, ATT acquiesced in the divestiture of its local telephone companies in exchange for the freedom to sell information services, equipment and software to final consumers. Its latest offerings are: (a) the Export Hotline (in partnership with General Electric), an online service providing exporters with current information on over 50 sectors worldwide; and (b) a real-time translation service for over 150 languages.

6.14   *Cross-Industry Entry*. Companies whose core business lies outside the information sector are taking advantage of their marketing, distribution and informatics skills

---

[2] This decision (decided in 1991) overturned Judge Greene's Modified Final Judgment (1983) that resulted in the breakup of ATT, and in the basic rules governing the regional telecom companies.

to compete with established information businesses. The US market provides a number of leading examples, but comparable industry restructuring is taking place across the OECD. Sears, no longer content to be a retail giant in a market where its competitive position is eroding, now co-owns Prodigy, the largest electronic bulletin board in the world. American Express and manufacturers like Westinghouse are major players in cablecasting, and online database services. Boeing and Ford sell time sharing services, while the General Motor's subsidiary EDS is a leader in the data-transmission and computer services market. As informatics pervades the manufacturing, financial and retail sectors, companies throughout the economy are turning their investment in information resources from cost into profit centers.

6.15   *Regulatory Change.* As the information sector has become more central to economic performance, governments have been forced to address the growing inconsistencies between policy and commercial/technological reality. The pressure for policy reform has not been restricted to the OECD countries, but is generating a more universal redefinition of public and private roles in supplying information and regulating its flow. In many countries, governments have sought to:

- liberalize information dissemination channels and reduce the government's direct role in the information industry;

- provide greater private access to public data; and

- regulate the growing information market.

6.16   As informatics has overcome technical constraints on the number of television and radio channels that can be broadcast without signal interference, the rationale for government monopolies over the airwaves has disappeared. In the past, television (and to a lesser extent radio) broadcasting was based on the terrestrial transmission of analog signals through the air. Radio spectrum limitations meant that only 6 or 7 television channels could be broadcast without interference. Today, the emergence of cable, satellite and data-compression technologies create the potential for simultaneous transmission of 40 or 50 channels, eliminating the scarcity premium. Similarly, the transmission and switching capacity of telecom networks has grown exponentially, providing a new medium for distributing a wide range of new information services. Policy reforms that respond to this technological change are being implemented in many countries[3/] and provide the benefits of increased consumer choice, greater competition, and an environment conducive to sustained innovation.

6.17   Public data is a vital resource for the private information industry (para. 6.02). Its dissemination is the key to efficiency and accountability in government, and to productivity in the overall economy (especially the effectiveness of finding, acquiring and using knowledge

---

[3/] These include both OECD countries (e.g., UK, Japan, Italy, New Zealand) as well as NICs, such as Mexico, Brazil, and Malaysia.

commercially). In the past, many governments adopted restrictive policies with regard to public data and information dissemination. Moreover, government data was stored in formats (often paper media) that make dissemination a costly and inefficient process. As informatics has revolutionized methods of data-collection, storage, retrieval and transmission, governments have recognized the potential benefits from policies that make public data-functions more demand drive. These include measures that: (a) expand private access to public data; (b) introduce cost-recovery mechanisms for data dissemination (where profits can be captured by the private sector); and (c) limit the public role to data dissemination in those cases where the private sector is better equipped as the information supplier.

6.18   As governments reduce their direct role in information markets, their regulatory role becomes correspondingly more important. The markets for information do not automatically generate competitive outcomes; and indeed the private supply of information is characterized by substantial imperfections, failures and asymmetries. Governments therefore have a legitimate interest in ensuring that information is supplied on a competitive basis, and that endogenous market imperfections are corrected. In practice, this typically results in two areas for policy activism. First, most governments are concerned to prevent the emergence of private sector information monopolies. They therefore develop detailed regulations regarding cross-media ownership, vertical integration within the information industry, and local concentration of media channels. Second, as advanced economies generate increasingly specialized information (and complex products with a high information content), standards play an important role in: (a) protecting consumers; (b) correcting information problems; and (c) diffusing best practice throughout the information industry. The evolution and internationalization of financial accounting standards and reporting requirements are a good example of developments in this area.

6.19   Governments that have failed to take these measures are (more and more) finding their restrictions and monopolistic practices rendered obsolete and ineffective by informatics. Satellite broadcasting has no respect for national boundaries or policies. Data transmission networks permit access to "off-shore" databases, bypassing theoretical restrictions on local information dissemination. Information that is censored in one country flows effortlessly to another country with less restrictive rules (and inevitably roundtrips back into the first country[4]). The main result of government information-based restrictions is a less attractive business climate, a loss of international competitiveness, and a private information services industry that is handicapped in its efforts to win global (or local) market share.

---

[4] A well-known example of this is the "novel" Spycatcher whose publication was banned in the UK (1988) because it contained government classified material; was subsequently published abroad, and rapidly found its way into UK book-selling chains.

Turkey - Sector Performance

6.20   The private information industry in Turkey has high growth potential. There is a large domestic market for information services. This market will grow rapidly on account of demographic factors, leisure-work substitution (as per capita incomes increase), and the information intensification of business and government. The communications infrastructure for an advanced information industry is being assembled through public investments in satellite, cable and data-transmission systems (see Chapter 5), and through private investments in terminal equipment (computers, televisions, satellite antennae, etc.). In addition, the Turkish information industry enjoys a natural competitive advantage in Turkic-speaking C.I.S. states. The uniqueness of the Turkish language, which in the past has fostered an inward-looking information industry, today provides the opportunity for exports and an international business perspective.

6.21   In the face of such attractive growth prospects, the immediate performance of the information industry has been disappointing. Accurate data is hard to obtain, but total industry revenues appear to be less than $2 billion (i.e., between 1% and 2% of GNP). The industry remains highly fragmented with no private company enjoying more than $100 million revenues. Gross advertizing income (which provides up to 50% of media income in other OECD countries) growing fast, but from a very low base. At present, advertizing expenditures amount to almost $500 million - equivalent to only $10 per capita (Figure 6.3). One quarter goes to the public broadcasting monopoly (Turkish Radio and Television - TRT); a second quarter to the "illegal" private broadcasters; and the remaining 50% to print media . There are few export sales; the overall quality and availability of commercial information on the Turkish market remains low; and the private consulting industry has yet to realize necessary economies of specialization. In general, information flows in Turkey are predominantly one-to-many; rather than the one-to-few flows that increasingly characterize more advanced economies. It is only in a few markets that the Turkish information industry has mirrored the dynamism of its foreign counterparts: in financial information services and "unauthorized" private broadcasting (para. 6.25). In other markets, the industry remains constrained by an unstable business climate, a high degree of information integration within the corporate and government sectors, persistent data problems, and policy distortions that crowd out and prevent entry by the private sector. As a result, the information industry in Turkey has been slow to benefit from the impact of informatics on productivity, market structure, and growth.

6.22   *Print Media.* Turkish *newspapers* operate in a relatively free and competitive environment, with a dozen national dailies vying for market share. Overall however, readership of the national papers has stagnated since the mid-1980s, although (given per capita income differences) Turkey's circulation ratio of 74/1000 is high compared to 47 for Portugal, 75 for Spain, and 99 for Italy. Circulation growth has been concentrated in the market for local rather than national newspapers. Small market size combined a fragmented industry structure is affecting profitability in the newspaper business, whose earnings quality has already been reduced by TV advertizing wars, special promotions, and unstable circulation. *Periodical*

Figure 6.3: Advertising Expenditures Per Capita Cross-Country Comparison, 1990

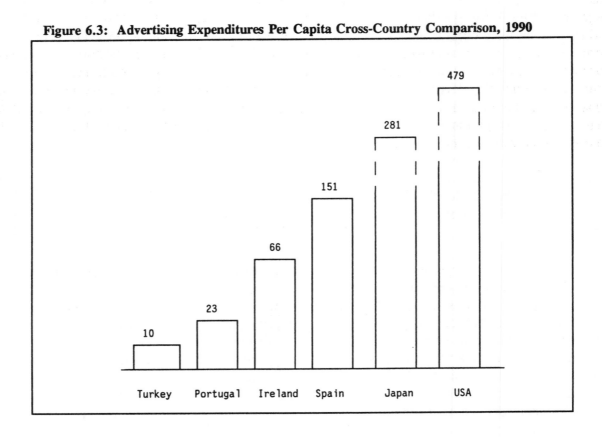

readership is also low, estimated at 6% of the population for weeklies and 4% for monthly journals. The largest periodicals are owned by the newspaper publishers, but represent only 5% of the total estimated $350 million market for newspapers/periodicals. In the long run, the newspaper periodical industry is likely to experience a phase of consolidation and also growth, spurred by demographic factors (e.g., higher literacy and urbanization rates) and by increased demand for more specialized periodicals (e.g., in computers, the retail grocery trade, and readywear export industry). However in the short run, a combination of price wars and increasing costs (labor, paper, and information technology) is encouraging the major publishing houses to look for diversification opportunities, particularly in the TV broadcast market (para. 6.25).

6.23   The market for *books* is largely controlled by the Government, which accounted for 70% of all publications in 1989, and (as a result of the transfer of some textbook printing to the private sector) 50% in 1991. The Government's dominance derives from the fact that 75% of the book market is composed of educational publications of which the government prints at least half and controls the content of the remainder. Much educational material is distributed free[5/] or at highly subsidized rates, making it difficult for the private sector to compete in main segment of the book market. It also distorts the economics of the whole book publishing industry since fixed costs (e.g., of printing presses, specialized human capital) cannot be spread across the market, but have to be charged against smaller and less stable component of demand for non-educational books. This market segment is small, comprising approximately 1500 new titles per annum. It is highly fragmented among numerous small publishers, and book runs are usually a maximum of 3,000. While productivity growth in the industry will require significant market restructuring and consolidation, this process is retarded by the preponderant public sector role in the educational book market.

Table 6.2: Cross-Media Ownership in Turkey

GROUP	NEWSPAPERS	PERIODICALS/CIRCULATION	TELEVISION	REVENUES
S. Simavi	Hurriyet/556,000 Meydan /324,000	Ekonomist / 35,000 Tempo / 21,000 Hafta Son / 96,000	Karacan TV Partners in show TV Sells Programs to TRT	$96m
Gelisim	Gunes / 45,000	Nokta / 25,000 Ekonomik / 19,000 Panorama Blue Jean / 3,000	INTV-pay TV Channel To be operational in 1992	
Karacan	Milliyet/464,000		Karacan TV Sells entertainment programs to TRT	
Sabah	Sabah /834,000 Bugun /363,000 Yeni Asir/47,000	Para / 8,000	Satel TV Partners in Show TV	$47m
Turkiye	Turkiye /595,000	Turkiye / 65,000 Cocuk	Vizyon Studios Completed To be operational in 1992	$28m

* : Average daily circulation March-June 1991.
**: 1991 average weekly circulation.

6.24   *Radio and TV Broadcasting*. TV Broadcasting is the market in which developments in Turkey most closely parallel the international trend towards increased competition and consumer choice. Legally, TV/Radio programming and transmission are public sector monopolies. Turkish Radio and Television (TRT) is responsible for programming while (under current arrangements) PTT provides all the transmission services. TRT has been

---

[5/] This practice was repeated in September, 1991 (just prior to the election) when the Government decided to distribute 26 million free textbooks.

aggressively increasing its programming efforts in anticipation of pressure to liberalize the market.   Until 1986, there was only one TV channel - TV1, which offered a mixed programming content. Since 1986, TRT has begun programming 5 other channels which offer more specialized content, and total program content have increased from approximately 12 to 42 hours/day. TRT is largely financed by advertizing with revenues increasing in real terms from $85 million in 1986 to $206 million in 1991; but are predicted to decline rapidly to $120 million in 1992! TRT advertizing revenues have risen more slowly than the number of broadcast hours, in part due to the more specialized audiences of the new channels but mainly because of increasing competition from the private sector (which today account for 50% of TV advertizing revenues).   Further liberalization of the TV broadcasting market would therefore need to be accompanied by a restructuring of TRT income to compensate for the foreseeable loss of advertizing revenues.

Box 6.1: Proposed TV and Radio Broadcast Legislation

The new Government is sponsoring legislation that will liberalize the TV and radio broadcasting regime. The draft legislation covers all radio and TV transmission systems, including terrestrial, cable and satellite channels. The policy would be implemented by the Supreme Council for Radio and Television Broadcasting (RTYK), which today supervises TRT. The main responsibilities of the Council would be to:

- review applications from private companies to establish TV and radio stations;

- monitor the ownership of private TV/radio stations for compliance with multi-shareholder provisions of the proposed law;

- ensure the conformity of programming with content rules (including rules governing local production, advertizing, live broadcasts, etc); and

- convene the National Consultative Committee to determine public opinion on program content.

Turkish Radio and Television will continue to broadcast its public TV/radio channels. However, as TRT loses market share, new sources of finance will need to be provided (largely from license fees and general budget allocations). Radio spectrum allocation will continue to be governed by the Radio Code (para. 5.45), and will be under the supervision of TGM. Certain aspects of the regulatory framework are still to be resolved. In particular, it is not clear whether: (a) the Council will have authority over PTT with regard to cable and satellite TV transmission; (b) PTT will retain its monopoly over all TV/radio transmission; (c) what pricing structure will be established for PTT's transmission function; (d) PTT entry into programming will be permitted; or (e) TRT will be required to give up some of its radio spectrum allocation.

6.25   Despite the continuing legal monopoly of TRT/PTT, the private sector has already entered the market and changes in the legislation are expected before the end of 1992 (Box 6.1).

Taking advantage of the opportunity created by high-power satellites with transmission footprints that include western Turkey, the development of cheaper antennae (capable of receiving direct satellite broadcasts), and a high television penetration rate (Table 6.3), a private sector station *Magic Box* broadcast into Turkey from Germany and effectively challenged the TRT monopoly. Given popular discontent with TRT programming, the Government decided against enforcing the 1924 law, which provides the basis for a public sector monopoly of TV/Radio programming and transmission.

6.26   Following *Magic Box*, Turkey's first private TV station, virtually all major publishers are planning to enter the market. These include: (a) a joint venture between the *Hurriyet* and *Sabah* groups; and (b) publishers of the dailies *Milliyet* and *Turkiye*. In addition, TV broadcasting is experiencing a wave of cross-industry entry that includes initiatives by: (a) *Erol Aksoy (Iktisat Bank)* station that is due to be broadcast from Paris, and aims to provide 24 hour entertainment targeted at the 15-44 age group; and (b) *Koc Holding/Time-Warner* joint venture that would primarily be a foreign movie channel. Aside from private companies, *Bosphorus University* has formed a joint venture with the Istanbul municipality, and *PTT* is rebroadcasting 10 foreign channels through its cable TV facilities.

Table 6.3: TV Penetration Rates

	TV SETS (1987) per 1000 people	Per Capita Income US$
Hungary	406	2240
Spain	368	6010
Poland	263	1920
Italy	257	10360
S. Korea	194	2690
Greece	175	4020
Turkey	172	1470
Portugal	159	2810
Thailand	103	840
Tunisia	68	1180
Indonesia	40	450

Source: UNESCO, World Bank Data.

6.27   *Radio* has so far attracted less attention, in large part because returns from overseas broadcasting (unlike the case of television) appear unattractive to private investors, and local broadcasts remain illegal. Nevertheless, a number of private ventures have been initiated, even in advance of legislation removing the government's monopoly. The expectation is that once this is done, a large number of local stations will emerge catering to highly differentiated audiences in Turkey's urban centers. One example is the Human Rights Association of Turkey, which is planning to establish a radio station that would cover metropolitan Ankara.

6.28   The *Electronic Information Services* business is concentrated in the financial markets. Reuters has approximately 500 clients, who are supplied with financial information (both local and international) through PTT leased lines. A local company Veritel has approximately 260 clients, and offers a range of online data services that are competitive with Reuters. In addition, the Bankers' Association is proposing to establish an online consumer credit database (with data-collection costs shared between participating banks). There are no local scientific or technical databases.[6/] However, researchers can link-up (indirectly) with foreign databases through TÜBITAK's TURDOC facility. Utilization of this facility remains low (Table 6.4) and is concentrated in the universities (which are charged on a cost basis). In the future, direct linkup may be possible through the proposed inter-university data transmission network. At present, there are no online public sector databases (e.g., from the State Institute of Statistics), although select SIS data is now available on diskette. Other institutions and universities that provide on-line information services include: (a) the General Directorate of Mineral Research and Exploration; (b) KOSGEB; (c) the Istanbul Chamber of Commerce; and (d) Bosphorus and Hacettepe University.

Table 6.4: Use of TURDOC On-Line Databases 1985-91

	Total Requests	Universities %	Government %	Private %
1985	3448	86	9	5
1986	2626	86	7	7
1987	3189	87	7	6
1988	2255	88	5	7
1989	1273	76	7	17
1990	1009	74	9	17
1991	1770	83	7	10

Note: Universities charged from April 1988 to June 1991

Source: TÜBITAK

[6/] Work is however, underway at TURDOC to establish on-line databases on Turkish scientists, scientific and technical events, and two bibliographical databases on S&T and medical information (published in Turkish journals). For further information, see Research and Development on Information Technology in Turkey (1992, TÜBITAK Working Paper).

6.29   *Consulting Services* remain a small subsector of the information industry. The total market for both activities (i.e., market research, and management consulting) is estimated at only $27 million in 1991.[7/] There are approximately 30 market research companies in Turkey, most of which specialize in consumer research. The average size of these companies is small: with an annual turnover of $300,000 and a permanent staff of 15 to 20 employees. Most firms are members of the Market and Public Research Association, which in turn claims that its members embrace the standards and ethical code of the European Society for Opinion and Market Research (ESOMAR). In practice, these standards are often neglected, particularly Article 13 pertaining to the mixing of market research with sales activities, and Article 24, concerning the confidentiality of client information. Only four of the companies have formal affiliations with foreign research companies (AGB, Yankelovich, Clancy and Schulman, GFK and Gallup). The Management Consultancy Association of Turkey has about 40 members. Of these, three are affiliates of international accounting firms, 16 are locally-based firms, and the remainder are representatives of manufacturing companies, banks and training companies.

6.30   *Endogenous Barriers to Growth.* Despite promising developments in the television broadcasting market, the information industry in Turkey is lagging behind international competition. Growth has been relatively slow; and the process of industry consolidation and integration has yet to emerge as the dominant trend. In large part, the gap between the Turkish and international information industry can be traced to differences in the policy environment (paras. 6.32 -6.50). But, policy distortions and public sector shortfalls are not the only problem. Rather, imperfections and failures in the private market for information add to the obstacles that retard industry modernization. First, specialized information services (including periodicals) are often uneconomic because the small size of the Turkish market cannot support their high fixed to variable cost structure.   Second, most large companies internalize delivery of their information requirements precisely to preserve the information gaps that are a source of profits. Third, consulting companies find it particularly difficult to capture the return on investment in staff development, since clients often poach high-performing consultants.   Fourth, the print industry suffers from significant free-rider problems, including rampant copying and unauthorized material duplication. In combination with the policy environment, these market-based problems reduce the scope for innovation and growth in the private information industry.

The Policy Environment

6.31   Almost all government policies either *directly* or *indirectly* affect the market prospects of the private information industry. Direct policies essentially define the respective roles of public and private sectors in the supply of information; and therefore govern: (a) the dissemination of public sector data; (b) public sector publishing activities; (c) private entry into TV and radio broadcasting; (d) private delivery of value-added services through the telecom

---

[7/] These estimates exclude the market for financial consulting services, which offer fee-based earning opportunities to the commercial and investment banks. Consulting services provided by the specialist merchant banks generated almost $10 million fees in 1990.

network; and (e) legal protection of privacy and intellectual property. On the other hand, indirect policies mainly affect the composition and volume of demand for information services. Indirect policies would include policy initiatives that increase the demand for accurate business information (e.g., elimination of directed credits), or that generate growth in consumer products advertizing (e.g., further trade liberalization).

6.32   During the 1980s, the Government's strategy for information industry modernization emphasized two main areas: investment in the communications infrastructure (Chapter 5); and the use of indirect policy instruments. The policies of economic liberalization and market development have had a profound (if slightly delayed) bearing on the demand for information. Before 1981, policies of import substitution, public investment in the traded goods sector, and government directed credit and investment sanctions limited market demand for information. Five Year Plans defined the sectoral investment strategy; the State Planning Organization provided the investment permit (in those cases where the private sector was to carry out the investment); and public sector banks provided the finance, so long as the paperwork was in order. Anti-competitive investment rules in the domestic market minimized the need for accurate information on the most efficient technological choice. There was little export activity, and correspondingly little intelligence on foreign market opportunities. Since 1981 however, the Government has progressively liberalized the main product and factor markets. Five Year Plans have become indicative rather than directive; the proportion of subsidized credit in the financial system has declined; and the decade has witnessed a three-fold increase in the volume of foreign trade. As the public sector continues to withdraw from direct intervention in the markets, producers, consumers, shareholders, and government regulators will all boost demand for reliable, timely and increasingly specialized information.

6.33   As the market for information grows, the next step for the Government is to review the supply-side impact of its policies. A number of initiative are already in process. First, there is a draft law that would liberalize the policy framework for television (including cable) and radio broadcasting. Second, the government has de-censored a number of books and publications, creating a much freer atmosphere for the print media. Third, an increasing percentage of government data is being released to the private sector, albeit subject to considerable time delays that reduce data value. Fourth, the Government is signatory to a number of OECD agreements on data confidentiality and transborder data flows.[8/] Nevertheless, there are four main areas in which further policy modifications will be essential if the private information industry is to meet the needs of the Turkish economy, and to become internationally competitive. These are:

- procedures and mechanisms for *public information dissemination*;

- *competitive entry* into the information industry;

[8/] These agreements have not yet been ratified through the introduction of enabling domestic legislation.

- *information standards*; and

- the *legal framework* for intellectual property and data privacy.

6.34   ***Public Information Dissemination***. Public data collection, management, and dissemination in Turkey is (on paper) the sole responsibility of the State Institute for Statistics (SIS). SIS may delegate this responsibility to specialized government agencies and departments, who SIS can authorize to gather statistical data "solely with the purpose of meeting their own requirements " (Article 24, SIS Law). All data published by the Government must (in theory) be cleared by SIS. This is true both for data that is to be disseminated to the private sector and for data that is to be shared between public sector agencies. Key SIS powers and responsibilities include:

- to collect, evaluate and issue all types of statistics related to economic, cultural, and social activities in Turkey;

- to establish and maintain a set of databases that will form the infrastructure for statistics in Turkey;

- to authorize other government departments to gather data for their own purposes;

- to request any information from public institutions, and to verify its accuracy; and

- to carry out the national census, and regular industry, household, and agricultural surveys.

6.35   To carry out these functions, SIS has departments for: (a) agriculture and industry statistics; (b) manpower, services, price statistics and indices; (c) social statistics; (d) national accounts; (e) research, studies and statistical techniques; and (e) statistical and econometric interpretation. These departments maintain SIS databases, and also provide technical support to other Government agencies that are developing their own data-functions (with SIS permission). SIS activities are 99% financed through general budget allocations (with 1% revenues earned through special projects). SIS is the archive for over two-thirds of public sector data. Development plans envisage a massive expansion in the databases that would allow SIS to play a role as the data-hub of Turkey's information society (Figure 6.4).

6.36   In practice, the system is not as centralized as the legal framework might suggest. First, SIS interprets its legal powers liberally, and aims to encourage investments by other agencies in data-functions related to their mission. In a number of cases, SIS is developing new databases in collaboration with the line agencies. For example, the proposed Geographic Information System (GIS) database is being developed together with the Ministry of Agriculture

Figure 6.4: SIS Proposed Data-Hub

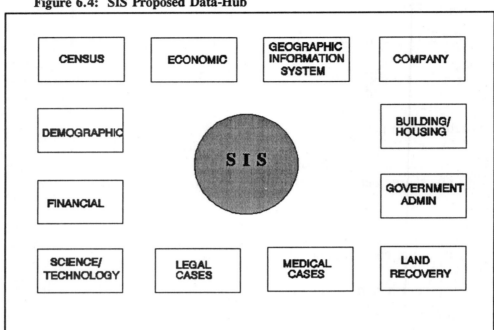

Agriculture,and TÜBITAK.   Second, SIS is not the primary data source for all data.   It frequently relies on data-collection and reporting by other agencies, to whom it has delegated responsibility.   For example, the Central Bank is the primary data source on monetary statistics; and provides its data to SIS, other Government agencies, and to the private sector.   Third, many agencies do publish and disseminate data (and information).   Publications are available to the public from the Central Bank, Treasury, State Planning Organization, and most of the line ministries[9].   Frequently, these publications contain overlapping information, and at times suffer from major factual inconsistencies.

6.37   Most of the information is disseminated in paper format, severely reducing its value for other government agencies and for potential private information retailers.   The main exceptions are: (i) SIS annual statistical volumes that can now be obtained in diskette format; and (ii) some Central Bank data that is supplied online to financial information suppliers (para. 6.28).   There is no online public access to SIS databases (which constitute the primary databank of the public sector).   Virtually all information provided to the private sector is free of charge, although SIS does charge for diskette-based data dissemination.   There is no obligation on

---

[9] For further material on information dissemination by agencies, see <u>Public Sector Information Dissemination</u> (1992, SIS Working Paper).

agencies (or on SIS) to provide information to the private sector on request. Although under no obligation, SIS can respond to a private request on a non-contractual basis (i.e., providing information for free), or on a contractual basis (provided that such information is statistical and does not reveal personal data). SIS has established a subsidiary,[10] which can sell information to the private sector at a price that covers costs of: (a) adding value to the primary data; and (b) distribution.

6.38   The public database system and framework for information dissemination was largely designed for a different set of economic and technological circumstances. At the time of its formulation, there was relatively little private sector demand for public data. Most information requirements could be met through the Five Year Plan. There were large technical economies of scale from the centralization of data-archiving and maintenance activities (whether there were held in paper format or on mainframe facilities). Dissemination could be easily controlled at the printing press or through restricted access to computing facilities. Limited demand pressure on the system kept recurrent costs low. Today, both the economy and the information technology has moved on; and it is less clear whether existing arrangements are well-adapted to the needs of an information-based economy. Within the public sector, investments in information technology have decentralized data-processing, created platforms for data-sharing, and provided the vehicle for multi-agency information dissemination. Efficient growth of a market economy is highly dependent on information flows, many of which are derived from public sector data. And as the system expands, the costs of government data-functions continue to demand an increasing proportion of scarce public resources. If Turkey is to take advantage of substantial public sector data (and information technology) resources, it will be necessary to develop policy and institutional arrangements that:

- facilitate demand-driven and coordinated investment in databases within the public sector;

- increase private sector access to public data; and

- improve system efficiency through cost-recovery mechanisms.

6.39   There is no national policy for *data-sharing* or for the coordination of *database investments* within the public sector. The result is significant waste of scarce technical and financial resources. First, there are problems in inter-agency data-sharing because of technical and administrative constraints. No data-communications network exists between the agencies. There are no clear procedures with regard to inter-agency data-sharing (and frequently no intra-agency procedures). Data-security procedures that are non-uniform across the agencies generate further barriers to data-sharing. Data standards, formats, storage media, and definitions differ from one agency to the next, generating substantial search, rekeying and quality control costs. One direct consequence of these costs is that many agencies prefer to duplicate database

---

[10] This subsidiary is a non-profit organization, established under the Revolving Fund legislation.

investments, to maintain control over their own information resources. Given the inter-agency data problems, it therefore comes as no surprise that public data dissemination to the private sector should fail to meet appropriate norms of timeliness, consistency and reliability. Second, there is no policy framework for prioritizing public sector investment in databases (or for avoiding duplication). Nor as yet is there the necessary market or analytic research program to establish: (a) the existing information resources of the public sector; (b) the information needs and priorities of government agencies; or (c) the composition of demand for public data from the private sector.

6.40   *Private sector access* to public data is today supply-driven. The public sector agencies essentially decide what they would like to disseminate, and then provide this information to the market at zero (or, at times, marginal) cost. Since SIS (in theory) is responsible for all data dissemination, other public agencies do not have clearly defined obligations with regard to this activity. Even SIS obligations are defined only in very general terms. There are no clear guidelines with regard to public information dissemination that would specify: (a) timeliness and frequency requirements; (b) data coverage; (c) distribution criteria; (d) media-choice (i.e., paper, on-line, CD-ROM, etc); (e) publishing standards and format; (f) copyright rules;[11] (g) confidentiality requirements; and (f) the extent to which agencies should "add electronic value" to disseminated data, or should leave this activity to the private information industry. The private sector agents has no automatic right of access to *statistical*[12] data collected by the government agencies (even though they pay the tax that finances its collection). Nor are there any guidelines that might define agency (voluntary) response to a private information request. In the absence of any system, private access to public sector data is dependent on personal relations, and is highly arbitrary.

6.41   Most public sector data dissemination takes place *without charge*. The implicit rationale underlying this policy are the public good attributes of most government data. Dissemination of public sector data is essential for economic productivity, and for an informed public debate over key policy issues. So long as dissemination activities remain limited and the data has large benefits for the economy as a whole, this policy makes good sense. However, as public data dissemination activities grow, they will impose a growing cost on the government budget. Moreover, an increasing proportion of the data will generate returns for specific businesses and private information retailers, rather than for the general economy. While information on e.g., medical research may generate mainly social benefits (and should therefore be distributed free of charge), public information on motor vehicle registrations is likely to have significant commercial value (and should therefore be sold). As the collection and dissemination

---

[11] At present, public sector data-publications not subject to copyright rules. As agencies begin to publish reports (that contain information and analysis, rather than data), they may be subject to copyright protection. However, the legal situation is not clear.

[12] Personal data collected by government agencies (where individuals can be identified) is of course not available to the private sector. For further information on data-confidentiality rules, see Legal Framework for Database Services and Management (1992, SIS Working Paper).

of public information becomes demand-driven (i.e., on a "need-to-know" basis), the government will therefore need to review existing pricing policy to ensure the system's equity and efficiency. Given the lack of a competitive market in this data (i.e., the government is a monopolist), many OECD countries appear to be moving towards a dual system: (a) marginal cost plus for government publications, to recover publishing and distribution costs; and (b) full cost pricing for agency responses to specific information requests, to recover variable personnel and computing time costs.   Box 6.2 explains the pricing policy of the US Government for its publications.

Box 6.2: Pricing Policy of the US Government Printing Office

The pricing formula used by the United States Government Printing Office is designed to recover the total sales program costs, i.e., both the direct and indirect costs involved in the program. The formula is based on the premise that the sales program should be self-sustaining and all incremental costs associated with it should be recovered.

Established in 1932 and refined in 1983 by a Task Force with a mandate to produce a simple pricing formula, the GPO's current formula is comprised of four central components: (1) Printing and binding costs calculated by applying a 30% discount to GPO in-house p & b rates. The discount reflects the higher costs incurred by GPO relative to commercial printers; (2) Handling costs are assessed in a manner to allocate all the direct and indirect costs of operating the GPO's sales program. The cost per publication is determined by multiplying the assessed charged by the number of square inches of material represented by that particular publication. The maximum charge which can be assessed against any one document for handling is US$15; (3) Postage costs set by using third class rates for publications of up to a pound with fourth-class rates used for those weighing more; (4) a 50% markup as required by law (Section 1708, Title 44, United States Code).

Accordingly, p & b, handling, and postage costs are multiplied by 50% to yield the sales price. This factor normally accounts for approximately 33% of the sales price. Finally, a rounding formula is used to compute the final price. Prices up to $4.99 are rounded to the nearest 25 cents, prices from $5.01 to $9.99 to the nearest half-dollar, and prices over US$10 to nearest dollar. A 25% discount is applied to bulk sales, however, this discount is not deemed adequate by commercial distributors and sales through this venue are limited.

6.42   At present, there is no explicit government policy with regard to public sector data collection, coordination and dissemination. SIS is itself aware of institutional and technical weaknesses in public sector information flows (paras. 6.37-6.41), and is reviewing options to make the system more demand-driven and to reduce its inefficiencies. The main objectives of this policy review are to determine what (if any) changes should be made to the SIS Law with the objective to: (a) strengthen the national information system and enhance coordination on technical issues; (b) reduce duplication of public investment in databases; and (c) develop a coherent pricing policy.

6.43   Modifications to the SIS Law would however, need to be coordinated with a complementary policy/legislative initiative addressing the overall framework for public data dissemination. The issues of SIS' role, pricing, and public investment cannot be resolved independently of clear *policy objectives* for public data dissemination. These objectives will need to balance the public interest in national security and data confidentiality with those of open government, freedom of information and market efficiency. As the latter interests acquire greater weight, the revised balance needs to be made operational through: (a) clear legislative intent to increase private rights of access to public data; (b) significant change in the institutional and procedural arrangements for public data dissemination; (c) operational targets for agency-based data dissemination; (d) a definition of the dividing line between public and private information services; and (e) design and enforcement of a framework for inter-agency data-sharing. These initiatives would help Turkey to unlock the underlying value inherent in substantial information assets of the public sector, and would catalyze development of the private information industry. Key first steps in revising the policy and institutional framework for public sector information system include:

- the development of meta-information on public sector databases and publications through establishment of an indexation system (that would be updated on a quarterly basis);

- market survey of public and private institutions to assess information requirements (data-content, format, pricing, etc); and

- establishment of a pilot information network that would provide on-line access to SIS data for: (a) key government users; (b) universities; and (c) leading private sector organizations.

6.44   *Competitive Entry*. The Government is already taking steps to open up the market for information services. New legislation has been proposed for television and radio stations (Box 6.1); there are a number of electronic information services supplied over PTT's network (Chapter 5); and there is somewhat greater dissemination of public data. As Government withdraws from direct intervention in the information industry, a key issue is whether market forces will automatically generate a competitive market structure. The role of Government becomes one of a pro-competition regulator, rather than a direct (or at least monopolistic) supplier of information. Experience from other OECD countries suggests that the information industry has a high probability of evolving towards a non-competitive structure. Already, a number of information markets have become quite concentrated (e.g., the music industry, financial information services). The radio spectrum is still a scarce resource and, if allocated solely according to financial criteria, might result in only a small number of information suppliers.   The economics of information create incentives for cross-media ownership, which may again reduce consumer choice and create barriers to competitive entry.

6.45   Many countries have therefore introduced regulations to prevent excessive industry consolidation.   In certain cases, anti-trust law is the most appropriate instrument to maintain competition in the information marketplace.   However, difficulties in defining the "market" (whether on a geographic or media basis) have led to the introduction of supplementary regulations tailored specifically to the information industry.   The objective of these regulations is (typically) to create a competitive supply of information, and to prevent domination of the local information industry by foreign suppliers.   For example, FCC rules in the USA prevent more than 20% foreign ownership of a public broadcasting TV station.

6.46   In Turkey, the Government has already recognized the importance of pro-competition regulations for the information industry.   The draft law for television and radio broadcasting spells out specific (and quite severe) shareholding limits for TV broadcasting stations.   Under Article 62 of the proposed law (February 1992 draft), no private or legal entity would be allowed to own more than 20% of a broadcast company; nor more than 5% of a company, which controls two or more stations.   The Supreme Council on TV and Radio would be responsible for ensuring compliance with these regulations.   Similar restrictions apply to foreign ownership.   However, the Government has not yet addressed the broader issues of concentration in the information industry.   First, there is no independent regulatory framework for the telecom network.   In the absence of institutional changes that are now under consideration (Chapter 5), PTT will be well positioned to play a dominant role in the information services industry; and is already investing in cable TV and in satellite broadcasting capability.   If PTT is to control all the main data transmission systems, then explicit rules limiting its lines of business and preventing excessive vertical integration are prerequisites for a competitive information market.   Second, there are no explicit provisions governing cross-media ownership.   Although antitrust legislation is now under consideration in Turkey, it is not clear whether the legislation will provide adequate safeguards in the information industry.   Already, the proposed broadcasting stations include a joint venture between Hurriyet and Sabah. In the future, further consolidation of the media can be expected, and legislation in this area needs to include competition as an explicit policy objective.

6.47   More generally, reform of the TV and radio broadcast sector offers new opportunities to create one-to-few (para. 6.21) flows of information, serving the needs of regions, local communities and special interest groups.   Government support for these more specialized flows - through the reservation of radio spectrum, TRT programming, licensing of new entrants, sectoral tax policy - will be essential if Turkey is to realize broader social benefits from the communications and information sector.   International experience suggests that transition from public monopoly to a commercially-driven broadcast system is not without costs. A significant gap between the social and private returns to program content (e.g., open university, farmer reports, health information) suggests that the Government (in particular, the Supreme Council on TV/Radio and Ministry of Culture) has an important policy formulation and regulatory role if TV/radio are to remain educational as well as entertainment media.

6.48   *Information Standards*.   An information-based economy needs accurate information. In part, competition in the market is likely to drive both greater information supply and improved quality. As investors, consumers and voters all become more sophisticated, public and private organizations will be under pressure to provide reliable information on business performance, product attributes, financial position, environmental impact, employment practices, etc.   In the long run, organizations that systematically under-supply information will lose competitiveness and will fail to meet the market test. Organizations that "have nothing to hide" are more likely to develop winning strategies in an information-conscious society.

6.49   Despite market and social pressures to disclose information, companies (and public agencies) also face incentives that may result in the supply of false or misleading information. There are many examples. In business, companies that are in financial distress frequently provide *false information* regarding their financial position. Even in more normal market conditions, *information gaps* can easily lead to misuse of shareholder funds by the management. Companies may seek to cover up environmental problems related to their business (which would result in costly clean-up bills); and *information asymmetries* between companies and consumers lead to repeated incidence of false product advertizing. It is often hard for consumers to assess the competing claims of manufacturers regarding e.g., the safety, nutrition content, or energy consumption of products. At times, the problem is not under- but *over-supply of information*. For example, it is extremely difficult for most consumers to understand insurance contracts or suppliers' guarantees and limited warranties. The average insurance contract is couched in obscure legal language, and contains a wealth of exceptions and limitations (making insurance product comparison very costly). Nor is it only private organizations that create information problems in the market. Government agencies also have a vested interest in restricting access to information that might expose agency problems, inefficiencies or policy mistakes.

6.50   As the Government reduces its direct intervention in the product, factor and information markets, its role as regulator becomes correspondingly more important. To a large extent, this regulatory function is an exercise in setting information standards and reporting requirements in markets that are not automatically efficient suppliers of information. As the economy becomes more integrated with the European Community and markets of other advanced trading partners, it will be necessary to harmonize standards on:

- financial accounting and reporting requirements (Box 6.3);

- consumer product information (including advertizing rules, product labelling, pricing, and manufacturers' warranties);

- occupational classifications and certification;

- legal documents for complex retail transactions including real estate, life and non-life insurance, consumer credit;

- retail financial products; and

- environmental conduct and performance.

In certain fields, the Government has already taken the initiative. For example, a project (supported by the World Bank[13]) will strengthen the system for metrology, testing standards and quality assurance (MSTQ). This system will help Turkish companies (particularly exporters) to provide material evidence regarding the technical specifications of their products, and to prove that they meet international quality standards. In other fields however, Turkey is lagging behind evolving international standards, and needs concerted action to catch-up.

Box 6.3: Accounting Practices in Turkey

Until the 1980s, Turkish accounting practices evolved largely as a matter of tax administration. The Turkish Commercial Code contained no principles regarding "fair disclosure"; nor did it provide a standards set of financial statements that companies were required to follow. Since most enterprises were either state or family-owned, there was little market pressure for accurate financial information.

Modernization of the accounting profession and financial disclosure rules became essential as soon as the Government decided to strengthen the role of capital markets in the economy. Once firms could turn to the public for funds through the stock exchange and issuance of negotiable debt instruments, the public needed to be informed about the financial position of these firms. After 1983, the Capital Market Board began to issue detailed regulations on accounting standards, proforma financial statements, qualifications of external auditors, and disclosure principles. In 1987, the principle of independent auditing was extended to the banking sector through a Central Bank directive. And in 1989, Turkey enacted its first law for the regulation of the accounting and auditing profession.

Nevertheless, the availability of reliable financial information on the corporate sector is weak. There are numerous problems with the financial accounts of the state enterprises. Financial accounting of unquoted (closely held) private companies is limited. And even in the case of publicly quoted companies and bank, there are significant discrepancies between Turkish and Generally Accepted Accounting Principles in the areas of: (a) inflation accounting; (b) consolidation of Group accounts; (c) hidden reserves; (d) foreign currency translation; and (e) valuation of intangible assets.

6.51   *Legal Framework.* The legal issues with regard to the protection of intellectual property (e.g., copyright provisions and enforcement) and data-confidentiality are addressed in more detail in Chapter 7. At present, the main problem appears to be with respect to the

---

[13] The Technology Development Project (Report No. 9079-TU), 1991.

enforcement of copyright. The absence of adequate measures to prevent unauthorized material duplication and product copying, while generating short term benefits for consumers, also reduces the incentive for suppliers to invest in: (a) easily copied information products (e.g., software, musical cassettes, videos); and (b) creation of product brands (which themselves play a valuable signalling role for consumers). Rather, it is more rewarding for suppliers to copy product ideas, and to compete on the basis of price rather than unique product attributes. This strategy may be successful if Turkey aims to remain permanently behind the international competition, However, if the goal is to increase share in more advanced (and higher value-added) markets, then exporters must first learn to increase the information-content of their products in the domestic market. The Government has already taken certain steps to improve the legal situation. In particular, *Law 3257 on Cinema, Video and Musical Works (1986)* has had some success in curtailing the piracy of video-cassettes. However, ambiguities within the law (e.g., with regard to software products) and more general problems in enforcing the intellectual property regime make further progress in this area desirable.

6.52   ***Conclusions.*** During the 1980s, modernization of Turkey's private information industry has lagged behind that of other sectors. Manufacturing, tourism, construction and the financial sector have all become more sophisticated and export-oriented. In large part, this is because of the tradeable (or in the case of tourism, quasi-tradeable) nature of the products. As the economy opened up, these sectors were well-positioned to take advantage of new market opportunities. However with the exception of the financial and tourism sectors, demand for information grew relatively slowly, since substantial efficiency gains could be achieved with only limited investment in better information. As a result, the private information industry faced a significant demand lag at home, had little incentive to increase productivity, and (because of language barriers) had few opportunities to enter foreign markets. In addition, the industry's modernization was delayed by a number of government policies and institutions that monopolized key sectors of the market (e.g., broadcasting), crowded out private competitors, and provided inadequate mechanisms for data dissemination.

6.53   In the 1990s, the private information industry can play a vital role in increasing competitiveness and productivity across the economy. As the easy efficiency gains (post liberalization) are exhausted, the productive sectors will need to intensify their investments in accurate and timely information. Competitive advantage in the market will rely increasingly on information about consumer preferences, technology, internal cost structures, competitors, suppliers, etc. And firms will need to practice their skills in the local market if they are to succeed abroad. Similarly, the quality of public-policy making will be a function of open debate, rather than being controlled behind closed doors. Increases in public sector productivity will require a well-informed citizen body, in which access to information is not monopolized by a few powerful interest groups. Policies that foster growth and modernization of the private information industry will therefore generate substantial economic benefits for the whole economy.

CHAPTER 7

THE LEGAL INFRASTRUCTURE

Introduction

7.01   Each stage of economic development has required investment in a complementary legal infrastructure. The shift from primarily agrarian to industrial economies created a new range of economic assets, relationships and risks that fell outside earlier legal categories. Initially, the legal system responded to that economic change (especially in common law countries) by modifying and extending existing concepts. However, this response soon proved to be inadequate; and legal system adapted to the reality of a mass-production industrial society by innovating and creating new concepts of:

- property: e.g., industrial property rights, joint stock companies, new financial assets;

- regulation: e.g., environmental, occupational health and safety, corporate governance, and strict product liability.

- crime: e.g., insider trading, money laundering, industrial espionage, false representation and illegal merchandizing.

In addition, the development of industrialized urban societies created pressure for new forms of civil liberty, including freedom of the press, freedom to form political parties and worker rights of association.

7.02   As advanced economies begin the transition from industrial to information-based economy, it is therefore inevitable that changes will also need to occur in the legal framework. First, economic transformation will increase the market value of information and knowledge. In the US, copyright income (on information assets) increased from 2% of GNP in 1954 to over 6% by 1990 - three times the contribution of agriculture! As other economies become more information-intensive, the re-specification of an appropriate set of property concepts (and the content of ownership rules) will be a critical task for the legal system. Second, the proliferation of computers and databases that contain vast amounts of personal sensitive individual creates many potential benefits for society, but also introduces new risks for the individual citizen. In principle, it has become much easier for organizations (both public and private) to use this personal data for unauthorized purposes, and thereby violate individual rights to privacy. Third, computerization has made society much more vulnerable to activities that destroy or violate the integrity of electronic data. Computer viruses, unauthorized entry into databases (e.g., computer "hacking"), and even deliberate breaches of physical computer security (e.g., terrorist attacks) all have the potential to impose enormous economic and social costs.

7.03   Across the OECD (and in more advanced NICs), the legal system is already responding to the new set of opportunities and problems. Many countries are strengthening their legal framework for the protection of intellectual property rights, and are now grappling with the complex issue of mixed public/private attributes of information (Chapter 6). The problem of data protection and privacy rights in an information economy has been explicitly recognized; and legislation passed to regulate public and private use of databases that contain sensitive information. New classes of crime have been developed (largely through statutory instruments even in common law countries) that provide sanctions against computer viruses, and other deliberate breaches of computer security. There has been less success however, in defining the agenda for civil liberties in societies where computer networks are displacing more traditional forms of communication. For example, in organizations that offer electronic mail facilities to their staff, the application of confidentiality rules (that govern privacy of telephone conversations) to electronic mail messages is highly uncertain. Civil libertarians are predictably concerned that the informatics era could, in the absence of adequate legal safeguards, result in a loss rather than enhancement of individual freedoms.

7.04   In Turkey, the Government has already taken certain steps to modernize its legal framework in line with changes in the economic basis of society. First, a number of initiatives are underway to strengthen the regime for industrial property rights (i.e., patents, utility models); and also for certain categories of information property (i.e., music, video-cassettes). Second, the Government is a signatory to the OECD Guidelines on data protection and transborder data flows, and domestic legislation for public sector databases also contains provisions on data protection and confidentiality. Third, a law on computer crime was passed in 1991.

7.05   Despite these positive steps, there are a number of areas in which further modernization of the legal system may be necessary. The legal framework for copyright protection remains very unclear, especially with regard to protection of software (Chapter 3). Turkey still lacks a more comprehensive system for data protection that would meet international standards, and prevent abuse of personal data. The new computer crimes in the Penal Code only cover a number of potential criminal activities, and is more of a signal to the computer-using community than a comprehensive approach to the problem. Further legal reforms will therefore be necessary to bring Turkey into line with her major trading partners (and as a prelude to possible EC entry).

7.06   This Chapter is organized in three main sections. Section one addresses the issue of intellectual property; and the benefits for Turkey from strengthening copyright legislation and its enforcement. Section two discusses the issue of data protection and privacy, and identifies key areas for further legal action. Section three reviews the adequacy of existing legislation on computer crime.

Intellectual Property Rights

7.07   The main objective of intellectual property rights (IPRs) is to increase the rate of technological progress and productivity growth. IPRs achieve this objective by protecting private returns on innovation in exchange for public disclosure and obligation to commercialize on the part of the innovator. The main forms of IPR are:

- *copyright* that protects the literary expression of an idea (rather than the idea itself) from unauthorized copying, subject to "fair use" provisions;[1]

- *patents* that protect not only the expression but also the useful features of a novel product or process; and

- *trade secrets* protected by contracts (e.g., employment contracts or commercial licenses) designed to ensure confidentiality on the part of the licensed user. Trade secrets are not publicly disclosed.

7.08   Information products are typically protected by copyright laws. Books, articles, music and films all receive some degree of copyright protection in OECD countries, and are covered by a number of international copyright conventions. More recently, copyright has been extended (either by statute or by common law judicial interpretation) to computer software products (Chapter 3). The economic rationale for providing copyright protection to software is that in its absence, private industry would find it uneconomic to invest in development of new software products. Software development costs are very high. The proliferation of personal computers has made software copying extremely easy (even in countries with copyright protection - Figure 7.1). Therefore, some level of copyright protection is in the public interest to permit a market-based supply of new software products and computer applications. In practice, software companies rarely test the limits of their copyright protection and accept that some unauthorized (i.e., non-commercial) copying takes place. But in countries where copying is now rampant, software houses - especially those based in the US - are becoming more aggressive and are pushing the Administration to impose trade sanctions on the worst offenders.

7.09   Until recently, the economic rationale for copyright protection of software (and other information products) has been less apparent in countries such as Turkey that are largely importers of information goods and services. First, copyright protection for software would have significant balance of trade implications. In the case of Turkey, it is estimated that legal reform in this area might generate foreign exchange costs of almost $100 million.

---

[1] Fair use provisions cover limited quotations and selective photocopying of journals, neither of which would require the authors' permission.

Figure 7.1: Illegally Copied Software in Use Cross-Country Comparison

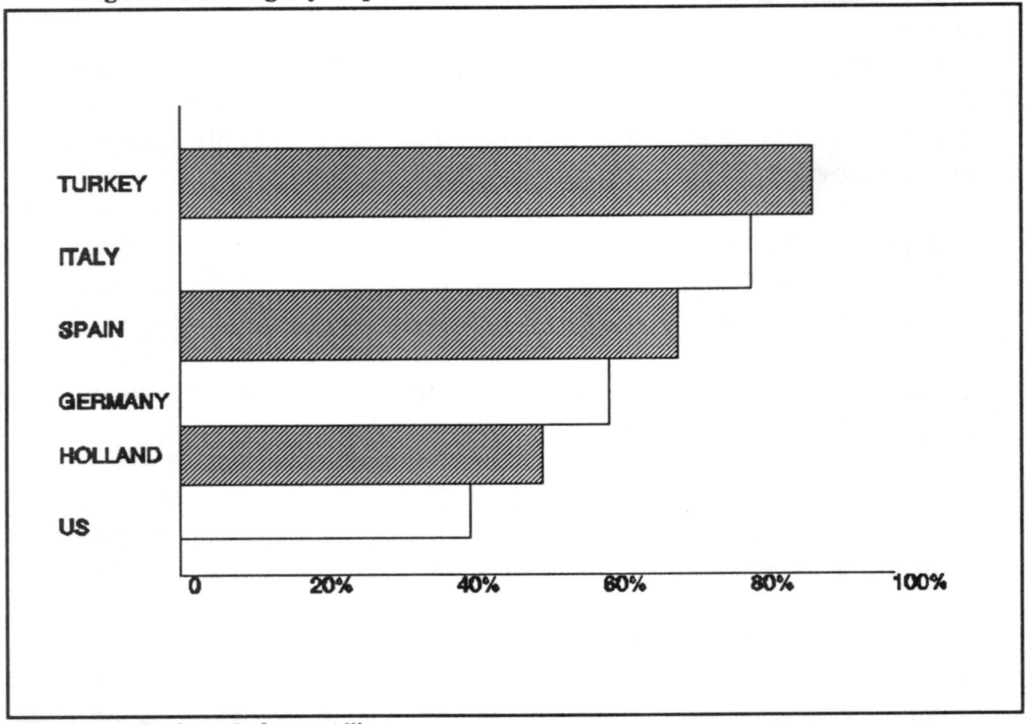

Source: Business Software Alliance.

Second, there is an argument[2] that marginal cost distribution of software is economically efficient. Since unauthorized copying is close to the marginal cost of distribution, there are economic benefits from a more permissive regime. This is particularly true in developing countries, where computer users may be more resource-constrained. These arguments have considerable merit especially in the short-run. Unauthorized software copying represents a massive opportunity for low-cost technology transfer, and probably helps to accelerate the time when developing countries can contribute to the global supply of computer software. It certainly avoids the problem - experienced in so many industries - where developing countries invest scarce resources in costly exercises of technology reinvention. Rather, unauthorized copying allows developing countries rapidly to access the international frontier for software technology, and to devote their intellectual resources to investment in new software products.

---

[2] This argument applies equally to software-producing nations. First best economics might support: (a) public financing through the tax system of software development costs; and (b) marginal cost distribution. In practice however, application of these principles might undermine the dynamism and innovativeness of the private software industry, and ultimately reduce rather than increase consumer welfare.

7.10   These economic benefits from a permissive legal framework for software copying are not inexhaustible, especially since leading software-producing countries have more restrictive IPR regimes.[3] In the limit, information and the know-how embodied in software are not a free resource. And declining marginal benefits from unauthorized copying need to be set against increasing marginal costs that result from the failure to develop a local software industry. Countries that host a strong software industry not only benefit in terms of employment and value-added creation; but they also become better computer users. Given the potential for computers to stimulate productivity growth across the economy (Chapter 2), failure to develop necessary complementary skills in a local software industry imposes a large (dynamic) opportunity cost on the economy. For Turkey, inadequate legal protection today compounds normal market risks faced by the software industry, discourages venture capital financing of software growth companies, deters foreign investment in the sector, and results in sub-optimal utilization of computers.

7.11   Software copying is rampant in Turkey, especially for imported packaged software such as Lotus 123, Wordperfect, Dbase II, etc. And the legal framework for software copyright protection is extremely unclear. There appear to be a number of legal avenues that could be pursued:

- some lawyers feel that the basic property laws can be interpreted to cover theft of computer software;

- other lawyers believe that the 1951 Copyright Law could be interpreted to include software, because the law covers languages and computer software can be construed to be a language; and

- others are quite sure that the 1991 amendments to the Criminal Code to cover computer crime (para. 7.32) against "automated databases" might also address software piracy. It appears that definition are broad enough that a judge could interpret the new law to cover hand-held pocket calculators, and personal computers as well as mainframes. The real question seems to be whether or not diskettes are covered, although in practice is may be difficult to prove that the alleged copying was done "without authorization".

---

[3] Global welfare gains might be maximized if copyright protection was: (a) provided at a level that creates competitive market conditions; and (b) consistent across countries. The policy problem that Turkey and other middle-income countries face is that neither of these conditions is fulfilled. There are significant differences in copyright protection even in the advanced economies. In addition, recent development in copyright and patent protection for software (especially in the USA) may be leading away from competitive market conditions. Within this second or third best environment, the welfare-maximizing approach for Turkey may be phased introduction of the minimum level of protection necessary to attract investment by foreign software houses.

Box 7.1: Software Copyright: Pro-Innovation or Anti-Competition

Copyright law tries to draw a distinction between the "idea" embodied in a piece of software and the "expression" of that idea. Ideas are free for everyone to use; expressions are protected. Thus one cannot copyright the idea of a numerical spreadsheet; but one can protect the expression of that idea in, for example, Lotus 123.

The European Commission is now trying to develop directives that will standardize copyright laws in the EC member nations. One of the main issues facing the Commission is the problematic distinction between expressions and ideas in the technical detail of "interfaces", which enable one program to work with another. More vexed still is the question of how much freedom would-be competitors should be allowed to pry into a protected piece of software in order to discover the unprotected, underlying ideas. Large parts of the computer industry relies on such freedom. Every IBM-compatible PC contains a piece of software that enables the machine to run the same application programs as IBM PCs.

The latest draft of the directive would permit programmers to read the underlying text of programs when they plan to write *complementary* but not *competitive* software. Most major software houses claim that this distinction is wide open to abuse; and would make it too easy for imitative rivals to steal their innovation. However, a number of European companies claim that any copyright system, which limits freedom to read the underlying text of software programs, will create huge barriers to entry. Too much copyright; and the law becomes an obstacle to competition and innovation. Too little copyright; and firms may lose the incentive to develop new products. The directive is still being revised.

In the USA, courts are grappling with the same issue: what does copyright protection really protect? Initially, protection applied only to the source code of programs; then to the object code; then to the flow diagrams that encapsulate the logic and sequence of the program; and now the courts are considering whether the "look and feel" of programs should be protected. The latest development is that software companies are seeking patent protection, on the basis that operating systems are analogous to any other industrial process.

Local software companies have initiated a number of law-suits (under a variety of legal headings) to combat piracy, and have organized in a collaborative effort to influence the statutory legislation. However, success in these cases is very uncertain given lack of prosecutor interest, and the difficulties experienced by judges in ruling on highly technical matters. In the meantime, venture capitalists as well as potential foreign partners have been inhibited from investing the Turkish software industry, the potential return on which may not be realized because of legal uncertainties and ambiguities.

7.12   Some software developers are also attempting to register their diskettes through the Ministry of Culture under the new Video Law[4/] which provides a procedure for identifying cassettes. Software owners or distributors must apply for a "distribution license". It has been reported that a license has been issued to some software companies. However, a unique number must be assigned to the software product, and stickers must be placed on the diskette bearing that number. So far, such stickers and numbers have not been supplied. This may be due to an uncertainty whether the Video Law really applies to software products, which are not explicitly mentioned in the legislation. Moreover, this procedure would constitute a considerable non-tariff barrier to software imports since most products arrive on the market shrink-wrapped from overseas factories. A local distributor would have to break the seal, place the sticker on the diskettes, and repackage the product.

7.13   Inadequacies in copyright protection for software products, although probably imposing the greatest economic costs, are not the only problem. Despite the introduction of the Video Law, film and video piracy is widespread. The Motion Picture Association of America (MPAA) estimates that 45% of films/videos in the cities. and as much as 65% in the villages, are pirated copies. Annual losses to authorized film distributors are estimated at $40 million. Another area of growing concern is publishing, especially of educational textbooks on scientific, medical and language-training. A large UK publisher of educational materials receives only a quarter of the income generated by sales of its university titles in Turkey. In November 1989, Turkey was identified by the US as a country with dubious intellectual property practices, although it was not thought to be a serious enough case to warrant placement on the priority watch roster. However, the influential US-based International Intellectual Property Alliance has recommended that Turkey be moved up to priority status.

7.14   Modernization of the Turkish economy over the past decade (and its integration into the world economy) has strengthened the case for protection of intellectual property rights. Industry is becoming more research-and-development intensive, and massive investment in computers and communications is accelerating growth in the information markets. Recognizing these trends and also seeking greater conformity with major trading partners, the Government has embarked upon an ambitious project of revising all its *industrial* property laws. Drafts of new statutes covering patents, industrial design, trademark and service marks have been completed (and are currently in the Parliamentary commissions). Copyright protection for software was also singled out as a priority by the Industrial Property Sub-Commission (State Planning Office: Science, Research, Technology Master Plan; para. 4.2.9.3).

7.15   However, the human resources to undertake this effort are limited. There is only one person in the State Planning Organization assigned to industrial property laws. As a result of timing conflicts with GATT talks in Geneva, this expert was unable to attend crucial discussions that took place simultaneously in Washington D.C. (Spring 1989) concerning the

---

[4/] Law 3257 on Cinema, Video and Musical Works (1986) was passed to curtail the piracy of music and video-cassettes (para. 6.50).

protection of semi-conductor chips.   Emphasis on industrial property laws together with inadequate human resources means that legislation to provide specific proprietary rights in semi-conductor chips,[5/] integrated circuits, computer software and databases (Box 7.2) has been necessarily postponed. With respect to computer software protection, the official position is that there will be no legislative initiative until the Uruguay Round of GATT negotiations is completed. However, continued delays in these negotiations combined with the initiative shown by the local software industry (which in 1992 sponsored preparation of draft legislation for Parliamentary review) suggest that Turkey should not hold essential legislative developments hostage to the GATT.

Box 7.2: Intellectual Protection for Databases

Draft legislation to provide EC-wide legal protection against the international piracy of electronic databases was recently approved by the European Commission. The latest directive would introduce a new type of intellectual property, protecting producers of databases - computerized lists or addresses, for example - from unfair copying of their databases for 10 years. The measure leaves aside the question of personal data protection, which is the subject of a controversial draft directive currently being discussed by the European Parliament. Database producers, which include large publishers and direct marketing organizations, believe that the directive will help to liberalize the $3 billion European market. It would allow competitors wishing to re-use such information commercially to obtain compulsory licenses "on fair and non-discriminatory grounds. The World Intellectual Property Organization (WIPO) is already considering amendments to the Berne Convention on intellectual property to cover databases, which are not seen as sufficiently original to qualify for normal copyright protection. Similar developments are taking place through the court system in the US.

7.16   The benefits from strengthened legislation for computer software protection (and for that of other specialized informatics products) are clear: stronger incentives for local suppliers and foreign investment. The costs from further legislative delay are growing, as computer users seek increasingly specialized services and software products. A key first step for the Government is to increase its investment in the human capital necessary to design, market and implement legislation in this area. Software copyright and legal protection for other

---

[5/] A semiconductor chip is an integrated micro-electronic device comprising thousands of electrical circuits, fabricated on a thin slice of semi-conducting material, on which patterns creating the elements of the circuits and their interconnections have been etched. These patterns are usually made from "masks" whose shadows define the circuit elements. The Semiconductor Chip Protection Act passed by US Congress in 1984 deals with intellectual property rights in these mask patterns. The law, which is administered by the Copyright Office, is a sui generis law adapted solely to the unique characteristics of the masked works. The term of protection is ten years. The conference held in Washington in 1989 was an effort to harmonize the protection offered to this new technology worldwide.

informatics products is a highly specialized discipline, requiring a blend of legal, economic and technical skills. Without adequate internal resources, there is an equal (possibly greater) risk that proposed legislation may err on the side of too much protection (and thereby prevent competition) as on the side of too little. Given the analytic and financial resources of large international software houses, a powerful lobby already exists in favor of anti-competitive excesses in copyright protection. The Government might therefore:

- establish a committee (with representatives from SPO, SIS, TÜBITAK, Ministry of Industry, key informatics suppliers and users) to develop policy for protection of informatics intellectual property (including but not limited to software copyright);

- commission a study of international developments in the legal protection of informatics intellectual property. (This study should also discuss differences between the legal position of US, EC and Japan);

- assess the requirements of the Turkish economy regarding the *scope* of intellectual property protection;

- design a *phased policy* for extending the scope of protection, and for improving enforcement; and

- prepare draft legislation.

7.17   A key principle of the intellectual property regime for the informatics sector should be explicit phasing in of greater protection. In the first phase, the law may seek to restrict software piracy and the strategy should emphasize improved enforcement by the courts. It is only in the second or third phase that Turkey should aim to tackle the more complex issues of copyright for technical interfaces and underlying program language. Premature over-protection of software may create a high barrier to the entry of new Turkish software houses; and would be inappropriate for an industry that is still significantly behind its competitors in other OECD/NIC countries. If the legislation (or implementing regulations) creates an explicit timetable for introduction of more stringent protection, this approach would: (a) strengthen incentives for entry by new companies at an early stage in the timetable; (b) provide clear signals to foreign investors and potential sources of risk capital;[6] (c) encourage existing software houses to strengthen in-house capabilities; and (d) provide a clear framework for medium term adjustment of the software industry.

---

[6] This is especially true for more complex software development projects that have lead times of two or three years.

Data Confidentiality and Privacy

7.18   Informatics has resulted in an exponential growth of databases containing personal and sensitive information. In the past, data-collection was a laborious process and, in most cases, individuals (and legal personalities) were active participants in the process of data-collection. In certain cases, individuals would be required by law (e.g., census law, company reporting, etc.) to provide certain types of information to the government. In other cases, commercial transactions (e.g., mortgages, job applications, business loans) would result in the voluntary provision of information as part of the contractual process. Today however, the situation has changed very significantly. First, there are an increasing number of transactions-generated databases in which individuals may have limited knowledge (or involuntary participation) in the data-collection process. In the US (for example), supermarkets are now able to collect precise information on customers' buying patterns at the check-out counter. Similarly, individuals that subscribe to magazines, charities or specialized clubs may find their names resold (many times) to other organizations. Second, the scope for abuse of computer files is much greater than that of manual files due to the speed and versatility of the computer. For example, data collected for one purpose can be easily adapted for another use or consolidated with data from another source. By overlaying the data available through thousands of information systems, it is now possible for organizations to create remarkably detailed profiles of most citizens.

7.19   Clearly, a significant percentage of this data-manipulation and reselling has the potential to increase economic efficiency. Indeed, the growth of a private market for this information (and specialized companies in the business of commercial information retailing) provides prima facie evidence that the information is economically valuable. There may be substantial welfare benefits from a market for detailed information about individual purchasing habits, or about the creditworthiness of individuals and corporations. However, the same data-collection and manipulation activities are also: (a) subject to a high rate of data errors that cause significant personal hardship e.g., from incorrect refusal of a mortgage application; (b) the source of discrimination in the employment, insurance and real estate markets (see Box 7.3); and (c) a risk to personal privacy through reselling information to multiple commercial organizations.

7.20   The growth of this private sector market in personal data has taken place in an environment that is unevenly regulated. Whatever regulations do exist (e.g., over credit bureau activities) have in many cases been superseded by technological developments that reduce the costs of data-collection and processing.[7] However, there are already indications that more rather than less regulation *is needed to stimulate* further market development. First, understandable fears about collection, processing and sale of personal data is resulting in a "citizen backlash". More and more individuals refuse to provide data on a voluntary basis, fearing the uses to which the data might be put and being uninformed as to who has access.

---

[7] Indeed, today much data is collected as a byproduct of other transactions (e.g., at a supermarket checkout counter) - at a very low marginal cost.

Box 7.3: US Markets for Data

Under US law, certain types of personal data can be collected without prior authorization and sold to interested organizations. For example:

a. A system of wholesale and retail *credit bureaus* keep detailed credit files on nearly 90% of American adults. All creditors (e.g., credit-card issuers, department stores, banks, mortgage companies) report the payment history of their clients to one or several credit bureaus. Each year 3 millions consumers go through the ordeal of trying to change their credit records because of incorrect or out-of-date information. Credit bureaus are protected by law from financial responsibility for "honest" mistakes. Under current regulations, anyone with a "legitimate business interest" is allowed to access the credit reports. This loose definition covers not just potential creditors; but also car salespeople, prospective employers or even dating services.

b. One company collects information on *medical mal-practice suits*; and today has a database of over 1 million records. People with a prior history of litigation can be made visible to hospitals, clinics and individual doctors. Because of this service, people who have been incompetently treated may, in effect, be black-balled by the medical community;

c. *Employers' Information Service* is one of several companies that report to employers about job applicants that have made on-the-job compensation claims. Another company keeps files on people that have been arrested, but not necessarily convicted, of a crime. The names are culled from newspaper stories. That information is then sold, mainly to perspective employers; and

d. In California and other states, data vendors maintain *records on tenants* who have been evicted or gone to court in a dispute with a landlord. That information is sold to other landlords, who use the reports to check on would-be tenants.

Privacy advocates are now trying to strengthen the law on data protection, especially with regard to credit bureau activities.

Second, data errors are difficult to identify or correct. Database vendors are not under any obligation to check data accuracy with the data-subject prior to sale; nor are they liable for "honest mistakes". There are only general principles that define database vendors' obligation to update data, or to provide access to the data-subject. Third, over-supply of personal data may (paradoxically) reduce efficiency in other markets. Not only does it generate a mountain of junk mail; but more seriously, it can cause a welfare-reducing bifurcation of insurance markets into good and bad risks. For example, if reputable insurance companies will provide auto-insurance only to drivers with completely clean records, drivers with bad records may have no (or a much reduced) incentive to improve their behavior. Over time, society will have to pay the cost of this incentive failure. A strong legal framework for data protection is therefore essential to reassure citizens about computers and make them more willing to give information about themselves for use on computer systems. Clear rules about data access, accuracy and content will benefit not only citizens; but ultimately database vendors, who have a strong interest in maximizing voluntary data-supply.

7.21   Citizen concerns and the perceived economic benefit of a strong framework for data protection has encouraged OECD nations to introduce a raft of legislation governing the use of personal data; and also the transactions-generated collection of data. Typically this legislation: (a) establishes a number of general principles regarding management of databases containing personal information (Box 7.4); (b) establishes rules about data protection during the process of data transmission; (c) defines the concept of authorized access; and (d) provides rules regarding the sale or export of database files. Certain countries (e.g., UK, Sweden) have also established national Data Protection Agencies, with which all databases containing personal data need to be registered. In addition, data protection and privacy is addressed separately in other specific pieces of legislation. For example, legislation governing Cable TV in the US and UK specifically prohibits cable-companies from developing databases on individual viewing habits (e.g., of blue movies). Similarly, there is pressure to develop clear legislation on the rights of companies to re-sell transactions-generated information without explicit prior consent from the

---

Box 7.4: General Principles of Database Management

Legislation in most OECD nations embody a set of general principles that are consistent with OECD Guidelines on data protection, and with UN Guidelines on Computerized Personal Data Files (1989). In Europe, legislation typically conforms with somewhat stricter rules established by the Council of Europe Convention on Data Protection and Privacy. These principles include that the personal data should be:

- obtained in a lawful manner;
- held only for one or more specified lawful purposes;
- held only to the extent necessary for the specified purpose;
- accurate and kept up-to-date; and
- held only for so long as necessary to achieve the specified purpose.

In addition, all legislation contains the "golden rule" that individuals have the right to: (a) be informed about databases on which he/she is a record; (b) access the data-record; and (c) where appropriate, have the data corrected or erased. Data-processing centers are also under an obligation to provide adequate security measures against unauthorized access to, disclosure or destruction of, personal data and against accidental loss or destruction of personal data.

subject individual.   Third, OECD governments are developing legislation that would limit the scope for creation of master-files that use relational database techniques to consolidate personal data from a number of different databases.

7.22   Data confidentiality has an important international dimension.   In particular, OECD and EC have played a coordinating role with regard to the issue of *trans-border data-flows* (TBDFs). Countries where data protection is in force are understandably reluctant to send their data abroad to places where the restrictions may be flouted. If data were exported to so-called "data havens", it could be misused there and so cause damage or distress to citizens of the originating country. This would defeat the whole object of the national statutes. To prevent such evasion of national laws, many countries have a clause forbidding the export of sensitive or personal data without the consent of the Data Protection Agency (or equivalent institutional arrangement).[8/] This Agency has the task of determining whether the receiving country is likely to misuse the data. Nations that do not possess an adequate legal framework for data protection will therefore miss out on the significant benefits of transborder data-flows, and may even lose certain types of business.

7.23   In Turkey, there has always been a strong emphasis on individual rights to privacy that are now being extended to the concept of data protection. Indeed, the personal quarters of the Sultans in the Harem of Topkapi in Istanbul contain a generous installation of fountains. These are reputed to have served not merely to satisfy requirements for cleanliness, but also to muffle the sounds emanating from the bed chambers so that the Sultan's private conversations could not be overheard. This penchant for privacy has been translated into a constitutional provision protecting the privacy of the individual and the assurance of secrecy in all communications (Articles 20 and 22). However, the overall legal framework for privacy is incomplete; and there appear to be significant gaps in data protection both with regard to public and private databases. Although Turkey is a signatory to the OECD Guidelines on data protection and transborder dataflows, there is no overall system for domestic implementation of these guidelines.

7.24   In the *public sector*, data protection is provided on an agency-by-agency basis. There are no equivalent of the UK Data Protection Act or of the US Privacy or Computer Matching Acts that impose common standards for data protection across the public sector. In certain cases, Turkish legislation contains quite comprehensive regulations on data protection. For example, the General Directorate for Judicial Records (Adil Sicil Genel Mudurlugu) maintains a highly sensitive database on the criminal records of Turkish citizens; and has data

---

[8/] It should be noted that there are substantial differences between US and EC law on data protection (with implications for transborder data-flows). First, US privacy laws follow a sectorial rather than the omnibus approach of the Europeans. Second, the US has adopted a "notice approach", whereby the user informs data subjects of his use of personal data about them and advises them of their right to object to such use. The EC directive proposes an "informed consent approach" i.e., a general prohibition against the collection or processing of personal data without explicit prior consent. Differences between US and EC privacy regimes may act as a barrier to TBDF between the two trading blocs.

protection standards similar to those of the EC (Box 7.5). The State Institute of Statistics Law also contains penal sanctions designed to protect the confidentiality of information obtained in the census or in other surveys. Individual information is not disclosed, and statistical data should not reveal any individually recognizable characteristics.[9] In other agencies and state-owned enterprises, the situation is much less clear. For example, the Labor Employment Office (IIBK) under the Ministry of Labor has very large databases containing personal information about skills, qualifications, and work experience. However, there are no explicit regulations regarding what information can be kept, who should have access or data-subject rights of correction. Similarly, the Ministry of Health is planning major investments in medical databases that would contain personal data. However, little consideration appears to have been given to the data protection and confidentiality aspects of this investment.

Box 7.5: Data Protection at the General Directorate for Judicial Records

The General Directorate has a mandate to maintain a sensitive database organizing all the judicial records pertinent to Turkish citizens, both living in Turkey and abroad. The General Directorate has no right to give out information to anyone other than the individual about whom the records pertain unless specified by law and upon a court order. Citizens have a right to inquire about their own records own identification with the ID issued by the National Population Office. Information can be obtained by other public agencies with a need to know, but any information illegally disclosed by officials of the General Directorate or by third parties can result in a prison term of 6 months to 1 year, and a substantial fine.

Individuals need to obtain a court order to have deleted wrongly recorded evidence of crime. Records are purged every five years for all except those who have been convicted of crimes that carry prison years of over 5 years unless they have received an amnesty. Records of Juveniles are sequestered and may not be obtained. Potential employers cannot obtain verification of criminal records.

7.25   In the *private sector*, the only sector where there is explicit legal protection for privacy is in banking. The Banking Act (Law 3182, Article 83) provides that bank personnel who disclose to those other than the authorities empowered explicitly by law, privileged client information shall be sentenced to imprisonment from 1 month to 1 year (and also fined). Employees leaving bank service are also required to maintain secrecy, but no time limit is specified. The Penal Code also contains a number of provisions that affect privacy of information. The Code: (a) requires bank employees to testify in court; and (b) specifies professionals who are permitted to maintain the confidentiality of their clients without disclosure as a witness. The Civil Procedure Code contains similar provisions, except that bank employees

---

[9] For further information, see Legal Framework for Database Services and Management (1992), State Institute of Statistics Working Paper.

have no obligation to testify in civil cases. More generally, data-processing centers in the private sector do not appear to have consistent standards (or professional codes of ethics) regarding data protection.

7.26   With regard to *privacy of communications*, the legal system is more explicit. Wiretapping is prohibited and all communication is secret as guaranteed by the Constitution (Article 22). The Ministry of Justice can get a court order to listen in on an unencrypted line, and courts may request and receive information transmitted by telegraph.[10] PTT Law also provides penalties of prison from five days to six months for intercepting "telephone and telegraph" lines or "disclosing the existence of the communication of a person". Although no court has so determined, there exists reasonable confidence that electronic data ("bilgi") on Turpak would be covered under this law. In addition, the prohibition against encryption of traffic on private leased lines was lifted in 1988. No filing of the encryption key is required.

7.27   *Conclusions.* Turkey may not yet be at the point at which data protection is a serious concern to citizens. The first credit bureau is only now being established by the banks. There has been little if any application of techniques for transactions-generated data-collection and direct mailing. Problems of data and systems compatibility in the public sector (Chapter 2) are likely to present a practical solution to the risks posed by computer matching techniques. Nevertheless, the case for a stronger privacy and data protection regime already exists. First, public and private investment in databases containing personal data will grow substantially over the next decade. In the absence of clear ex ante regulations (modelled on best international practice), this investment may not be consistent with broader social objectives and may generate unnecessary economic costs (para. 7.20). Ex post regulations will be too late, especially since database vendor lobby will be well-positioned by that time to bias the political debate. Second, further integration of the Turkish economy into world trading patterns requires elimination of potential barriers to transborder data-flows (TBDF). At present, Turkish standards for data-protection are behind those of both the EC and US (though they more closely resemble those of the US). Data protection legislation in many EC countries might prevent companies from exporting to or importing data from Turkey, if Turkish protection of personal data is viewed as inadequate. Turkey therefore has an immediate economic interest in strengthening its legal framework in this area.

7.28   There is no single right model for data protection. US and European practices differ widely; and there is only limited harmonization of regimes within the European Community. In principle, the key areas that require legal initiative and strengthening are:

- protection of personal data collected by the public sector. As SIS gives up its de jure monopoly (Chapter 6), the issue is what general regulations should ensure data confidentiality, and how should they be enforced;

---

[10] Telegraph and Telephone Law No. 406 (1924); section 9 of Chapter 2.

- protection of personal data collected by the private sector. As computer databases proliferate in the private sector, should the legal framework (as in Europe) provide general protection through establishment of a regulatory agency and registration requirement, or is the decentralized US approach preferable in Turkish conditions? and

- ownership rights over personal data. The EC Data Protection directive implicitly assumes that data-subjects own the data; and therefore must give consent to the collection and processing activities of database vendors. The US law assumes the reverse: that the database vendors are the primary owners, and provides a residual right of objection to data-subjects. Turkish law will need to determine which model to follow.

Turkey can take advantage of its latecomer status to data-protection law; and can build on its Constitutional safeguards to reconcile social benefits of databases containing personal data with individual rights to privacy.

Computer Crime, Security and Liability

7.29   Electronic Databases are increasingly central to the smooth functioning of organizations and the whole economy. The databases represent a massive and rapidly growing investment; and cover almost every aspect of economic life. They are also subject to a number of risks that include:

- computer viruses that scramble the data and can destroy the value of the database investment;

- unauthorized access to the computer databases; and

- unauthorized modification of the database contents.

In many countries, these activities are no longer viewed as merely civil offenses. Rather, they are classified as criminal offenses because of: (a) the economic damage that they can cause; and (b) the threat they pose to public confidence in computers. This confidence underpins the use of computers in banking, the health sector, public administration, weather forecasts, etc.

7.30   Developments in informatics technology and management are the first line of defence against these risks. As computer users have become more sensitized to scale of their potential vulnerability, they have created a market for a range of products including: (a) virus-hunting and destroying software; (b) encryption keys that code data during transmission procedures; (c) built-in passwords and access codes; and (d) physical computer security devices.

At the same time, data-processing centers have strengthened measures to prevent unauthorized access within the context of standards for total quality management. Nevertheless, the management of computer security is becoming a more complex task as data-processing capability becomes distributed throughout organization. Ten or fifteen years ago, computer security was largely a question of maintaining the physical integrity of mainframe installations. Today, it is much harder to guarantee as changes in computer architecture and information flows create networks of personal computers and multiple sources of risk.

Box 7.6: The Cost of Computer Security Breaches in the UK

Breaches of computer security cost UK business $2 billion annually, according to a recent survey of 900 private corporations. The main conclusions of the survey are that:

- at least half of the companies had suffered from a significant security breach over the past 5 years;

- estimated losses from physical breaches (which include theft, electrical and equipment failure, fire and flooding) amount to approximately $850 million annually (for the surveyed companies);

- estimated losses from logical breaches (e.g., computer hacking, software viruses) amount to $800 million; and

- most companies are still reluctant to inform the police about logical or physical breaches of security.

These costs do not include: (a) substantially larger sums that are spent each year by companies on preventive measures; and (b) widespread but unreported time costs incurred by PC users in restoring data that has been destroyed by computer viruses. In Turkey, it is estimated that breaches of computer security may cost up to $100 million annually.

Source: National Computing Center Survey (1991).

7.31   Initially, the legal response to breaches of computer security was to interpret existing criminal statutes (developed for a different purpose) to cover various categories of computer crime. Prosecutors used charges of criminal damage, forgery, trespass, telecommunications misuse and even abstraction of electricity, but with varying degrees of success. These criminal charges were somewhat blunt instruments to deal with a set of destructive activities that had not been envisaged by the criminal laws. In addition, it was frequently difficult for the criminal justice system (both police and courts) to understand the complex nature of the crimes, and to develop adequate preventive measures and deterrent sanctions. Governments across the OECD/NICs have responded to this problem by passing legislation that explicitly recognizes certain categories of computer crime.   In the UK (for example), Parliament passed the Computer Misuse Act 1990 that addresses:

- the offence of deliberate unauthorized access to computer programs or data, including access by authorized users that goes beyond their level of authorization;[11]

- the more serious offence of deliberate unauthorized access to computer programs or data, with ulterior intent to use the information to commit a further crime (e.g., electronic fraud of bank accounts or blackmail); and

- the offence of deliberate unauthorized modification of the contents of any computer (e.g., by releasing a computer virus).

Given that these offenses can be carried out from remote (i.e, non-UK) locations, the Act specifically claims jurisdiction whenever the offence affects a UK-based computer even if the offender is not UK-based.   Similar legislation has been implemented in most advanced economies.

7.32   In Turkey, the Government has also recognized the problem. In 1991, with the expectation that no computer system is 100% secure, a new law has been put in place to penalize unauthorized use and tampering with the data.[12] This law is considered by legal scholars as a "good start" in reforming the law to accommodate informatics, functioning primarily as a "cultural message" that such behavior will not be tolerated. In addition, it is possible that existing provisions of the Penal Code may cover certain activities - e.g., theft of automated data or even unauthorized use of computer time (as theft of electricity).

7.33   However, there are a number of unresolved issues within this legislation; and also certain categories of computer crime that are not explicitly addressed. First, it is not clear whether the new amendments cover unauthorized copying of software residing on a *diskette* as opposed to software residing in the computer system itself. Legal opinion is undecided and, in any event, this activity was not the primary motivation behind the new provisions. Second, the offence specified in the law is couched in the language of "unlawful acquisition of programmes and data from an electronic data system". It is again uncertain whether this offence covers the activity of "unauthorized access" (i.e., trying a number of computer system passwords) as well as unlawful acquisition. If the latter, it may be difficult in practice to prove the offence. The law does not stipulate whether acquisition implies physical removal of the programmes or data,

---

[11] It is estimated that 70% - 80% of unauthorized access offenses are carried out by "insiders".

[12] Law No. 3756, enacted 6 June 1991, amending Turkish Criminal Code No. 765.

or merely copying (leaving the originals intact). Moreover, the law does not deal with the more prevalent activity of unauthorized access to a computer system in which there may be no acquisition of programmes or data; but in which the owner of the computer system may suffer significant expense in ascertaining whether any damage or theft has in fact been caused. Third, the law does not appear to cover those cases in which unauthorized individuals are able to log-in to a computer system, and gain benefit through "computer eavesdropping" without either acquiring or copying the data. Fourth, it is not clear whether the amendments cover computer viruses that neither destroy data nor disable the system; but rather e.g., deny certain users access or clog up the computer's memory. In the judicial interpretation of the new amendments, it will therefore important to clarify their meaning. At a later point, further revisions to the Penal Code may need to be introduced that deal in more general terms with offenses of unauthorized access and computer viruses.

7.34   One defect of the amendments is that they do little to influence the behavior and management of data-processing centers. Since the amendments focus on data acquisition or modification, they do not provide implicit standards of appropriate computer security to prevent unauthorized access. In Turkey, the main risk to computer security is not deliberate hacking or data-theft. Rather, it is the lax standards of computer security that are applied in many public and private organizations. Few electronic data-centers appear to have: (a) specialized computer security staff; (b) well-defined and documented procedures to reduce the risk of logical and physical breaches of computer security; (c) procedures for back-up systems in case of e.g., an electrical failure; (d) internal rules to prevent the use of virus-infected diskettes on e.g., networks of personal computers; or (e) electronic log-books to detail the use of computer systems by authorized users.[13] As yet, there is no standard for computer security in the public sector (although a specialized working group has been established under the Prime Ministry). Passage of the new amendments to the Penal Code need to be complemented by a program of public information on the proper management of computer security. Best-practice procedures for computer security should be included in the computer standards effort, proposed in Chapter 2 of this Report. The high ex post economic cost of breaches of computer security (even when no actual destruction or modification of data) make it essential that organizations take preemptive action rather than relying on penal sanctions as a deterrent.

7.35   *Liability for Computer Failures.* As economies become increasingly dependent on information technology, issues arise not only of criminal but also of civil liability. The classic example is that of the telephone network. Failure of the telephone network has the potential to impose enormous economic costs (as happened recently in the New York metropolitan area - Box 7.7). More generally, problems in data transmission or simple data errors have significant economic implications. Data errors by e.g., computerized credit bureaus may result in a false denial of credit (or equally a false approval). Errors in data transmission may result in mistaken funds transfers in the absence of proper controls for authentication; or they may cause bugs in software programs that have been transferred electronically. While these

---

[13] This is related to the lack of charge-back systems for computer budgeting (Chapter 2).

problems are relatively rare in Turkey, progressive computerization of the banking system, credit approval procedures, and also of transactions in the product markets creates potential issues of civil liability. The economy is already dependent on the telephone system; and at present there are no objective standards of quality to which PTT must aspire.

Box 7.7: Economic Vulnerability in the Information Age

On January 4, 1991, an AT&T fiber-optic telephone cable connecting New York and Newark to the rest of the world was severed at peak time by a workcrew removing outdated cables in New Jersey. Immediately blocking 60% of all calls on AT&T's New York long-distance network, the accident also affected 40% of New York City's phone communications. The area's three airports effectively shut-down for over an hour while vital air traffic data made available through the AT&T network was rerouted. Hundreds of flights were delayed or cancelled with the effects cascading throughout the Northeastern air corridor and beyond as Chicago O'Hare, Miami International and others announced substantial delays.

The stock exchanges which have their own communication networks remained relatively unaffected but both the Commodity Exchange and the New York Mercantile Exchange chose to close for several hours. Similarly, while most large firms which rely on several long-distance carriers and/or have their own satellite, microwave and cable networks escaped down as did many dependent on AT&T for their 1-800 and 1-900 businesses. MCI and Sprint were also indirectly affected as they lacked capacity to immediately respond to the overflow from AT&T, with demand for their services increasing by seven-fold on occasion before the peak time crunch eased in the afternoon.

Legally, neither AT&T nor any of the other communications are obliged to compensate customers. Regulators have traditionally discouraged firms from filing rates which included compensation for loss of services. The concern was that costly law suits would result and that businesses would benefit from such compensation at the expense of residential customers. While business customers at US Sprint have some clauses in their agreements covering reliability, the firm does not provide compensation for service problems. Larger companies have already taken the route of starting their own satellite communication systems or laying private lines to the switching centers of long distance companies. Similar ventures which would join numerous smaller firms are yet another option being studied to reduce dependence on outside carriers.

7.36   As in other OECD countries, Turkey is only now beginning to address the issue of allocating civil liability for computer and communication errors. At present, PTT accepts no liability with respect to messages transported by telegraph or telephone, although correspondents may receive a refund of the transmission charge for telegrams that do not reach their destination or are distorted to the point of being unable to serve their function. In parallel with most OECD countries, there is no civil liability imposed on PTT for economic costs associated with loss of business for e.g., telephone system break-downs or for failure to e.g., correct faults or install new lines within an appropriate time-frame. Insofar as the private data-vending industry (including credit bureaus) has not yet developed in Turkey, civil liability for data-errors has not yet become a major issue. Within the context of: (a) regulatory reform of the communications sector; and (b) introduction of data protection legislation, initiatives that the Government might consider on the issue of civil liability are:

- definition of quality of service targets for PTT as a responsibility of the regulatory agency, and specification of penalties for failure to meet those targets. These quality of service targets would in effect substitute for broader civil liability, and would serve as an objective yardstick that PTT is acting in a non-negligent manner (Chapter 5); and

- definition of standards of care that data-vendors must meet in maintaining the accuracy of data, and specification of data-subjects' rights to claim economic losses in cases of data-error (where data-vendors have fallen short of the standard).

7.37   *Conclusions*. The legal system faces a complex challenge over the coming decades in adapting to the informatics era. First, informatics has created a range of activities (e.g., electronic bulletin boards) that do not fall into the conventional categories of telecom, printed material, or broadcasting. Issues therefore arise as to whether, how and by whom the content of such bulletin boards should be regulated. Second, informatics has also created a class of assets to which conventional concepts of intellectual property apply at best uneasily. For example, it is not clear whether the public interest is served by providing copyright for technical software interfaces (Box 7.1), or whether such information should be in the public domain as a shared resource. Third, informatics is posing new risks to civil liberties. Legal regimes for data protection straddle a conflict of principles between freedom of speech and individual rights to privacy; while new categories of computer crime may impose unnecessarily severe restraints on the legitimate freedom of "computer hackers". In the US, concern that computer crimes do not adequately distinguish between malevolent and benign computer hacking has led to the formation of the Electronic Frontier Foundation, a nonprofit organization concerned with the application of civil liberties to electronic media. As electronic networks become more ubiquitous in advanced societies, it will be essential to define a set of basic freedoms and rights analogous to those that govern the press and telecom sectors.

7.38   Turkey cannot afford to lag behind the international community in modernizing its legal system. Informatics is essentially a technology that transcends national boundaries. Data can flow from one country to another without much public control. Satellites already broadcast television programs into Turkey from private stations despite the legal monopoly in principle enjoyed by the state. Turkish universities are today members of international computer networks and electronic bulletin boards; and their participation is governed by the trans-territorial rules of those networks rather than only by Turkish law. Differential legal regimes for intellectual property rights and data protection may create a barrier between Turkey and other OECD nations in precisely those information-intensive activities that will be crucial to further economic modernization.   Computer crimes have very little respect for national boundaries; and indeed are likely to originate in those countries that have the lowest sanctions.

7.39   The benefits to Turkey of bringing its legal framework into line with that of its OECD partners (and selecting best practice where there are intra-OECD conflicts) are substantial: a more vibrant informatics industry, public confidence about computerization of society, and greater access to international knowledge and databases.   A concerted effort to update the laws, to train lawyers and judges in the legal aspects of information-based economy, and to use informatics to raise productivity in the judicial system, could win support among a key constituency for the IBE agenda. The economic costs of legal modernization - e.g., foreign exchange costs for software imports - are real but in the medium term unavoidable. By acting independently of external pressure (e.g., Uruguay Round of GATT), the Government will be better positioned to develop a legal framework and to phase its implementation in a manner that makes most sense for Turkey.

CHAPTER 8

ACTION PLAN AND THE ROLE OF GOVERNMENT

Introduction

8.01   Turkey's strategy for an information-based economy (IBE) should be based on policy action in four main areas:

- *private sector development*: to foster an internationally competitive supply of information technology, goods and services (especially in the communications sector);

- *human capital formation*: to align human resource strategy and education delivery mechanisms with the needs of an IBE;

- *public sector management*: to increase productivity and innovation in public sector services through better use of informatics; and

- *information regulation*: to safeguard civil liberties and consumer rights against risks created by informatics.

A public-private sector partnership that tackles this agenda can make informatics a catalyst for Turkey's economic modernization and a potent source of international competitiveness (Figure 8.1). This Chapter has two main sections. Section one draws upon the recommendations of the Report to outline an action plan for Turkey. Section two addresses the question of institutional arrangements for effective implementation.

An Information-Based Economy Action Plan

8.02   *Private Sector Development*. To accumulate informatics technology, attract foreign direct investment, and develop innovative information and communications services (more rapidly than competitors), the Government should:

- reduce and progressively eliminate state monopolies in telecom, and television/radio broadcasting;

- ensure competitive supply of key technologies through open market policies and legal reform; and

- stimulate improved technological capability in local industry.

Figure 8.1: Action Plan for an Information-Based Economy

Private Sector Development	Human Capital Formation	Public Sector Management	Information Regulation
* eliminate state monopolies in telecom and broadcasting	* strengthen university supply of informatics professionals	* implement national databases and information policy	* modernize legal framework for informatics
* foster technology development in private sector	* mobilize private resources for training	* improve key aspects of government computerization (procurement, standards, training risk management)	* introduce consistent regulatory framework on information content
* ensure competitive and open informatics markets	* diffuse computer literacy through-out workforce		* prepare and enforce better information standards

8.03   Tackling the state monopolies in telecom, TV and radio should be a priority item on the Government's informatics agenda. The process is already well-advanced in the television and radio field with a proposed Constitutional amendment (to remove the state monopoly), and with new legislation to license the private broadcast industry. However, reform in the telecom sector needs to be accelerated if Turkey is to remain competitive and to harmonize institutional arrangements with major trading partners (including the European Community). Key changes that are required include: (a) preparation of new policy and legislation for liberalization of the communications sector; (b) separation of mail from telecom services; (c) establishment of an independent regulatory body for the sector with the involvement of TGM and RTYK; (d) restructuring of the mail business; (e) corporatization of Turkish Telecom; and (f) progressive privatization of Turkish Telecom subsidiaries, starting with the value-added services (paras. 5.34 - 5.51).

8.04   Greater effort is also needed to create a transparent regulatory, legal and policy framework for competitive informatics markets. First, explicit copyright protection for software should be phased in over the next 5 years (paras. 7.07 - 7.17). Second, unproductive non-tariff barriers to trade (i.e., Ministry of Industry approval of computer imports) should be eliminated,[1] and tariff rates adjusted to create a level playing field between imported and domestically assembled PCs (para. 2.43). Third, product certified by accredited international

---

[1] There is no evidence of constrained consumer choice or an information problem in the computer market that would justify a regulatory government intervention.

organizations as conforming with network standards should be exempted from PTT type approval and conformance testing procedures (para. 5.27). Fourth, regulations on minimum lease-life need to be revised from three to two years in line with conditions in the computer leasing market. And fifth, an appropriate regulatory and tax framework for the venture capital industry should be introduced (following passage of the new Capital Markets law) to improve external financing sources for the software industry (para. 3.35).

8.05   Given a competitive market framework, there are a number of steps that the Government can take to build technological capability in the local industry. First, public sector procurement of informatics goods and services should be overhauled (paras. 2.30, 3.52). As an interim measure (para. 8.12), a working committee should be established (possibly with reactivated leadership of the Prime Ministry) with an explicit mandate and technical resources to define consistent procurement standards that include: (a) best practice tender specifications; (b) separate bidding on hardware, software, training and maintenance components; and (c) rigorous evaluation mechanisms. These standards should be mandatory across the public sector, with an exceptional review process for special cases (para. 8.12). A second action area is standards for software and total quality management of computer facilities. TSE should coordinate a public-private joint program to: (a) introduce international standards and best software engineering practices to Turkey; (b) provide training for the industry; (c) launch a Software Quality Initiative; and (d) develop conformance testing capability (para. 3.54). Third, additional support should be provided for software development through explicit grant and contract mechanisms (e.g., the Technology Development Foundation) (paras. 2.49 - 2.51).

8.06   *Human Capital Formation*. Building an information workforce is the most important challenge confronting the Government. Turkey's young population is potentially the nation's greatest competitive asset, but only if the education system works efficiently, is responsive to market demand and can be properly funded. To create the talent and skill-base central to an information-based economy, action is needed today to:

- enhance the pivotal role of universities in informatics skills supply;

- mobilize private resources for the training system; and

- create an enabling environment for general skills formation in informatics and information-handling.

8.07   Universities are the primary source of high calibre professionals for the informatics sector and for academia. To meet market demand over the next decade, three main actions are proposed (paras. 4.47 - 4.51). First, the leading universities should establish separate Informatics Faculties, responsive to market demand for graduate output with multi-disciplinary skills in software engineering, computing, organizational behavior, project management, etc. These Faculties should be able to: (a) offer competitive remuneration to staff and graduate students; (b) develop strong linkages with business; and (c) invest in adequate technology platforms and inter-university networks. Second, the Government should support efforts - initiated by the Turkish Informatics Association and TUBISAD - to establish a private Informatics Institute. This Institute is intended as a strategic investment for the sector: to improve the human capital base, create a critical mass of expertise, and put Turkey on the map as a competitive location for foreign investment in informatics research, design and manufacturing. Key steps to implement this proposal include: (a) establishment of a public-private working group; (b) preparation of detailed cost estimates; (c) market survey to determine curriculum content and Faculty composition; and (d) creation of a Foundation (vakif) to mobilize private and public financial resources, and to manage the implementation program. Third, Yök should initiate a program to: (a) integrate informatics into non-engineering disciplines; (b) determine the investment and resource implications of this curriculum change; and (c) assess the potential for informatics to raise productivity of university support functions (i.e., information services, administration).

8.08   Improvements in the higher education system are a necessary but insufficient condition for Turkey to close its informatics skill deficit over the next decade. Measures are also necessary to improve the functioning of the informatics labor market, and to raise efficiency in the private computer schools (paras. 4.52 - 4.58). First, the Ministry of Labor (IIBK) should finalize establishment of an Occupational Standards Commission, and prioritize introduction of standards for the informatics profession and corresponding test procedures. Second, SPO (with the Turkish Informatics Association) should publish a detailed annual survey of conditions in the informatics labor market. Third, the Ministry of Education should eliminate non-productive regulations on the private computer schools (e.g., on curriculum changes, staff qualifications), introduce an objective framework for school certification based on international standards of professionalism, and end the collusive practice of minimum fee-setting by the computer schools association. Finally, the Government could increase the incentive for firms to invest in their employees' training through the introduction of: (a) trade secrets legislation; (b) certification procedures for training and refresher courses that qualify as corporate tax deductions; and (c) a national award scheme for company training.

8.09   Turkey is not investing enough in diffusing computer skills throughout its younger generations (paras. 4.59 - 4.63). In the short run, implementation of the computer-assisted education program (CAE) under the Ministry of Education needs to be strengthened, especially with regard to: (a) teacher training; (b) curriculum development; and (c) relevant software availability. In the medium term however, the CAE program should be complemented by investment in the infrastructure - "Bilgitel" - for a national information market-place. The Bilgitel program would aim to accelerate mass computerization of households (and businesses), to support network development for data-communication, and to create a range of public domain educational software, knowledge-bases, and information services. The potential benefits of Bilgitel are very large: as an educational tool to familiarize children with computers, as a communications system, as a vehicle for innovative government services, and as a national project to differentiate Turkey from the competition. However, the risks and coordination costs are also substantial. The Government (with PTT, TÜBITAK and SPO leadership) should therefore: (a) carry out a detailed study to review the economics of Bilgitel (including determination of appropriate PTT tariffs); (b) assuming Bilgitel is commercially viable, define a pilot project to test the program; (c) establish an implementation vehicle together with private sector capital/management; and (d) execute and review results of the pilot project.

8.10 ***Public Sector Management.*** The Government has invested massively (over $500 million) in computer systems over the past decade, but with limited results in terms of public sector productivity and innovation. Performance improvement in government computerization requires two initial steps:

- design and implementation of a national database and information policy; and

- establishment of a mechanism to tackle inter-agency problems of computerization and related training requirements.

These actions will complement the program to increase efficiency (and spill-over benefits) of government informatics procurement (para. 8.05).

8.11 The State Institute for Statistics (SIS) should take the lead in formulating, coordinating and monitoring implementation of national policy for public sector databases and public information dissemination (paras. 6.34 - 6.43). This policy should address:

- standards for data-format, content, confidentiality and communication in the public sector;

- procedures for inter-agency data sharing;

- coordination of database investments;

- decentralized data dissemination by public agencies;

- guidelines on data dissemination;

- private sector rights of access to public information;

- pricing policy for public data; and

- guidelines for value-added information supply by the public sector.

The first step should be an audit (and development of an indexation database) of information already available in the public sector. This initiative implies a significant modification to the SIS law, and the implementation of a new policy that rebalances the public interest in national security and data-confidentiality with those of open government, freedom of information and rational decision-making in the market. This initiative is essential to improve the efficiency of information-processing in the public sector (its main activity), and to catalyze information flows in the private sector more consistent with market efficiency.

8.12   As computers become increasingly central to the government function, there will be substantial benefits from dealing with systemic issues of requirements planning, procurement and broader computerization objectives (including quantifiable performance targets). In the medium term, it may also be desirable to reorganize public sector computing into independent "informatics hubs" rather than agency-specific data-processing centers. These hubs could achieve substantial economies of scale over existing arrangements, and would create a critical mass of informatics expertise. This is however a longer term task, and would require support from the highest levels of Government. As a first step (paras. 2.29 - 2.31), the Government should begin preparation of a small independent agency with the following functions: (a) to provide technical assistance to the agencies on informatics procurement and design of tender specification; (b) to negotiate special government prices for standard IT products and services; (c) to standardize public sector occupational streams for informatics professionals, and provide training support; (d) to perform a technology watch function for the government; (e) to review exceptional cases that fall outside standard procurement rules; and (f) to promote inter-agency coordination on informatics strategy. Once the agency has succeeded in this mandate, it could assume broader responsibilities on issues of procurement practices (para. 8.05), and capacity planning for the public sector information system. The agency should have a small technical staff, broad public/private representation in the shareholder assembly, and an independent revenue source (possibly a 1% fee on public sector informatics procurements).

8.13   *Information Regulation*. The transition towards an information-based economy creates potential welfare losses as well as gains. Technological change always poses new social and economic risks, and informatics is no exception. Basic measures to preempt these risks include:

- a stronger legal framework for informatics, particularly in the areas of data-confidentiality and computer crime;

- a consistent regulatory framework on issues of information content; and

- better information standards in the market.

8.14   Further action is needed to modernize the legal framework. First, regulations on data-protection are behind those of the European Community and US (though they are closer to the US model) (paras. 7.23 - 7.28). In particular, there are no rules governing the operation of private sector databases containing sensitive financial and employment data. This incompatibility between the data-protection regime in Turkey, and that of her major trading partners creates a potential trade barrier, and therefore an immediate economic case for strengthening the law. Second, the restrictive formulation of the 1991 law on Computer Crime to "unauthorized acquisition" of electronic data appears to limit its usefulness to deal with more prevalent offenses of unauthorized access, copying of diskettes, computer viruses that clog up computer memory rather than destroying data, or computer eavesdropping. Further revision should therefore be made to the Penal Code to address computer crime in more general terms (paras. 7.32 - 7.34).

8.15   In the next few years, a proliferation of new (private) TV and radio stations is expected, together with the introduction of cable TV, electronic information services across the telecom network (e.g., 1-900 numbers), and potentially a national computer network (Bilgitel). While diversification of information resources for the public presents many potential advantages, it also creates a challenge for Government to develop a consistent framework for regulation of information content. A priori, there is no reason why cable TV or electronic bulletin boards should be subject to different content standards from television broadcasts. As part of the proposed reform of the television sector, the jurisdiction of the Supreme Council on TV and Radio Broadcasting should therefore be expanded over the whole range of electronically transmitted information services (para. 5.46). The Supreme Council should: (a) carry out a review of best practice in other OECD countries;[2] (b) prepare and disseminate clear guidelines for the electronic information services industry; and (c) develop a training program to strengthen personnel in line with new responsibilities and functions.

8.16   Information standards in Turkey are not yet consistent with the requirements of market efficiency (paras. 6.47 - 6.49). As the Government continues to reduce its direct intervention in product and factor markets, its role as an information regulator becomes correspondingly more important. Today, Turkey lags behind its OECD trading partners in enforcing information standards in financial markets, consumer retailing, industrial products, occupational classifications, etc. These standards play a crucial role in protecting society from the costs of false or misleading information. They also help to promote fair competition, to spread awareness of best practice, and to enhance incentives for product and quality development. Concerted action is therefore required from a number of agencies (e.g., TSE, Ministry of Industry, SIS, Capital Markets Board) to strengthen the design of standards, progressively bring them into line with OECD norms, and enforce them in the market-place.

Implementing the Plan

8.17   At present, Turkey possesses a decentralized institutional framework for implementing informatics policy. Almost every agency is involved in implementing various aspects of what in practice is an *implicit* informatics policy. Since a vast range of policies affect

---

[2] Practice to be studied would include the guidelines and their implementation for: (a) review of applications for broadcasting; (b) monitoring observance of ownership rules; (c) ensuring conformity with program content rules; and (d) definition and enforcement of pricing formulae.

the speed and process by which Turkey's economy is becoming more information-intensive, this institutional decentralization is a natural (and desirable) outcome. Indeed, it is essential that each agency understand the implications of informatics for its own mission, and develop a corresponding set of programs and initiatives. As a result, policy design and implementation appears to have been more effective in those cases that require relatively limited inter-agency coordination (e.g., network modernization, import regulations, computer crime legislation). However, in other cases (e.g., government computerization, procurement policy, public information policy, human capital development), policy implementation has been severely constrained by coordination failures. These issues must be tackled on a collective basis if Turkey is to accelerate her transition towards an information-based economy.

8.18   Governments in a number of other countries have recognized the benefits of a coordinated policy response to informatics, and have introduced explicit policies and corresponding institutional arrangements (Figure 8.2). The justification for this approach is to: (a) solve coordination problems; (b) create a critical mass of expertise in the public sector; (c) raise general awareness about the social and economic consequences of informatics; (d) increase the efficiency of government computerization; and (e) launch specific projects that cut across agency lines in the fields of infrastructure development, standardization, human capital formation, and technology support for the private sector. Especially in countries with an explicit set of policy and institutions, informatics is perceived as an enabling set of technologies whose application raises productivity and competitiveness across the whole economy. These are the countries that are most likely to capture the economic benefits from informatics investment, to build complementary assets especially in human capital, to attract the local and foreign capital into the sector, and to reposition their economies for future international competitiveness.

8.19   In Turkey, development of an over-arching framework for informatics policy is likely to be a long-term task. In the short run, what may be more practical is the implementation of specific projects (contained in the Action Plan). These projects will by themselves generate much of the coordination necessary for effective action in the informatics sector, and will provide demonstrable concrete benefits for the economy. Additionally, a Steering Committee could be established (preferably by Government Decree) with public and private representation to: (a) set annual targets for implementing the Plan; (b) review progress; (c) update the Plan and Report; and (d) disseminate major findings and recommendations to the broader informatics community. Logical candidates for secretariat to such a Committee would include TÜBITAK, SPO, SIS, Treasury and/or a representative organization selected from the private sector.

8.20   In the longer run, if additional coordination proves to be necessary, the Government has a number of possible vehicles including: (a) establishment of a Ministry for Communications and Informatics; (b) enlarging the scope of the proposed agency for government computerization (para. 8.12); or (c) creation of a National Informatics Board with a broad mandate for coordinating sectoral initiatives. However, the case for such institutional change

Figure 8.2: National Informatics Policies

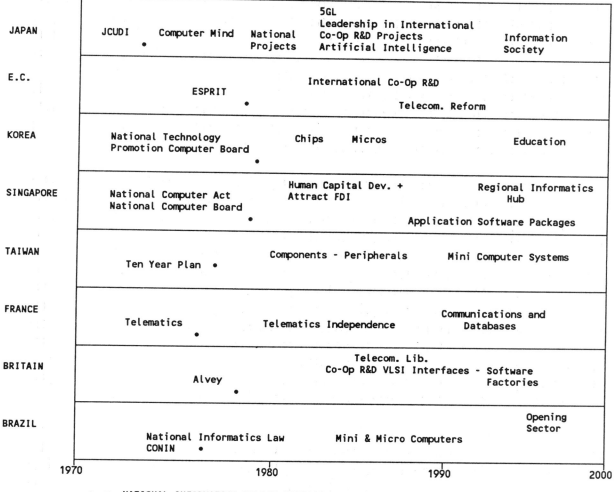

• = NATIONAL INFORMATICS POLICY INITIATED

is not yet overwhelming; and there are significant risks that investment in creating new bureaucratic structures would substitute for real action in the sector.

8.21   Implementation of the proposed Action Plan cannot take place overnight. Many of the proposals require legislative changes, significant institutional adjustment and the development of more detailed project proposals. Nevertheless, there are a number of actions that should be initiated to launch the program. The priorities include:

- translation of the Action Plan into Turkish, and wide dissemination of the Report's major findings;

- passage of legislation on private TV and Radio broadcasting;

Figure 8.3: Major Benchmarks in IBE Action Plan

	Action	Year	1	2	3	4	5
1.	Liberalization of Broadcasting		●				
2.	Telecom Reform						
	. Mail Separation		--------●				
	. Regulatory Agency		----●				
	. Liberalization			- - - - - - - - - - ->			
	. Privatization			- - - - - ->			
3.	Higher Education Reform for Informatics						
	. Private Institute		----●				
	. Informatics Faculties			------------●			
	. Informatics Integration Review		----●				
4.	Government Computerization						
	. Procurement Updating		●				
	. Specialized Agency		----●				
	. Legal Change		----●				
	. Technical Implementation			- - - - ->			
	. Informatics Hubs			- - - - ->			
5.	Software Industry Initiative						
	. Standards		●				
	. Certification		------------●				
	. R&D/Copyright		-------------------------->				
6.	National Database and Information Policy						
	. Indexation Study		●				
	. Market Survey		●				
	. Legal Changes		------------●				
7.	Bilgitel Computer Infrastructure						
	. Market Research		--------●				
	. Program Design		--------●				
	. Pilot			-----------●			
	. Roll-out					----------->	
8.	Action Plan Review						
	. Mid-term Update			●			
	. 5 Year Retrospective						●

Figure 8.4: Responsibility Matrix for IBE Action Plan

	Prime Ministry	SIS	TÜBITAK	PTT	MOT	Ministry of Culture	YÖK	Supreme Council on TV	TSE	MPM	PSIR	SPO	Treasury	Other
1. Liberalization of Broadcasting				✓	✓	✓		*			✓	*		
2. Telecom Reform				✓	*							*	✓	
3. Higher Education Reform		✓					*			✓	*	✓		MOE
4. Government Computerization	*	✓	✓	✓	✓				✓	✓	✓	✓	✓	MOF State Procurement Office
5. Software Industry Initiative		✓	*			✓			*		✓	✓		State Procurement Office
6. Database and Information Policy	✓	✓	✓	✓		✓			✓			✓	✓	KOSGEB
7. Bilgitel Computer Infrastructure		✓	✓	*	✓						✓	✓		
8. Action Plan Review	✓	✓	✓	✓	✓		✓	✓	✓		✓	*	*	

Note: * = Candidate for Lead Agency
       ✓ = Main Related Agencies
       MOF = Ministry of Finance
       MOT = Ministry of Transportation
       MOE = Ministry of Education
       PSIR = Private Sector Informatics Representatives

- preparation of draft legislation (and action plan) for the separation of mail and telecom, and establishment of an independent regulatory authority;

- design and implementation of standards for public sector procurement of informatics goods and services;

- establishment of a working group (and timetable) for the private Informatics Institute;

- SIS coordination of preparatory work on the National Database and Information Dissemination Policy;

- a Software Industry Initiative that would embrace the introduction of standards, phased legal protection for software copyright, changes in procurement practice, and the provision of software development support grants.

Once the short-term program has been launched and implementation is underway, additional medium term initiatives include: (a) establishment of Informatics Faculties in the leading universities; (b) preparation and implementation of the Bilgitel project; (c) progressive privatization of Turkish Telecom; (d) organization of the proposed agency for government computerization; (e) further legislative change in the areas of computer crime and data-confidentiality; and (f) an inter-agency effort to improve information standards. Figure 8.3 suggests a possible timetable for implementing the Plan.

Conclusions

8.22   During the 1980s, Turkey succeeded in taking a short-cut to a more information-based economy. A relatively liberal import regime provided Turkish organizations with access to the latest informatics technology. A greater emphasis on market forces and competition intensified demand for information, and for information-processing and management skills. Public sector investment in the communications infrastructure overcame earlier deficiencies in the telecom network, and efforts were made to improve the supply of informatics professionals. Even in the absence of an explicit informatics policy and accompanying institutions, Turkey appears to have made substantial progress. Indeed, it is likely that market and technological forces over the next decade will reinforce this trend without any significant change in government policy! A high rate of productivity growth in the informatics sector, greater experience in applications, the opportunity to catch-up with international practice, and competitive pressure in the market will be enough to ensure that informatics plays an increasing role in the Turkish economy.

8.23   However, all OECD and middle-income countries are likely to benefit from these same market and technological forces. At best, the absence of an explicit informatics policy and action plan implies that Turkey will continue to lag behind the leaders and may fall further behind those countries that have targeted informatics as a strategic sector for overall economic performance.   If Turkey aims to accumulate information assets at a faster rate than the competition and to catch-up with more advanced economies, then a more dedicated approach is essential. Turkey today has a choice: either to include the information-based economy as an explicit objective in the national development agenda or to make it a residual outcome of policy. The central message of this Report is that Turkey has the potential to become an active player in the informatics revolution and an information hub in the global economy. Realizing this potential will require a long-term partnership between enlightened government policy and private entrepreneurship.

ANNEX 1

HARDWARE TECHNOLOGY AND POTENTIAL GROWTH AREAS

1.   Hardware is the most visible component of the informatics sector. This annex provides background on the terminology of hardware, and an assessment of Turkey's supply opportunities

The Development of Informatics Hardware

2.   Historical evidence of organized business records indicates that organized information has been a part of business practice since business began. Records in the form of transaction logs have been found on cuneiform tablets and remain in current use. Improvements over using logbooks as the only form of business record have been few: the invention of double-entry account keeping in the 15th century, the file folder, first used in the last century, the punched card, invented shortly after the file, and finally the computer.

3.   The introduction of the computer in business, which occurred in the early 1950's, is often considered to have made great changes in business, but it did not. The first commercially successful computer, the IBM model 650, functioned only as an addition to an existing collection of punched card processing equipment, which had been in common use in large corporations for some time. Indeed, mainframe computing did not change the way work was done in most companies until very recently. Computers typically replaced large groups of clerical staff, which were already centrally located in most large businesses, especially those in financial services. The real potential to change the way business was organized did not exist until the development of what is called on-line or real-time systems, which allowed the mainframes to communicate directly with those who were performing front-line business functions. The technology to support this form of data processing did not become effective until the early 1980's. Shortly afterward the personal computer began to take the attention of the business world and the trend to implementing on-line systems slowed.

4.   Today the use of technology hardware is in a confused state. The capabilities of the hardware are moving so rapidly that business can not find effective ways to use it. Developing software, long the bottleneck in technology use, is no longer the principal challenge. The simple business transaction, which began as a line of symbols describing an acquisition of sale, is no longer the only concern. Text, graphics of various kinds and decision parameters are important, but do not fit into the old systems architectures. The automated use of these forms of data are the domain of the personal computer, but supplying a computer to each worker gives up the central management and control of the mainframe and presents new communications problems. Underlying the proliferation and rapid advancement of the hardware is the practice of designing and marketing hardware based upon its own capabilities, such as speed and capacity, rather than on the ability of the hardware to solve business problems.

5.   This section discusses the state of the art in hardware in the various categories in which it is usually sold, although the classifications are rapidly blurring. Also covered is the issue of compatibility, the most difficult technical problem presented by hardware at this time.

Mainframe Computer Technology

6.   Mainframe computers are large and expensive; they require special environments and special skills are required to maintain, program, operate and manage them. Mainframes are made by a small number of manufacturers in a few countries, but are used throughout the world. They are vital to our society.

7.   The mainframe computer is made in four parts: a central processor or group of processors, a communications controller, a central fast-access memory and a group of disk drives used for large capacity memory. There are myriad components in a mainframe installation, but most belong to those four functional groups. The trends in computing can be viewed as changes to these four groups. The processors, of course are being made faster. There is a trend toward using increasing numbers of them (2 to 6, at present). The disk storage facilities (called disk farms) are also gaining in capacity and number, as is the central storage facility. These changes have been occurring over many years and were easily predicted. The communications control group, however, is undergoing significant and unpredicted change as the computing world moves into networking. Some communications controllers rival central processors in capability and cost. They are computers in themselves, reflecting the trend in the use of mainframe facilities.

8.   When personal computers were first marketed by IBM corporation, about ten years ago, some analysts predicted that these machines would replace mainframes by 1995. They based their opinions on the prediction that PCs would be as fast as mainframes within that time, a prediction disputed by many other analysts. Long before 1995, PCs did achieve mainframe speeds, and their sales exceeded mainframes greatly, but a clear trend showed that the use of mainframes was continuing to increase. It seems that the use of PCs stimulated such great demand for information, that mainframe demand was considerably increased.

9.   The role of the mainframe, however, is being changed by the increasing use of desktop computers. The mainframe now serves as a central data repository, and as a communications hub, rather than as a number manipulator. The movement to this new role is limited by the availability of technology components to make PC/mainframe links more useful and by the large inventory of applications software programs on the mainframes which can not be moved to PCs quickly. The target architecture, not yet technically feasible, is one in which the PC does the processing and stores local data, and the mainframe stores corporate data. It is called client-server architecture, with the PC being the client and the mainframe acting as a database server. A mini computer can also be used to store departmental data.

PC (Micro-computer) Technology

10.   The personal or micro computer has found its way into every part of business. It is generally acknowledged, however, that the PC has not been used to its full potential, because few users have changed their basic approach to work to take advantage of the power that the PC makes available.

11.   Currently there are two levels of PC technology in common use. The first is the use of IBM-compatible PCs under the DOS operating system as word processors, terminal emulators or for spreadsheet work. Most of the users at this level have a principal use for the machines which accounts for almost all of their use. For this purpose, the earliest forms of PC technology will suffice: the Intel 8086 and 8088 based systems, running the DOS operating system, although the use of a hard disk drive provides a great increase in function beyond the earlier reliance on floppy disks. The second level is the use of a graphical user interface (GUI) to integrate software systems for the user. Users habitually switching among applications find great utility in GUI's. The three GUI environments are Microsoft Windows, running with DOS, IBM's OS/2 and Apple's Mackintosh. Of the three, Macintosh provides the most stable and easily used environment. Business has great difficulty making decisions regarding the cost benefit of all of these alternatives, even when convinced that some type of PCs are invaluable. The other difficult decision regarding PCs is the use of networks.

12.   The work that PCs do is not the same as mainframe work. In general, PCs are not used for transaction processing. The PC is also not a very secure device, both in the sense of privacy and also form the viewpoint of protecting data from accidental destruction. Only when better client/ server tools are made available, will significant parts of transactions systems be built on PCs.

13.   Although PCs have not proven to be a substitute for mainframes (in many applications), they play an important complementary role. The desktop work that most commercial PC software is designed to support is important enough to motivate a very large industry and to produce rapidly increasing demand for more powerful PCs.

Mini-computer and Workstation Technology

14.   Mini-computers were very popular when they were first sold (the DEC PDP8 was the first successful mini: 1968). It was before the introduction of PCs and the mini-computer allowed processing capability to be moved closer to users. It also enabled organizations that needed computing support, but were much too small to support a large computer to obtain a their first machines. The early uses of minicomputers, as stand-alone support for small operations have long since ceased, except process control. The mid-sized computer has gone in two directions: becoming an intermediate computer in a multi-layered network architecture and becoming a super-powerful mainframe on the desktop.

15.　　　　Some mini-computers, notably DEC, run proprietary operating systems, but many of the mid-sized machines, almost all of the desktop workstations are running UNIX, the machine independent operating system developed by Bell Labs. Members of the workstation family include the Next, the IBM6000, and the market leading Sun SPARC Workstations. Using UNIX, these machines offer more software compatibility than other processing systems. The Next has its own GUI; the others can use the X-Windows standard interface. These machines all offer increased processing power and upgrade capability to applications that require more than PCs can offer. Common uses of workstation are in education, science and engineering. It is also possible to use either a mini-computer or a UNIX workstation as a departmental computer to support a business operation.

Information (Data) Communications and Networking Technology

16.　　　　Data communications is growing more rapidly than any other form of communication. Some recent developments have closed long-standing gaps in communications capabilities, but many remain. Communications is generally considered to provide the greatest technical challenge to corporate informatics staff due to its inherent complexity. Indeed, it is so complex that it is difficult to discuss without an agreed upon framework. The most widely accepted of the communications frameworks is called the OSI model, and it is only applicable for networking, as opposed to communications in general. This model defines seven layers into which network standards fall, with physical transmission media at the bottom and the end user's work (applications) at the top.

17.　　　　As useful as the OSI model has been to networking, there are few organizations which have built networks using products which comply with the OSI standards. Current networks use products built to a mixture of OSI and vendor standards. DEC's DECnet and IBM SNA are in common use, usually implemented with Ethernet and/or Token Ring as local area network (LAN) standards - both of which are now OSI standard.

18.　　　　The utility of communications to end-users is often overlooked when discussing the technology. To an end user, there are is a limited number of functions offered:

- *File Transfer*:　the ability to move files from one system to another;

- *Terminal Emulation*:　making one computer (generally the end-user's PC look like a terminal to another computer;

- *Program-to-Program*:　having a program one computer communicate data and commands to a program running in another (this requires a standard interfacing language understood by both programs, even though each program may be written in a different language and run on a different computer);

- *Message Transfer*: the transfer of highly defined packets of data under very strictly controlled conditions (this is not the same as electronic mail, although e-mail can use message transfer to send its data from one machine to another);

- *Host Switching*: giving the end user transparent access to a distant computer through the user's own computer, even though the computers are not of the same type;

- *Virtual Files*: making a remote storage facility seem to be another hard drive on the end-user's PC;

- *Electronic Mail*: not really a communications service, but an application built upon communications, e-mail implies either message transfer, file transfer or terminal emulation and requires a directory facility;

These services are rather primitive. The concept that an end-user unexposed to communications has is a set of applications services, such as is offered by All-in-1, DEC's electronic office support system or Compuserve. The vision is one of access to unlimited data, immediate connection to anyone who has a PC, and the ability to develop cooperative, client-server applications. All of these are beyond the scope of communications itself and some will not be feasible in most business environments for some time.

Compatibility and Interoperability

19.   Compatibility is hardware's most difficult problem; it is difficult to understand and discuss as well as solve. There are two classes of compatibility which have very different characteristics: plug compatibility and interoperability. The first, called plug or instruction set compatibility compares two hardware products as being interchangeable from the applications viewpoint. Fully plug compatible equipment will run the same machine language code. A variation is systems which can run each other's programs, but which require recompilation of the source language (or which run from source language directly). All UNIX machines should be compatible in this way. In general, the mainframe equipment sold as plug compatible today actually is highly compatible. The one caveat is that the IBM plug compatible competitors do not support very new features of IBM operating systems.

20.   Interoperability refers to the ability of two machines to cooperate with each other. There are many forms of this type of compatibility, most controlled by some form of standards, either issued by one vendor (such as IBM SNA and SAA) or by an independent body (such as ISO Open Systems Interface standards -- OSI). Most vendors of equipment intended to interoperate with others state compliance with the standard. The Corporation for Open Systems supplies software to test compliance with some standards. However, compliance with the

standard does not guarantee interoperability. Interoperability must be tested on a case by case basis to assure success.

21.　　　　These limitations also apply to PC hardware. Plug compatible PCs are called clones and they generally perform identically to the IBM PS2. Desktop computers now support only a few real computing platforms: PC DOS, PC DOS with Windows, IBM OS/2, Mackintosh and various forms of UNIX. Today, they can all read the PC DOS file structure (called "FAT") on 3 1/2 inch floppy disks. They all can communicate on common LAN's, but not on all LANs. Personal computers continue to increase in compatibility, so that only minor details and advanced functions will not move from one platform to another.

22.　　　　Complete compatibility in informatics hardware will never be achieved. Vendors will continue to develop new functions faster than the standards and interchange capabilities of the systems can make them compatible. Otherwise, vendors will be competing on price alone, which is unlikely.

Potential Hardware Growth Areas

23.　　　　This section describes the product areas that have potential for growth in the next ten years. Some of them may be opportunities for Turkey, given a stable macroeconomic environment and the elimination of policies that distort private investment decisions. Given the rapid pace of technological change in informatics, only the markets will be flexible enough to "pick winners". Government interventions are unlikely to be successful in second-guessing market and technology trends.

24.　　　　*Personal Computers*: are the most visible of all informatics hardware products. For the past decade they have also been the largest part of the market. Growth has been as spectacular as the increases in performance of the machines. They are now as powerful as the mainframes of only a few years ago. There does not appear to be any diminution of the PC market in the foreseeable future. The personal computer's immediate future is more concerned with software than hardware, however. The role of hardware improvements, especially performance improvements, would appear to be dedicated to the support of better software and improved networking capability. The most promising hardware niche market related to PCs is most likely special purpose add-on boards that supplement the software's new capabilities.

25.　　　　The one area in PCs that has a high potential for immediate, rapid expansion is the very small portable PC, often referred to as a personal input device (PID). The size of portable computers has been reduced continually for the past five years, while their capabilities have increased. In a short time a 1.5 kilogram, 20 millimeter thick portable will be sold with a color monitor. When the machines become that size, they will sell very well indeed. However, the technologies required to build color monitors and batteries for small computers is not generally available as components. It is questionable whether the PC market a good one for Turkey. The market is very competitive; there is a PC assembly industry in many countries.

The probability of new entry into market niches is small. The more basic technologies required for PCs require large investments. However, it may be advantageous for Turkey if some basic chip technology production was started, but not to support the production of personal computers so much as the products that will be developed from this basic technology.

26.   *Workstations*: are very powerful desktop computers that are used to support scientific, engineering and complex business work. They usually run the UNIX operating system. These machines are growing in popularity. It is possible that the PC and the workstation will have a joint future, when they are both very much more powerful than today and can run the PC and UNIX operating systems together at high levels of performance. Another probable trend is that workstations will become the basis for workgroup computing in networks with less powerful PCs and will find a place in process control, essentially usurping the role of the minicomputer. This technology is promising and should be watched by Turkish industry, but the rate of expansion of the market does not currently provide entry for new producers.

27.   *Minicomputers and Mainframes*: The mainframe and minicomputer markets have been more or less saturated for many years. With the exception of a few new accounts in developing countries, all of the industries that can support mainframes bought them by 1980, leaving only new businesses and conversions as the only targets for new mainframe sales. The saturated market continues to be a source of large revenues for a few manufacturers who can produce increasingly powerful machines that will run huge investments in existing corporate software. There are only two reasonable ways to enter this market: (1) make plug-compatible equipment, competing with IBM, Hitachi and Fujitsu; or (2) buy and sell used equipment.

28.   In addition to saturation, the mainframe market is in danger of extinction. Not, as is often supposed, due to the rise of PCs, they seem to have increased the need for mainframe capacity, but due to the eventual convergence of PC, Workstation, Minicomputer and Mainframe technologies into a computing environment based completely on a single chip. In less than two decades, it is likely that all computing will be based on configurations of a single, very powerful chip. Desktop computers (PCs), minicomputers, mainframes, workstations and new computer types, such as communications servers and database servers will be distinguished only by the number of these chips that they incorporate, their storage capacity, their throughput bandwidth and the operating systems software that they run. As the shift to this technology begins, the opportunity to enter the market will arise.

29.   Turkey may be in a better position to enter the mainframe market of 2010! Even then it may not be advisable to compete directly with the companies that produce large computers now, but the technology of 20 years hence promises many more types of equipment in the mainframe category, including niche products such as specialized servers sold with pre-written applications software and constructed from commonly available basic components. The basis for building this new industry exists in Turkey today.

30.   *Peripheral devices*: currently include disk drives, tape drives, printers, optical scanners, optical disk storage devices and other special purpose equipment which can be directly attached to computers of all sizes. The market is a thriving one in which many middle size businesses compete successfully with the large mainframe vendors. In the future, peripheral devices will be based upon more commonly available basic components than they are today. The desktop laser printer industry has already reached this stage: only a few microprocessor chips and laser printing engines are the basis for all of the dozens of laser printer products sold throughout the world. Within a few years, arrays of PC-size disks will become the most cost-effective storage for mainframe computers, and optical disk technology is being developed this way from the onset.

31.   While the composition of peripheral device products simplifies, the number of products will increase geometrically. This class of informatics hardware may result in the largest growth in product numbers and new revenues in the next two decades. It is primarily through the use of these devices, and hand-held computers that will have the same capabilities built in, that informatics will expand its overall services. An example might voice and speech recognition interfaces, which have been experimented with for many years. When they become serious business tools, they will be constructed mainly from off-the-shelf components. Peripheral devices will offer, therefore, an excellent example of the effect of the opposing trends of component convergence and product proliferation. This class of hardware might be a good one for development in Turkey. A majority of Turkish exports have been classed a peripheral devices in the past, and the basis for future efforts is with Turkey's capabilities.

32.   *Communications*: Communications hardware obviously represents Turkey's main short-term opportunity in the informatics hardware marketplace. This class of hardware is already being successfully manufactured in Turkey and successfully marketed domestically and exported. The question that may be asked however, regards future trends in this classification of informatics hardware.

33.   There are several ways to divide communications hardware into subclasses. The first is into two classes, voice and data, but the separation of the two is rapidly disappearing. The second is by the scope of the network: local and wide area. The distinction between these two is also becoming blurred. Also, the bulk of LAN concerns are becoming software issues. Another possible classification is market product classes: (1) switches, all sizes and types; (2) communications servers, which can be described as very intelligent switches for data and include mainframe communications front-end processors, LAN gateways and routers and other network devices (3) network protocol devices including network cards for PCs, protocol converters and bridges and other in-out devices (4) media and support equipment including wires, plugs, adapters, radio and light spectrum transmission and reception equipment. Much of the equipment in all of these subclasses will also become dependent upon common component construction. Furthermore, even these classes may merge; there is already some overlap, pointing out the lack of any need to single out product lines for future attention. Turkey is already in this market and market forces are likely to generate further proliferation of products.

34.   ***Multi-media Technologies***: combine traditional data forms with text, voice and images to provide a more complete, flexible informatics capability. The number of new products that will be marketed in support of this new technology will be very large. Because it pervades the entire informatics spectrum, these new products will appear in computing hardware, information storage, all phases of communications and software of many types. Although multi-media technology has been anticipated for at least five years and has been recently implemented in a few impressive business applications, multi-media technology is developing slowly. Until a threshold of utility is reached, it will not become a market dominating capability and will not provide a significant market demand. While Turkish industry should not be advised to move into multi-media technology markets, the technology should be watched closely, since it is a key to the direction of the informatics hardware marketplace.

35.   ***Components and Basic Technologies***: A key question related to informatics hardware manufacture is whether or not the manufacture of basic technology components, such as chips, should be among the ambitions of Turkish industry. The research, development and manufacture of these technology components is some of the most complex and expensive work being done anywhere, and the organizations that are doing it are very well supported, either by massive informatics revenues or government subsidies.

36.   It is unlikely that Turkey will enter this industry without some government incentive. The profit risks are too great to attract private sector investment. However, the long-term interests of the country might be well served by having some modest basic technology development capability within either the borders or ownership of Turkey. Such a capability would assure a degree of engineering depth that might otherwise not be readily available to Turkish research and development efforts. Another consideration is that without this capability in Turkey, other countries may exert damaging pricing and/or availability pressures on informatics hardware components to give advantage to their own industries. There is also a chance that a basic technology discovery might occur in Turkey, giving great advantage to Turkish informatics industries for a short time, and, even that the possibility of basic discoveries would provide a source of continuing motivation. The cost of the facilities for basic technology research makes it impossible to make a firm recommendation for the pursuit of this class of technology, but consideration for some facility or foreign partnership is suggested.

Figure A1.1: Market Opportunities Through 1995
Products and Technologies

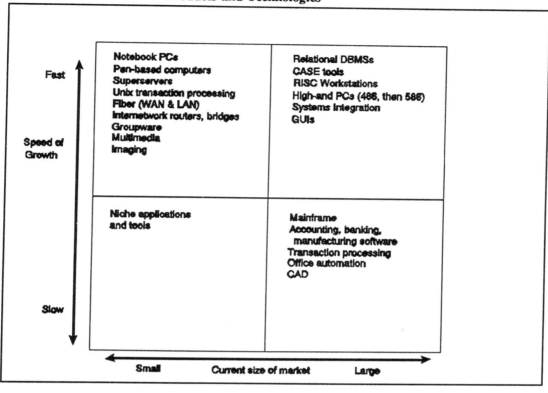

ANNEX 2

OVERVIEW OF THE WORLD MARKET IN SOFTWARE

1.　　　　Software is a booming sector, and is growing faster than most industries. The market for computer software and services is global, intensely competitive, fast-changing and fast-growing. The world software market was approximately US$110 billion in 1988, and is expected to double in size in 1993 to US$225 billion, and to US$400 billion in 1995.[1] In the United States, it is estimated that US$10 billion is spent each year on producing marketed software, which amounts to about 1% of gross national product. The cost of in-house software development (a non-marketable activity carried out mostly in large systems suppliers and in large and medium sized user firms and organizations), may be in the range of US$150 billion to US$200 billion.

2.　　　　The software and services market worldwide is forecast to grow at a rate of 15% a year over the next four years. The rate of growth has slowed from about 20% over the past five years.[2] The Europeans and Japanese expect their software industries to grow faster than that of the United States; however, the United States will still total nearly half of the world market in 1993.

3.　　　　Software sector employment has expanded rapidly in many industrialized countries, often during sluggish employment growth in other sectors. In the United States, for example, employment in the sector increased by over 238% during the period 1978-87, compared to only 36% and 44% for the hardware sector and the entire economy respectively. In the state of Massachusetts, the over 800 software firms provide nearly 46,000 jobs in the state and roughly 300,000 jobs worldwide.[3] In Japan, employment in software increased by 157%

---

[1] Consultronique/Sema Group, "Export Development Opportunities in the Software and Services Sector," Paris, April, 1990. Systematic data on sales of software and services exist only for the United States and Western Europe, and even these data are suspect. The lack of government and sector statistics make it practically impossible to make cross-country comparisons. And the measurement of software sales and services (including customized software, systems support, timesharing, documentation, and data base access) is made even more difficult by the parallel phenomena of consolidation and overall sector growth that are blurring the distinction between the software, service, and even hardware market segments. Software firms are expanding the service parts of their businesses, and services and hardware companies are increasingly stepping up their software efforts in order to build stronger bases and provide more utility to end users.

[2] Due to several factors, including general economic conditions in the maturing U.S. computer market, and confusion over software standards, which in turn has led to slower growth of personal computer sales over the past year.

[3] Sivula, C., "Massachusetts Miracle Goes Soft(ware)," Datamation, August 1, 1990, pp. 33-46.

during the period 1978-86, compared to an increase of only 12% in total employment during the same period.[4/]

Two Key Markets: Products and Services

4.   Software packages and systems integration are the fastest growing segments of the sector, as illustrated in Figure A2.1. Software packages will experience the highest growth rates until 1993, mostly due to the demand for microcomputer-based software packages--operating system packages, relational data bases, and generic and vertical applications packages. It is also due to the increasing availability of packaged software for ever more markets such as multiuser environments, data communications, and cooperative processing.

Figure A2.1: Worldwide Software and Services Market by Segment

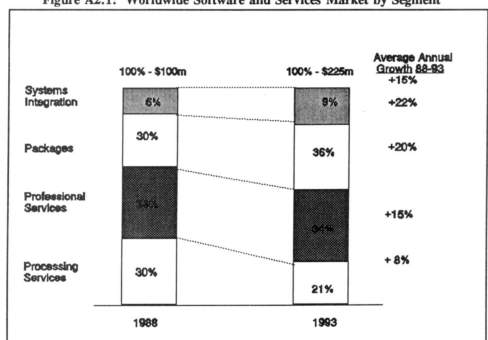

Source: Consultronique/Sema Group (1990).

5.   The systems integration services segment of the market--which can include project management, requirements analysis and design, contract programming, subsystem integration, education and training, and ongoing system support and maintenance (illustrated in Figure 1) is expected to increase at an average annual growth rate of 22-28% over the next five years. The

---

[4/] Japan Information Service Industry Association, "Today and Tomorrow of the Japanese Information Service Industry," Tokyo, March 1988.

systems integration market is quite concentrated, with the top 10 systems integration firms accounting for almost two-thirds--or about US$3.8 billion--of the US$5.9 billion US market. Most current subcontracting by the leading systems integrators is for contract programming, custom software design, and education and training. Systems integration is of special importance to a country like Turkey since these services can become the focal point for developing a capability to effectively use electronics and associated technologies such as communications networks, on-line transaction systems multi-vendor computer systems, geographical systems, just-in-time manufacturing, agency-wide and multi-national systems. Systems integration has already become a primary sales channel for both hardware and software products, and an important source of subcontracting work for software companies.[5]

Sector Dynamics

6.   In virtually all software industries in the developed world, there has been a trend since 1979 toward the production of packaged, "shrink wrapped," software--producing new products, adding new features, and customizing these products to customer requirements--and away from customized programming services. Packages offer economies of scale to vendors, who can focus on a few market areas and then meet growing demand for more sophisticated technical and support services related to the product. On the demand side, customers prefer packages because of the scarcity of experienced human resources and the risks in custom development projects--risks that are becoming much greater as information systems become larger, more integrated, and more complex.[6]

7.   If one can identify "historical trends" in what is still very much an *industrie nouveau*, one might classify countries according to the degree of their software sector output accounted for by packaged software. It is clear that the United States is far ahead of other countries when this comparison is made, with packaged software accounting for over 40% of sector revenues in 1990; whereas in Europe, the corresponding percentage in the same year was about 38%, as shown in Table A2.1.

8.   Another major trend in the software and services sector is the verticalization of the market. This has occurred because each sector has its own characteristics in terms of data processing expenditures, environment, level of information intensity, and importance of vertical applications. For example, most large banks require an effective management information system on a global basis to assess profitable and nonprofitable sectors, to monitor risk via centralized

---

[5] It should be noted that a considerable amount of know-how is required to undertake systems integration projects, and that the experience of major players in this market indicates that the assimilation of technological know-how does not occur over night; in most cases it has evolved as a result of considerable experience in large projects.

[6] The "horror" stories are now legion, though they have largely been ignored. See Ackoff, R., "Management Misinformation Systems," Management Science, Vol. 14, No. 4, December 1967; Boehm, B., "Understanding and Controlling Software Costs," IEEE Trans. Software Engineering, Vol. 14, No. 10, October 1988.

**Table A2.1: Worldwide Packaged Software Market by Country
($ millions, 1989-94)**

	1989	%	1990	%	1994	%
U.S.A.	15,830	43.1%	18,020	41.9%	32,040	39.7%
Japan	3,334	9.1%	3,901	9.1%	7,726	9.6%
EC*	12,520	34.1%	15,152	35.3%	29,127	36.1%
Mid-Income Industrial**	941	2.6%	1,175	2.6%	3,072	3.2%
Other	4,108	11.1%	4,782	11.1%	8,717	11.4%
TOTAL	36,733	100.0%	43,030	100.0%	80,682	100.0%

Note:
*:   EC consists of Germany, U.K., France, Italy, Netherlands, Spain, Belgium,
      Denmark and Norway.
**:   Middle Income Industrial consists of Brazil, Mexico, S. Korea, Venezuelan, Taiwan,
      Malaysia, Hungary, Singapore, Hong Kong and Thailand.

Source: International Data Corporation, 1989

systems, and to support 24-hour trading. Traditionally, end-user sectors have been segmented into: financial services, manufacturing, services, and government and defense, each representing about a quarter of the market. But this segmentation is also changing, as other subsectors become attracted to developing software, such as transportation and communication. Further, as information technology takes up an increasing proportion of corporate budgets, there is the attraction of turning parts of that investment into a revenue stream, or of turning programs into products. This drive to commercialize software has spawned not just products but entire companies. In the United Kingdom alone, Datasolve, IMI, Istel, and a few public sector spinoffs were born of non-information technology parents with a mission to exploit a wider market.

Changing Skill Requirements

9.   Software development is not an easy task since there is no simple set of rules or methods that work under all circumstances. There is a general agreement within the software community that experience plays a very large role in the development of a good software engineer. Research and development efforts in software engineering have produced new methods that show promise for improving programmer productivity and software reliability. But the "software crisis" still remains. On the one hand, software applications are becoming more complex due to increasingly large projects that require the coordinated work of many teams (often in different locations), stringent requirements (e.g., for reliability in performance and

integrity of the data used), the need to support a range of interactions with the environment in real time, and/or certain structural features. On the other, software development is still a craft sector, which depends on talented people--perhaps the most important element in any software organization--and on the software organization's approach to and management of the entire software process.[7]

10.   In the foreseeable future, there is therefore likely to be a long-term decline in the numbers of routine or low-level programmers required, and a rise in demand for higher-level computer, software, and communications expertise, with business know-how. Rather than programmers, the sector will need well-educated managers and project leaders,[8] electronic and communications engineers and technicians, software and systems engineers and technicians, creative end-users (for example, computer-aided design and manufacturing users and management information systems analysts), and routine end-users (e.g., basic word processing or routine systems).[9] The growing shift toward simplified information systems development offered by software packages and fourth generation languages will fuel the growth in end-user computing.

Software "Success" Factors

11.   Like many businesses in their early stages, software firms have had and continue to have their share of successes and failures. The industry has too frequently been swept along by a tide of optimistic enthusiasm during the "wild" success of certain products, or by enthusiasm for new hardware and software capabilities. Certainly not all players are successful. Indeed, it is becoming increasingly difficult to achieve success in the software sector through luck or accident.

12.   The history, however, of certain software firms, and interviews with numerous companies in different countries, reveal what may be considered "success" factors in this sector. Table 2 provides a list of these factors which, it should be noted, pertain mostly to areas or regions where software development is already highly developed and firms are clustered, and where a legal framework exists protecting intellectual property combined with active and effective enforcement. It would appear that successful software industries benefit from the synergy that comes from a concentration of firms, which can be seen, for example, in states

---

[7] As Marcus Bolton, managing director of the U.K. software developer, System C, put it: "You cannot replace one bright individual with a team of adequate ones." See Financial Times "Personal Computers and Software Survey," September 25, 1990, p. viii.

[8] See Angell, I.O., and S. Smithson, "Managing Information Technology: A Crisis of Confidence?" Working Paper Series 20, London School of Economics and Political Science, Department of Information Systems, 1989.

[9] See IT Strategy Services, "The State of the UK IT Skills and Training Market," Mimeo, London, IT Strategy Services, 1988.

such as Massachusetts, Washington, and California in the U.S.[10] The availability of support services, the presence of universities in the area, communications networks among players, and the balance of information technology infrastructure requirements all serve to increase success in software. The continuous enhancement of the supply of inputs, in particular well-trained software engineers, however, was considered most important in the ratings and rankings of software firms interviewed for the study.[11]

Box A2.1: Key Factors Present for Successful Software Innovation and Development

Skilled Labor

- Students
- Well-trained software engineers
- Management commitment and understanding

Economy

- Extent of computerization in industry
- Standards
- Computers in Schools

Universities

- Research and development
- Software engineering curricula
- Direct interactions with industry

Funding

- Venture capital markets
- Government contracts and grants
- Banks that understand software

Support Services

- Telecommunications infrastructure
- Disk duplicators
- Printers
- Mail/express services

Communications Networks Among Players

- Engineers
- Managers
- Marketers
- Funders

Attractive Environment

- Entrepreneurial, problem-solving
- Low cost rents, labor services

Access to Market Channels

- Joint ventures
- Cooperative arrangements

Source: Adapted from John Whitman, "Key Factors for Software Success," Draft prepared by the Oakland Group, Inc. 675 Massachusetts Ave., Cambridge, MA, November 20, 1990.

---

[10] As John Whitman, Former President of Oakland Group, put it: "Competition and egos notwithstanding, software executives tend to communicate and share experiences." See J. Whitman, "Key Factors for Software Success," Mimeo, Oakland Group, Cambridge, Massachusetts, December 26, 1990, p. xi.

[11] The study is described in the paper by John Whitman, "Key Factors for Software Success," Mimeo, Oakland Group, Cambridge, Massachusetts, December 26, 1990.

ANNEX 3

LEGAL PROTECTION FOR SOFTWARE BY COUNTRY[12]
EXHIBIT I. LEGAL PROTECTION FOR SOFTWARE BY COUNTRY[1]

Nation	Copyright	Convention Memberships	Nation	Copyright	Convention Memberships
Argentina	Probably	B.U.P	Macau	No	None
Australia	Yes	B.U.P	Malaysia	Yes	P
Austria	Maybe	B.U.P	Mexico	Probably	B.U.P
Belgium	Maybe	B.U.P	Netherlands	Probably	B.U.P
Brazil	Yes	B.U.P	New Zealand	Probably	B.U.P
Brunei	Unknown	None	Nigeria	Yes	U.P
Bulgaria	Yes	B.U.P	Norway	Probably	B.U.P
Canada	Yes	B.U.P	Oman	No	None
Chile	Maybe	B.U	Pakistan	Unknown	B.U
China (PRC)(21)+	No	P	Panama	Unknown	U
Colombia	Yes	B.U	Peru	Maybe	B.U
Costa Rica	Maybe	B.U	Philippines	Yes	B.P
Czechoslovakia	No	B.U.P	Poland	Maybe	B.U.P
Denmark	Yes	B.U.P	Portugal	Maybe	B.U.P
Dominican Rep.	Yes	U.P	Romania	Maybe	B.P
Ecuador	Maybe	U	Saudi Arabia	Yes	None
Egypt	Maybe	B.P	Singapore	Yes	Bilateral Copyright
Finland	Maybe	B.U.P			
France	Yes	B.U.P	South Africa	Probably	B.P Bilateral Copyright
Germany (Dem Rep)	No	B.U.P			
Germany (Fed Rep)	Yes (7)	B.U.P	South Korea	Yes	U.P
Greece	Unknown	B.U.P	Spain	Yes	B.U.P
Guatemala	Unknown	U	Sweden	Yes	B.U.P
Hong Kong	Yes	B.U.P (as extended pursuant to the UK's memberships)	Switzerland	Maybe	B.U.P
			Taiwan (ROC)	Yes	Bilateral Copyright
			Thailand(21)+	No	B
			Turkey	Maybe	B.P
Hungary	Yes	B.U.P	USSR	No	U.P
India	Yes	B.U	UAE	No	None
Indonesia	Yes	P.Bilateral Copyright	United Kingdom	Yes	B.U.P
			United States	Yes	B.U.P
Ireland	Maybe	B.U.P	Uruguay	Yes	B.P
Israel	Yes	B.U.P	Venezuela	Maybe	B.U
Italy	Probably	B.U.P	Yugoslavia	No	B.U.P
Japan	Yes	B.U.P			
Luxembourg	Maybe	B.U.P			

Notes:

[1]: Copyright indicates whether subject matter protection is available for software under the national copyright law of the specified country. If it is, the list under Convention Memberships shows whether there is an applicable mutual membership or bilateral agreement between the US and that country. If there is, subject matter protection is probably available.

---

[12] F. Greguras, G. Rebach, J. Riff, "Software's Legal Protection Around the World," Information Strategy, Fall 1990. p. 24.

B: Berne Convention

Maybe: Subject matter protection may be available based on favorable lower court opinions, views of commentators, or registry of software in the country's copyright office.

No: No substantial case law precedent supports subject matter protection.

P: Paris Convention

Probably: Significant case law precedent supports subject matter protection.

U: Universal Copyright Convention

Unknown: Information not identified.

Yes: Protection for software available pursuant to legislation or presidential decree expressly protecting software.

ANNEX 4

INCENTIVES TO PROMOTE SOFTWARE INDUSTRIES
IN SELECTED COUNTRIES

France
- Accelerate Depreciation of hardware used in development or testing of software (proposed).
- Write-off of software R&D expenditures (proposed).

United Kingdom
- Software Products Scheme (1972-1985)(SPS). L47m ($65m) in direct, non-recoverable grants for up to a third of development and marketing costs of software products.
- Support for innovation (SFI) (1985-present). L4m indirect, non-recoverable grants for 25% of development and marketing costs. SPS was incorporated into SPI in 1985.

Japan
- Long-term low interested loans for software development through Information Technology Promotion Agency.
- Reserve account established for software companies to cover cost modifying programs.
- 50% of income on packaged software sales set aside as tax-free reserve for four years to cover future software development costs.
- $50m retaining grants for programmers.

Taiwan
- Five year tax holiday for software and systems design services firms; 25% max. corporate tax rate thereafter.
- Credit guarantee fund and export guarantee and insurance systems planned.

Singapore
- Producers of sophisticated software packages may receive ten year tax holiday.
- Firms exporting software above $1 million (Singapore) receive 20% concessionary tax rate.
- Six free trade zones.

Hungary
- Exemptions from corporate tax for 1st 5 years of a joint venture.

- No import tariffs on equipment for local production and development.

Ireland
- Employment grants for jobs created.

- Capital grants

- Training Grants

- 10% tax on profits

- R&D grants up to 50% of project cost

- Venture capital program for software developers

- Industrial Development Authority planning and financing international marketing.

Israel
- 0% tax on investment

- 40% grants for building costs

- Loan guarantees

- 50% joint venture funding

- R&D Support

Mexico
- Bancomext lead bank for export financing
  - Trade fair organization
  - Capital goods

- Tariffs reduced to average 10%.

Philippines
- 5-10% tax credit on net earned

- 100% exemption from taxes and duties on imported capital equipment.

ANNEX 5

OCCUPATIONAL STRUCTURE OF THE INFORMATICS PROFESSION (1991)

HARDWARE PROFESSIONALS:

Job Title	*Job Description*
Communications Specialists (Example: Telecommunications Engineer, Communications Network Engineer	Those who translate requirements involving combination and software aspects of telecommunications and who are able to integrate and network them into properly engineered and tested communication services.
Field Engineers	Those who engage in the hardware aspects of IT and who are able to install, perform diagnostic tests to identify the source of equipment failure and to perform repair and preventive service on user's equipment on demand and/or to agreed schedule.
Hardware Specialist (Example: Eletronics Engineer Design/Product Development Engineer, Hardware Engineer, IC Design Engineer	Those who expertise lies primarily in the hardware/electronics area of IT and who are able to develop and/or translate hardware requirements into properly engineered tested hardware assemblies as part of an overall information systems.

SOFTWARE PROFESSIONALS:

Job Title	*Job Description*
System Analysts/Designer	Those who engage in the analysis and design of application systems encompassing the development, modification and translation of user's requirements into user oriented solutions.
Application Programmers (including Analyst/Programmer)	Those who create, modify and code computer software into working, debugged, and documented programs.
System Engineers	Those who make technical recommendations concerning the configuration and operation of products to meet defined systems requirements.
Systems Programmers	Those who monitor and tune hardware and software performance of the computer systems in operation to optimize processing response times.

MANAGERIAL:

Job Title	*Job Description*
Development Managers	Those who manage and direct the overall application systems development functions and activities from the definition, planning, feasibility study and analysis, design, construction through to the evaluation phases.
Project Leaders	Those responsible for the development, management and control of specific information systems projects.
EDP Managers	Those who manage a group which coordinates their organization's information processing activities including applications development and the operation and control of the organization's own computer installation or selection and control of outside facilities.
Operations Manager	Those with the overall responsibility to plan, manage , co-ordinate and optimize computer operation from data entry, production control, post-processing to resource allocation.

MARKETING AND SALES:

Job Title	*Job Description*
Marketing Representatives	Those who co-ordinate the activities leading to the sale, installation and on-going utilization of products to meet customers' stated requirements.

SERVICES AND SUPPORT:

Job Title	*Job Description*
Computer Operators	Those who carry out the full range of practical tasks associated with operational computing and peripheral equipment in accordance with the workload, service priorities and deadlines as defined in the daily production schedule. Liaise with Systems Programmers to determine cause of failure and dislocations and corrective action requires. Liaise with maintenance programmers to resolve operation application program concerns and abnormal terminations.
Consultants	Those who offer advisory services to management of other organizations with respect to the definition, planning, analysis, design, implementation and evaluation of information systems.

Research & Development Specialists	Those who are involved in the technological scientific research and development work in one or more aspects of the specialized fields of IT.
Lecturers/Teaching Associates	Those who plan, prepare and conduct formal courses in one or more aspects of the field of IT to educate, train/ or upgrade future or current information workers.
Knowledge Engineers	Those whose expertise lies in the area of artificial intelligence and expert systems and who apply such knowledge in developing applications for end users.
Information Analysts	Those who plan, design and advise on the installation of database systems to support management control and decision making activities and assist executive management in the analysis, modelling and development of enterprise information requirements.
Quality Assurance Specialists	Those who are responsible for developing and enabling the application of quality Assurance techniques, methodologies and standards to the development and operation of information systems.
Security Specialists	Those who develop methods and procedures for foiling unauthorized usage and ensure the integrity of the information in maintained/protected.
Database Specialists (Example: Database Administrator, Database Designer)	Those who develop, administer, maintain, control, operate and ensure the integrity of the database management information system, including the preparation and enforcement of standards for use and the security of information in the databases.
End-user Support Specialist	Those who advise, assist and train all levels of user/client in the development of end-user applications.

Source: NCB, Singapore.

ANNEX 6

UNDERGRADUATE PROGRAM, ODTÜ (1991)

First Year

First Semester
Calculus I
General Physics I
General Chemistry
Introd uction to Computer
   Engineering I

Second Semester
Calculus II
General Physics II
Introduction to Computer Engineering II
Applied Linear Algebra

SECOND YEAR

Third Semester
Programming Languages I
Data Structures
Probability & Statistics in
   Comp. Science I
Electrical Circuits
Differential Equations

Fourth Semester
Programming Languages II
Probability & Statistics in Comp. Science II
Discrete Computational Structures
Digital Logic Systems II
Basic Electronics

THIRD YEAR

Fifth Semester
Computer Organization
Microprocessor & Microcomputers
Data Management
Numerical Analysis I
Operational Mathematics
Intro to Business Administration

Sixth Semester
Systems Programming
Database Management Systems
Numerical Analysis II
Computer Graphics
Principles of Economics
Summer Practice (30 Working Days)

FOURTH YEAR

Seventh Semester
Operating Systems
Data Communications
Informatics Systems Analysis
   and Design
Formal Languages and Abstract
   Machines
Senior Seminar
Fundamentals of Operational
   Research

Eighth Semester
Language Processors
Information Systems Engineering
Artificial Intelligence
System Simulation
Parallel Architectures and Computing
Graduation Project
Summer Practice II (Min. 30 Working Days)

Source: Department of Computer Engineering, ODTÜ.

ATTACHMENT

TURKEY: TOWARD AN INFORMATION-BASED ECONOMY
OBJECTIVES, STATUS AND PROPOSALS

CHAPTER	POLICY OBJECTIVE	STATUS	PROPOSED ACTIONS
2A.	SUPERIOR COMPUTER MANAGEMENT	1. Liberal policies permit access to frontier technology 2. Latecomer status results in computer park; but 3. Systemic inefficiencies in public use 4. Slow use of networking technology 5. inadequate standards	1. strengthen public procurement process - oversight on requirements planning - standardized IT tender documents - uniform prices for standard products - unbundle contract components 2. Improve public IT management - classification of IT occupational stream - best practice IT management standards - training and advisory service - technology watch function 3. Commercialize communications sector - see policy objective 5 4. Create skills in technology management - changes in university curriculum - business-university links 5. Introduce standards - use public procurement to promote OSI - adoption of national standards - capacity for standards revision - user-driven standards preparation

TURKEY: TOWARD AN INFORMATION-BASED ECONOMY
OBJECTIVES, STATUS AND PROPOSALS

CHAPTER	POLICY OBJECTIVE	STATUS	PROPOSED ACTIONS
2B.	INCREASED SUPPLY OF LOCAL TECHNOLOGY	1. Limited assembly of PCs 2. Growing consumer and communications electronics industry	1. Target applies R&D to key user segments - ED/I for textile sector - educational software - agricultural information systems - communications - competitive niche analysis 2. Introduce framework for venture capital - eliminate double tax problem - introduce regulatory framework 3. Promote competition - eliminate trade distortions - change leasing rules - strengthen IPRs - improve public procurement - avoid new incentives - programs to attract DFI in sector

TURKEY: TOWARD AN INFORMATION-BASED ECONOMY
OBJECTIVES, STATUS AND PROPOSALS

CHAPTER	POLICY OBJECTIVE	STATUS	PROPOSED ACTIONS
3.	MORE PRODUCTIVE SOFTWARE APPLICATIONS	1. Small but rapidly growing industry; still at low productivity levels 2. No foreign investment or exports 3. Lack of legal protection 4. Lack of standards 5. Public procurement discriminates against independent suppliers 6. Limited tax incentives 7. No sources of external finance 8. Human capital constraints	1. Strengthen public procurement process - unbundle software component - certification of qualifying suppliers - training of Ministry staff - percentage reservation of contract for independent houses 2. Develop software standards - introduce quality assurance standards - provide specialized training - develop certification resources - Software Quality Initiative 3. Phase in legal protection - provide copyright for software - see Policy Objective 7 4. Expand human resources - reorient university curriculum - upgrade existing skill-base 5. Provide support for R&D - target software through Technology Foundation - precompetitive research grants - attract foreign software houses

TURKEY: TOWARD AN INFORMATION-BASED ECONOMY
OBJECTIVES, STATUS AND PROPOSALS

CHAPTER	POLICY OBJECTIVE	STATUS	PROPOSED ACTIONS
4.	HIGH-SKILL INFORMATION WORKFORCE	1. Lack of informatics specialists 2. Quality not in line with market demand. 3. Universities not responding adequately 4. Private training poor 5. Lack of general informatics skills	1. Strengthen university performance - separate informatics departments - endowed university chairs - company sponsored computing facilities - curriculum reform - integration of IT across disciplines - university-business councils - university computing network - private Informatics Institute 2. Foster private training industry - occupational standards - certification and accreditation - labor market information - training fund for SME employees 3. Enable in-house private training - trade secrets legislation - certified refresher course - award scheme for in-house training - non-profit training consortia for SMEs 4. National Computer Program (BILGITEL) - design low-cost intelligent terminal - ensure competitive terminal supply - partial funding for low-income HHs - public domain software - PTT coordination

TURKEY: TOWARD AN INFORMATION-BASED ECONOMY
OBJECTIVES, STATUS AND PROPOSALS

CHAPTER	POLICY OBJECTIVE	STATUS	PROPOSED ACTIONS
5.	COMPETITIVE COMMUNICATIONS NETWORK	1. Rapid network expansion 2. Latest digital technology 3. Public sector monopoly 4. High prices: cross subsidies; excessive overhead costs 5. Barriers to private entry 6. Semi-liberalized CPE market 7. Deteriorating mail performance	1. Establish independent regulatory body - interconnection and market access rules - restriction of PTT service range - further liberalization of CPE market - quality of service targets - radio spectrum allocation - coordination with TV/radio regulation 2. Separate mail and telecom - liberal policy framework for mail - separate accounting entities - separate physical facilities - financial restructuring of mail - phaseout PTT cross-subsidies - reduction in over-staffing - investments in mail to increase productivity 3. Improve commercial performance of telecom - separate value-added services (VAS) - corporatize and privatize VAS - develop joint ventures for international market - place telecom under commercial law - long run privatization

TURKEY: TOWARD AN INFORMATION-BASED ECONOMY
OBJECTIVES, STATUS AND PROPOSALS

CHAPTER	POLICY OBJECTIVE	STATUS	PROPOSED ACTIONS
6.	BETTER INFORMATION	1. Small private information industry 2. Private industry mainly in newspapers; but growing cross-media integration 3. Government main source of primary data; but dissemination restricted and uneven quality 4. SIS legal monopoly over public information dissemination; but de facto multi-agency info-flows 5. Public monopoly (legal) over TV and radio being revised 6. Inadequate information standards	1. National Database & Dissemination policy - SIS as oversight agency - standards for data and networking - procedures for inter-agency datasharing - coordinated database investment - decentralized data dissemination - guidelines for data dissemination - private access rights to statistical data - pricing policy for public data - guidelines for value-added information supply by public sector 2. Liberal Framework for TV and Radio - regulatory agency - clear rules for private entry - changes in PTT role - restructuring of TRT revenues - prevention of media concentration - reallocation of radio spectrum - unified regulation of info-content - policy on non-commercial programming 3. Strengthen Information Standards - financial accounting & disclosure - consumer product information - job information - standardized legal documents - standardized insurance contracts - standardized retail financial products

TURKEY: TOWARD AN INFORMATION-BASED ECONOMY
OBJECTIVES, STATUS AND PROPOSALS

CHAPTER	POLICY OBJECTIVE	STATUS	PROPOSED ACTIONS
7.	SUPPORTIVE LEGAL FRAMEWORK	1. High rate of software piracy 2. No clear legal protection of software 3. Signatory of OECD Guidelines on data protection; but no domestic legislation 4. Legislation on computer crime; but incomplete	1. Strengthen software copyright - review international practice - develop phased legislation - explicitly extend copyright to software - restrict anti-competitive use of software 2. Introduce Data Protection legislation - guidelines for database management - private rights of access and correction - registration requirements - determine primary ownership of personal data 3. Extend Computer Crime definition - unauthorized access - computer security standards

SELECT BIBLIOGRAPHY

Chapter 1. Vision, Strategy, and Constraints

Bell, D. The Social Framework of the Information Society.

Cline, W. Informatics and Development: Trade and Industrial Policy in Argentina, Brazil and Mexico (Washington, DC: Economics International, 1987).

Dertouzos, M. Building the Information Marketplace (Technology Review, January 1991).

Englebrecht, H. The Japanese Information Economy: Its Qualification and Analysis in a Macroeconomic Framework (with Comparisons to the U.S.) (Elsevier Science Publishers, 1986).

Guile, B. and Brooks, H. (eds.). Technology and Global Industry: Companies and Nations in the World Economy (Washington, DC: National Academy Press, 1987).

Hanna, N. The Information Technology Revolution and Economic Development. World Bank Discussion Paper No. 120 (Washington, DC: The World Bank, 1991).

Hon, W. S. A Developing Country Strategy for Using Information Technology: Case Study of Singapore. Singapore National Computer Board (September 27, 1990).

Jonscher, C. Information Resources and Economic Productivity (Elsevier Science Publishers, 1983).

Katz, R. The Information Society (Praeger, 1990)

OECD. Information Technology and New Growth Opportunities (Paris, 1989).

Pool, I. Technologies of Freedom (London: Harvard University Press, 1971).

Roach, S. Services under Siege: The Restructuring Imperative (Harvard Business Review, September 1989).

Scientific American. Communications, Computers and Networks (Special Issue, September 1991).

Stiglitz, J. Economics of Information and Theory of Economic Development (NBER Working Paper No 1566).

Williamson, O. Economic Organization (New York: New York University Press, 1986).

The Economist. Information Technology: The Ubiquitous Machine (June 16, 1990).

Chapter 2. Creating Computer Advantage

Commission of European Communities. The European Situation: An Overview (Washington, DC: 1991).

Dahlman, C. Electronics Development Strategy: The Role of Government. World Bank Industry Series Paper No. 37 (Washington, DC: The World Bank, June 1990).

Department of Trade and Industry. Evaluation of the Alvey Programme for Advanced Information Technology (HMSO, 1991).

Flamm, K. The Computer Industry in Industrialized Economies: Lessons for the Newly Industrializing. World Bank Industry Series Paper No. 8 (Washington, DC: The World Bank, February 1989).

Frischtak, C. Specialization, Technical Change and Competitiveness in the Brazilian Electronics Industry (IBRD, Industry Series Paper No. 15, 1990).

International Data Corporation (IDC). Worldwide Information Technology Spending Patterns, 1990-1995: An Analysis of Opportunities in Over 30 Countries. Report No. 5996, IDC (Framingham, MA: October 1991).

National Research Council. The National Challenge in Computer Science and Technology (Washington, DC: National Academy Press, 1988).

Office of Management and Budget. A Five-Year Plan for Meeting the Automatic Data Processing and Telecommunications Needs of the Federal Government (Washington, DC: 1990).

Strassman, P. The Business Value of Computers (Cannan, CN: Information Economics Press, 1990).

Chapter 3. Competing in Software

Coopers and Lybrand. Computing Services Industry 1986-1996: A Decade of Opportunity -- 1989 Update. Report to the U.K. Department of Trade and Industry (London: 1989).

Data Resources. The Impact of the Computer Software and Services and Computer Hardware Industries in the U.S. Economy (Arlington, VA: ADAPSO, 1989).

Kopetz, H. Chances and Issues in Software Production in Developing Countries. IPCT. 144 (Vienna: United Nations Development Organization, 1991).

National Research Council. Keeping the U.S. Computer Industry Competitive: Systems Integration (Washington, DC: National Press, 1992).

OECD. Information Technology Standards: The Economic Dimension. ICCP Policy Paper No. 25 (Paris: OECD, 1991)

OECD. Software Engineering: The Policy Challenge (Paris, 1991)

OECD. Venture Capital in Information Technology (Paris, 1985)

Rappaport, A. and Halevi, S. The Computerless Computer Company (Harvard Business Review, July 1991).

Schware, R. Software Industry Entry Strategies for Developing Countries: A "Walking on Two Legs" Proposition. World Development, Vol. 20, No. 2 (1992).

Schware, R. The World Software Industry and Software Engineering: Constraints for Newly Industrialized Economies. World Bank Technical Paper No. 104 (Washington, DC: The World Bank, 1989).

Chapter 4. Human Capital for an Information Economy

Career Associates. Career Choices for the 90's for Students of Computer Science (New York: Walker & Co., 1990).

Ducatel, K. and Miles, I. New Information Technologies and Working Conditions in the European Community (PREST/SPRU 1991).

Jacobs, J. Training the Workforce of the Future. Technology Review (August/September, 1989).

National Computer Board. IT Manpower Survey (NCB Singapore: 1989).

Sako, M. Enterprise Training in a Comparative Perspective: West Germany, Japan and Britain: A Report Prepared for the World Bank (London: London School of Economics, July 1990).

Thomas, P. et. al. Job Preparation of IS Graduates: Are They Ready for the Real World?. Journal of Systems Management. Vol 42, No. 8 (August 1991).

Wanda, O. and Baroudi, J. Better Jobs? Occupational Stratification and Labor-Market Segmentation in the United States' Information Labor Force. Information Society, Vol. 7, No. 2 (1990).

Chapter 5. The Communications Network

Ambrose, W. et. al. Privatizing Telecommunication Systems: Business Opportunities in Developing Countries. IFC Discussion Paper No. 10 (Washington, DC: 1990).

Bruce, R. Restructuring of Telecom Sector: An Overview of the Experience in Some Industrialized Countries and Some Lessons and Implications for Policymakers (Washington, DC: April 1991).

Crandall, R. After the Breakup: US Telecom in a More Competitive Era (Brookings Institute, 1991).

Department of Trade and Industry. Competition and Choice: Telecom Policy for the 1990s (HMSO: 1991).

European Community Commission. Green Paper on the Development of the Common Market for Telecoms Services and Equipment. (Brussels, 1989).

European Community Commission. Green Paper on Satellite Communication in the European Community (Brussels, 1990).

Huber, P. The Geodesic Network (Washington, DC: U.S. Department of Justice, 1987).

National Telecom and Information Administration. NTIA 2000: Charting the Course for the Next Century (US Department of Commerce: 1988).

OECD. Telecommunications Network-Based Services: Policy Implications (Paris: 1989).

OECD. Structural Characteristics and Change in Communications Services (Paris: 1988).

OECD. Performance Indicators for Public Telecom Operators (Paris, 1990).

Office of Technology Assessment. Critical Connections: Communications for the Future (GPO, 1990).

Pool, I. <u>Technologies without Boundaries: On Telecommunications in a Global Age</u> (London: 1990).

Wellenius, B. et. al. <u>Restructuring and Managing the Telecom Sector</u> (IBRD Symposium, 1989).

Williams, F. <u>The New Telecommunications: Infrastructure for Information Age</u> (New York: The Free Press, 1991).

World Bank. <u>Turkey: Telecommunications Sector Memorandum</u>. Report No. 5691-TU (Washington, DC: The World Bank, June 26, 1983).

Chapter 6. Reducing Uncertainty - The Role of Information

Dunn, A. D. and Fronistas, C.A. <u>Economic Models of Information Services Markets</u> (Stanford, CA: Stanford University).

European Community Commission. <u>The Market for Value-Added Services in Europe</u> (Scion Networks, 1989).

Financial times. <u>The New Face of British Broadcasting</u> (October 1990).

Kahin, B. <u>The NREN as Information Market: Dynamics of Public, Private, and Voluntary Publishing</u>. J.F. Kennedy School of Government.

Office of Technology Assessment. <u>Informing the Nation: Federal Information Dissemination in an Electronic Age</u> (Washington, DC: OTA, October 1988).

Office of Technology Assessment. <u>The Role of Federal Scientific and Technical Information: Helping America Complete</u> (Washington, DC: 1990).

Perritt, H. <u>Government Information Goes On-Line</u>. Technology Review (November/December 1989).

Chapter 7. The Legal Infrastructure

Branscomb, A. <u>Law and Culture in the Information Society</u> (Information Society, 4, 4, 1986).

Consumer Reports. <u>What Price Privacy?</u> (May 1991).

Elbra, T. A Practical Guide to the Computer Misuse Act (NCC 1990).

OECD. Computer-Related Crime: An Analysis of Legal Policy (Paris: OECD, 1986).

Office of Technology Assessment (OTA). Finding a Balance: Computer Software, Intellectual Property and the Challenge of Technological Change (Washington, DC: OTA, 1992).

Rubin, R. Personal Privacy in an Information Society: Information Economics and Policy in the United States (Littleton, CO: Libraries Unlimited Inc.).

Subramanian, A. The International Economics of Intellectual Property Right Protection: A Welfare-Theoretic Trade Policy Analysis. World Development, Vol. 19, No. 8 (1991).

Wolfgang, S. et.al.,(eds.). Strengthening Protection of Intellectual Property in Developing Countries: A Survey of the Literature. World Bank Discussion Paper 112 (Washington, DC: The World Bank, 1990).

Distributors of World Bank Publications

ARGENTINA
Carlos Hirsch, SRL
Galeria Guemes
Florida 165, 4th Floor-Ofc. 453/465
1333 Buenos Aires

**AUSTRALIA, PAPUA NEW GUINEA,
FIJI, SOLOMON ISLANDS,
VANUATU, AND WESTERN SAMOA**
D.A. Books & Journals
648 Whitehorse Road
Mitcham 3132
Victoria

AUSTRIA
Gerold and Co.
Graben 31
A-1011 Wien

BANGLADESH
Micro Industries Development
   Assistance Society (MIDAS)
House 5, Road 16
Dhanmondi R/Area
Dhaka 1209

   Branch offices:
   156, Nur Ahmed Sarak
   Chittagong 4000

   76, K.D.A. Avenue
   Kulna 9100

BELGIUM
Jean De Lannoy
Av. du Roi 202
1060 Brussels

CANADA
Le Diffuseur
C.P. 85, 1501B rue Ampère
Boucherville, Québec
J4B 5E6

CHILE
Invertec IGT S.A.
Americo Vespucio Norte 1165
Santiago

CHINA
China Financial & Economic
   Publishing House
8, Da Fo Si Dong Jie
Beijing

COLOMBIA
Infoenlace Ltda.
Apartado Aereo 34270
Bogota D.E.

COTE D'IVOIRE
Centre d'Edition et de Diffusion
   Africaines (CEDA)
04 B.P. 541
Abidjan 04 Plateau

CYPRUS
Center of Applied Research
Cyprus College
6, Diogenes Street, Engomi
P.O. Box 2006
Nicosia

DENMARK
SamfundsLitteratur
Rosenoerns Allé 11
DK-1970 Frederiksberg C

DOMINICAN REPUBLIC
Editora Taller, C. por A.
Restauración e Isabel la Católica 309
Apartado de Correos 2190 Z-1
Santo Domingo

EGYPT, ARAB REPUBLIC OF
Al Ahram
Al Galaa Street
Cairo

The Middle East Observer
41, Sherif Street
Cairo

FINLAND
Akateeminen Kirjakauppa
P.O. Box 128
SF-00101 Helsinki 10

FRANCE
World Bank Publications
66, avenue d'Iéna
75116 Paris

GERMANY
UNO-Verlag
Poppelsdorfer Allee 55
D-5300 Bonn 1

HONG KONG, MACAO
Asia 2000 Ltd.
46-48 Wyndham Street
Winning Centre
2nd Floor
Central Hong Kong

INDIA
Allied Publishers Private Ltd.
751 Mount Road
Madras - 600 002

   Branch offices:
   15 J.N. Heredia Marg
   Ballard Estate
   Bombay - 400 038

   13/14 Asaf Ali Road
   New Delhi - 110 002

   17 Chittaranjan Avenue
   Calcutta - 700 072

   Jayadeva Hostel Building
   5th Main Road, Gandhinagar
   Bangalore - 560 009

   3-5-1129 Kachiguda
      Cross Road
   Hyderabad - 500 027

   Prarthana Flats, 2nd Floor
   Near Thakore Baug, Navrangpura
   Ahmedabad - 380 009

   Patiala House
   16-A Ashok Marg
   Lucknow - 226 001

   Central Bazaar Road
   60 Bajaj Nagar
   Nagpur 440 010

INDONESIA
Pt. Indira Limited
Jalan Borobudur 20
P.O. Box 181
Jakarta 10320

IRELAND
Government Supplies Agency
4-5 Harcourt Road
Dublin 2

ISRAEL
Yozmot Literature Ltd.
P.O. Box 56055
Tel Aviv 61560

ITALY
Licosa Commissionaria Sansoni SPA
Via Duca Di Calabria, 1/1
Casella Postale 552
50125 Firenze

JAPAN
Eastern Book Service
Hongo 3-Chome, Bunkyo-ku 113
Tokyo

KENYA
Africa Book Service (E.A.) Ltd.
Quaran House, Mfangano Street
P.O. Box 45245
Nairobi

KOREA, REPUBLIC OF
Pan Korea Book Corporation
P.O. Box 101, Kwangwhamun
Seoul

MALAYSIA
University of Malaya Cooperative
   Bookshop, Limited
P.O. Box 1127, Jalan Pantai Baru
59700 Kuala Lumpur

MEXICO
INFOTEC
Apartado Postal 22-860
14060 Tlalpan, Mexico D.F.

NETHERLANDS
De Lindeboom/InOr-Publikaties
P.O. Box 202
7480 AE Haaksbergen

NEW ZEALAND
EBSCO NZ Ltd.
Private Mail Bag 99914
New Market
Auckland

NIGERIA
University Press Limited
Three Crowns Building Jericho
Private Mail Bag 5095
Ibadan

NORWAY
Narvesen Information Center
Book Department
P.O. Box 6125 Etterstad
N-0602 Oslo 6

PAKISTAN
Mirza Book Agency
65, Shahrah-e-Quaid-e-Azam
P.O. Box No. 729
Lahore 54000

PERU
Editorial Desarrollo SA
Apartado 3824
Lima 1

PHILIPPINES
International Book Center
Suite 1703, Cityland 10
Condominium Tower 1
Ayala Avenue, Corner H.V. dela
   Costa Extension
Makati, Metro Manila

POLAND
International Publishing Service
Ul. Piekna 31/37
00-677 Warzawa

For subscription orders:
IPS Journals
Ul. Okrezna 3
02-916 Warszawa

PORTUGAL
Livraria Portugal
Rua Do Carmo 70-74
1200 Lisbon

SAUDI ARABIA, QATAR
Jarir Book Store
P.O. Box 3196
Riyadh 11471

**SINGAPORE, TAIWAN,
MYANMAR,BRUNEI**
Information Publications
   Private, Ltd.
Golden Wheel Building
41, Kallang Pudding, #04-03
Singapore 1334

SOUTH AFRICA, BOTSWANA
For single titles:
Oxford University Press
   Southern Africa
P.O. Box 1141
Cape Town 8000

For subscription orders:
International Subscription Service
P.O. Box 41095
Craighall
Johannesburg 2024

SPAIN
Mundi-Prensa Libros, S.A.
Castello 37
28001 Madrid

Librería Internacional AEDOS
Consell de Cent, 391
08009 Barcelona

SRI LANKA AND THE MALDIVES
Lake House Bookshop
P.O. Box 244
100, Sir Chittampalam A.
   Gardiner Mawatha
Colombo 2

SWEDEN
For single titles:
Fritzes Fackboksforetaget
Regeringsgatan 12, Box 16356
S-103 27 Stockholm

For subscription orders:
Wennergren-Williams AB
P. O. Box 1305
S-171 25 Solna

SWITZERLAND
For single titles:
Librairie Payot
1, rue de Bourg
CH 1002 Lausanne

For subscription orders:
Librairie Payot
Service des Abonnements
Case postale 3312
CH 1002 Lausanne

TANZANIA
Oxford University Press
P.O. Box 5299
Maktaba Road
Dar es Salaam

THAILAND
Central Department Store
306 Silom Road
Bangkok

**TRINIDAD & TOBAGO, ANTIGUA
BARBUDA, BARBADOS,
DOMINICA, GRENADA, GUYANA,
JAMAICA, MONTSERRAT, ST.
KITTS & NEVIS, ST. LUCIA,
ST. VINCENT & GRENADINES**
Systematics Studies Unit
#9 Watts Street
Curepe
Trinidad, West Indies

TURKEY
Infotel
Narlabahçe Sok. No. 15
Cagaloglu
Istanbul

UNITED KINGDOM
Microinfo Ltd.
P.O. Box 3
Alton, Hampshire GU34 2PG
England

VENEZUELA
Libreria del Este
Aptdo. 60.337
Caracas 1060-A

DATE DUE

DEMCO NO. 38-298